TEENAGE PREGNANCY

Recent Titles in
A World View of Social Issues Series

TEENAGE PREGNANCY

A GLOBAL VIEW

Edited by
Andrew L. Cherry,
Mary E. Dillon,
and Douglas Rugh

A World View of Social Issues
Andrew L. Cherry, Series Adviser

Greenwood Press
Westport, Connecticut • London

Library of Congress Cataloging-in-Publication Data

Teenage pregnancy : a global view / edited by Andrew L. Cherry, Mary E. Dillon, and Douglas Rugh.
     p.   cm. — (A world view of social issues, ISSN 1526-9442)
     Includes bibliographical references and index.
     ISBN 0–313–31195–1 (alk. paper)
     1. Teenage pregnancy. 2. Teenage pregnancy—Cross-cultural studies. I. Cherry, Andrew L. II. Dillon, Mary E. III. Rugh, Douglas. IV. Series.
HQ759.4.T431848   2001
306.874'3—dc21   00–069130

British Library Cataloguing in Publication Data is available.

Library of Congress Catalog Card Number: 00–069130
ISBN: 0–313–31195–1
ISSN: 1526–9442

First published in 2001

Greenwood Press, 88 Post Road West, Westport, CT 06881
An imprint of Greenwood Publishing Group, Inc.
www.greenwood.com

Printed in the United States of America

The paper used in this book complies with the Permanent Paper Standard issued by the National Information Standards Organization (Z39.48–1984).

10 9 8 7 6 5 4 3 2 1

CONTENTS

SERIES FOREWORD

Why are child abuse in the family and homelessness social conditions to be endured or at least tolerated in some countries while in other countries they are viewed as social problems that must be reduced or eliminated? What social institutions and other factors affect these behaviors? What historical, political, and social forces influence a society's response to a social condition? In many cases, individuals around the world have the same or similar hopes and problems. However, in most cases we deal with the same social conditions in very dissimilar ways.

The volumes in the Greenwood series A World View of Social Issues examine different social issues and problems that are being faced by individuals and societies around the world. These volumes examine problems of poverty and homelessness, drugs and alcohol addiction, HIV/AIDS, teen pregnancy, crime, women's rights, and a myriad of other issues that affect all of us in one way or another.

Each volume is devoted to one social issue or problem. All volumes follow the same general format. Each volume has up to fifteen chapters that describe how people in different countries perceive and try to cope with a given problem or social issue. The countries chosen represent as many world regions as possible, making it possible to explore how each issue has been recognized and what actions have been taken to alleviate it in a variety of settings.

Each chapter begins with a profile of the country being highlighted and an overview of the impact of the social issue or problem there. Basic policies, legislation, and demographic information related to the social issue are cov-

ered. A brief history of the problem helps the reader better understand the
political and social responses. Political initiatives and policies are also dis-
cussed, as well as social views, customs, and practices related to the problem
or social issue. Discussions about how the countries plan to deal with these
social problems are also included.

These volumes present a comprehensive and engaging approach for the
study of international social conditions and problems. The goal is to provide
a convenient framework for readers to examine specific social problems, how
they are viewed, and what actions are being taken by different countries
around the world.

For example, how is a problem like crime and crime control handled in
Third World countries? How is substance abuse controlled in industrialized
countries? How are poverty and homelessness handled in the poorest countries? How does culture influence the definition and response to domestic
violence in different countries? What part does economics play in shaping
both the issue of and the response to women's rights? How does a national
philosophy impact the definition and response to child abuse? These questions and more will be answered by the volumes in this series.

As we learn more about our counterparts in other countries, they become
real to us, and our worldview cannot help but change. We will think of
others as we think of those we know. They will be people who get up in
the morning and go to work. We will see people who are struggling with
relationships, attending religious services, being born, growing old, and dying.

This series will cover issues that will add to your knowledge about contemporary social society. These volumes will help you to better understand
social conditions and social issues in a broader sense, giving you a view of
what various problems mean to different people and how these perspectives
impact a society's response. You will be able to see how specific social problems are managed by governments and individuals confronting the consequences of these social dilemmas. By studying one problem from various
angles, you will be better able to grasp the totality of the situation, while at
the same time speculating as to how solutions used in one country could
be incorporated in another. Finally, this series will allow you to compare
and contrast how these social issues impact individuals in different countries
and how the effect is dissimilar or similar to our own experiences.

As series adviser, it is my hope that these volumes, which are unique in
the history of publishing, will increase your understanding and appreciation
of your counterparts around the world.

                                                              Andrew L. Cherry
                                                              Series Adviser

PREFACE

This volume is an attempt to treat in a compact and objective manner the dominant individual, social, political, and economic aspects of adolescent and teenage pregnancy in 15 contemporary nations. The countries in this volume were selected because they represent differences and similarities that—when organized in one volume—bring to light an extensive picture of adolescent pregnancy around the world. Presented in this way, we hope that important social aspects of the issue can be synthesized and better understood.

Sources of information used to write the chapters in this volume include scholarly books, journals, and monographs; official reports of governments and international organizations; and numerous periodicals. The Internet was an extremely useful tool in locating information. References appear at the end of each chapter. In all, the authors have sought to adhere to accepted standards of scholarly objectivity.

As such, this volume represents the analysis of the editors and authors. Conclusions and suggestions for policy should not be construed as an expression of support for any official government or private foundation policy on adolescent/teen pregnancy.

We dedicate this book to the teenage girls around the world who have had the burden of the world's future thrust upon their shoulders. When will their true value be realized by an aging world?

INTRODUCTION

No collective event in human experience creates such joy, celebration, and astonishment as the birth of a child. The celebration of a birth comes to us so easily and is so natural. Most of us cannot resist the primal/instinctual forces that are released within us when we are near a newborn. The birth of a child is a familiar yet surreal event—one that we can never become accustomed, one that could never be ordinary. The birthing process strengthens our bond to the child, to each other, to our past, and to our children's future. Somehow, we seem to know intuitively that every child is a small part of ourselves, our link to eternity. This is why understanding the experiences of children born outside our own community is so important. Teenage pregnancy is one of those situations that affects the celebration of life for the child, for those around the child, and in many countries. It affects society in general.

Today's adolescents, the largest generation of 10- to 19-year-olds in human history, are coming of age in a world that is very different from the one in which their parents came of age. Although the pace of change varies among regions of the world, societies around the world are in a state of widespread and rapid transformation, creating a dizzying array of new possibilities and new challenges for teenagers and young adults. This volume isolates one of those challenges and a common social phenomenon in all countries: teenage pregnancy.

Imagine a 13-year-old walking out of her apartment building in a modern city to catch a city bus to school. She stops to buy a pastry with the money her mother gave her. She leans against the brick and watches the cars inch their way downtown. She thinks about the boy that she will invariably see in a few hours. He is older, and she is afraid that she may be pregnant. Now imagine a 13-year-old carrying water back from the spigot at the edge of town. She is barefoot, muddy, and the flies are bothering her as they land on her arms and legs. Her parents had introduced her to a much older man, and now she is afraid that she may be pregnant. These two girls, although separated by a great distance and surroundings, share one thing in common: Their future will be irreversibly altered with the birth of their first baby.

As you will discover in the following chapters, adolescent girls who become mothers have fewer options for their future. Early childbearing often limits school and job possibilities for these girls, which helps explain why so many of the world's young mothers and their children live in poverty. Teenage mothers are also more likely to have problems in pregnancy and delivery.

In the developed and developing countries used to portray a worldview of teen pregnancy in this volume, you will find that teen pregnancy is directly associated with many of the chronic social problems experienced by teens around the world, including poor health, inadequate shelter, lack of education, violence and crime, and substance abuse.

Complex physical, familial, and cultural factors that are often poorly understood by those involved determine who will marry and when; who will begin sexual activity before marriage; who will begin childbearing during adolescence; and who will bear children outside of marriage. The available data demonstrate that while the needs and experiences of adolescents vary around the world, there are similarities that traverse national and regional boundaries.

Teen pregnancy accompanies the initiation of sexual activity at increasingly younger ages. The United Nations Children's Fund (UNICEF) estimates that 15 million children throughout the world are born to adolescent mothers every year. In other words, enough children are born each year to populate a city the size of Mexico City (Alan Guttmacher Institute, 1998).

At least 60% of the children born to adolescents worldwide are the result of unwanted pregnancies, according to the U.S.-based Alan Guttmacher Institute (1998). In the developing countries of Africa, Asia, and Latin America, women who have their first child before they are 18 years old have an average of seven children throughout their lives. This is double the number for women who have their first child after age 25. In most of the world, the majority of young women become sexually active during their teenage years.

You will also discover that in some societies women begin having sex during adolescence because they are expected to marry and begin childbearing at an early age. In other societies, marriage typically occurs later, but premarital sex is common. Regardless of the convention that influences adolescent girls, pregnancy during the teenage years carries certain risks. For example, girls who marry young often have little say in fertility-related decisions and limited opportunity to obtain education or job-related skills. Unmarried women who become pregnant may have to decide whether to obtain an abortion or try to support their child out of wedlock. Both married and unmarried women are vulnerable to sexually transmitted diseases, and those who bear children very early or frequently risk impairing their health. Early marriage and, especially, childbearing can have a profound and long-lasting impact on a woman's well-being, education, and ability to contribute to her community.

The timing of a first union is strongly associated with a woman's educational attainment. In much of sub-Saharan Africa, Latin America, and the Caribbean, rates of early marriage among women with less than a basic education are roughly three times those among women with at least seven years of schooling. As access to education increases and the benefits of postponing childbearing have become more widely known, adolescent childbearing has declined in some countries where it once was common.

When examining teen pregnancy across 15 countries, it is clear that delaying marriage beyond adolescence has advantages for women but leaves them vulnerable to certain hazards as well. A woman who postpones marriage may be able to pursue her education further, may have a greater role in deciding when and whom she will marry, and may have more influence over what happens within her marriage and family. However, she also may become more likely to engage in premarital sexual behavior, which carries the risk of unintended pregnancy and infection with sexually transmitted diseases (STDs). When faced with an unintended pregnancy, a woman who is unmarried must decide whether to bear a child out of wedlock or to seek an abortion. In countries where induced abortion is illegal or not easily accessible, many women will resort to clandestine abortions, and many will die from botched abortions.

You will find that in most countries covered in these chapters adolescents who wish to use contraception face many obstacles when seeking a method. Teenagers who value birth control may not know where to obtain it. This is a greater problem in rural rather than in urban areas. Additionally, in some countries where sexual activity among unmarried adolescents is commonly viewed as wrong, immoral, against religious standards, or against the law, girls' and young women's access to contraceptive services is legally restricted. Despite their frequently low levels of contraceptive use, throughout the world teenagers today are more likely than those of the 1970s to be using a modern method of birth control. Increases in the use of contraceptives are most notable among married teenagers in the developed Asian countries. Prevalence has doubled or tripled in Indonesia, the Philippines, and Thailand, and it has increased tenfold in Bangladesh (Alan Guttmacher Institute, 1998).

HEALTH RISKS

The risks of early pregnancy are numerous. Every day at least 1,600 mothers die worldwide from complications of pregnancy or childbirth—the equivalent of four jumbo jets crashing every day with no survivors. At least 99% of maternal deaths take place in the developing world. Nearly half of all deliveries in developing countries take place without the help of a skilled professional. Less than one-third of new mothers get postnatal care, even though most maternal deaths occur soon after childbirth. And for each death between 30 and 100 more women suffer short- or long-term illnesses related to pregnancy and childbirth. Teenage girls by and large bear the burden: Eleven percent of all births (15 million a year) are to adolescent girls. Moreover, girls aged 15 to 19 are twice as likely to die from childbirth as women in their 20s. Girls under age 15 are five times more likely to die from childbirth (Alan Guttmacher Institute, 1998).

The toll on children from the death or illness of their mother is immense. In developing countries, a mother's death often means death for her infant. The children who survive their mother's death are up to 10 times more likely to die within two years than are children with two living parents. In addition, when mothers die in childbirth, their surviving children are less likely to attend school regularly, to complete their education, or to receive sufficient health care.

Adolescent girls also face a set of complex barriers to obtaining reproductive health care. In many countries, laws prohibit unmarried young people from receiving family planning information or services, and even where there are no such laws, health care providers often are judgmental about sexually active young women and deny them access to available services. Getting to and paying for services are beyond the reach of most adolescents.

Confidentiality is another barrier. In small villages, young women are often shy about seeking family planning services. They worry about the stigma to themselves and their families, should it become known that they are sexually active. This is the case despite the fact that a majority of women and men become sexually active by the age of 20—in developed and developing countries alike. Finally, most reproductive health services are designed for adult women only and often fail to meet adolescent girls' needs such as intensive case management, financial aid, and parental education.

Another threat to an adolescent's health lies in the decision to terminate an unwanted pregnancy by abortion. Where abortions are illegal or difficult to obtain, adolescents will seek out people who perform abortions clandestinely. Too often, these practitioners are unskilled and work in unsanitary conditions that can lead to serious complications, permanent injury or damage such as sterility, and even death.

There are cultural practices that are also associated with reproductive health risks among adolescents. In some societies, many girls undergo female genital mutilation, in which part or all of the genitalia is removed. Complications can occur from the cutting itself, and lifelong effects may include chronic pain during intercourse, recurrent pelvic infections, and difficult labor.

Finally, young people throughout the world experience sexual abuse, incest, and rape. In many regions, young people, particularly those who are poor or homeless and who lack the skills to compete for nonexploitative employment, are victims of sexual exploitation and work for the lowest of wages.

GENERAL SOLUTIONS

Most countries recognize the necessity and value of education for young women. In comparison with women who have had no formal education, women who have at least had a primary education delay marriage and childbearing by approximately 18 months. Girls with a secondary education postpone childbirth even longer. Education also contributes to the health of a woman's children and family and facilitates her use of information and services. Governments and other social institutions therefore must find new ways to enable families to enroll girls in school and to encourage young women to stay in school and complete their basic education.

Pragmatic, straightforward sexuality education has reduced teen pregnancy and STDs in western Europe. Countries such as France, Germany, and Sweden have responded with strong sexuality education programs and adolescent contraceptive services, coupled with mandatory confidentiality. Due in part to public and political resistance to such measures, the United States lags behind other developed countries in the extent to which teenage fertility has declined.

Young children and teenagers often learn about sexual matters from peers, siblings, parents, and the media, but the information they obtain through these channels is usually limited and may be erroneous. Formal instruction, tailored to the age and background of the youth involved, is an important source of accurate information about sexuality, pregnancy, childbearing, contraception, and STD prevention. Formalized curricula are common in developed countries. Sexuality education is much less prevalent in developing countries and typically is not implemented at the national level. Furthermore, given the short duration of schooling common in many countries, and the high dropout rates among disadvantaged adolescents, community-based educational programs are a necessary supplement to school initiatives.

Comprehensive sexuality education programs not only cover biological facts but also provide young people with practical information and skills regarding dating, sexual relationships, and contraceptive use. Although programs often encounter religious or political opposition, most studies show that they do not encourage sexual activity; rather, they are associated with the postponement of first sex and, among young people who are sexually active, with the use of contraceptives.

In many developing countries, services for pregnant and parenting women of any age are inadequate. Adolescents in particular, however, need to be informed about the importance of prenatal care, and services need to be made accessible to them. They also need social support during pregnancy and after giving birth. They need support and health care for themselves and their infants. Teenage mothers may require breast-feeding instruction, advice about nutrition, or information about immunizations. Many will need contraceptive counseling and services to help them delay their next pregnancy.

Some young women who experience an unwanted pregnancy will seek an abortion, whether or not it is legally available. In countries where it is, services must be financially and geographically accessible to all young people. Postabortion care should include contraceptive counseling to help women avoid another unwanted pregnancy.

Today's adolescents are the next generation of parents, workers, and leaders. To fill these roles to the best of their ability, they need the guidance and support of their families and their communities. Moreover, they need a government committed to their development and well-being.

REFERENCES

Alan Guttmacher Institute. (1998). *Into a new world: Young women's sexual and reproductive lives.* New York: Author.

BBC. (1999, June 11). Published at 16:03 GMT; 17:03 UK.

Save the Children. (1999). Retrieved August 19, 2000, from the World Wide Web: http://www.savethechildren.org.

1

BRAZIL

Andrew L. Cherry

PROFILE OF BRAZIL

Brazil is the largest country in South America. It covers almost half of the South American continent. It stretches from north of the equator to south of the Tropic of Capricorn. The country covers a total of 8,550,000 square kilometers (3,300,000 square miles). Brazil has three primary geographic areas: the Brazilian Highlands, a vast highland region in the southeast; the Amazon River Basin with its lowlands, forests, floodplains, and swamps; and the Guiana Highlands in the far northeast and northwest.

One of the great rivers of the world, the Amazon River is almost entirely within Brazil. Oceangoing ships can navigate the Amazon for 3,700 kilometers (2,300 miles) inland. The Atlantic coastline of Brazil is a narrow strip with a backdrop of beautiful mountains (Hudson, 1998).

Although Brazil is becoming a major economic power, social conditions for the rural and urban poor remain primitive. The government and social service providers recognize the existence of a number of serious social problems such as domestic violence, street children, child abuse, and husbands murdering wives and girlfriends. Teenage pregnancy is also a serious problem. To date, federal funding has not provided for any substantial programming to prevent teenage pregnancy (Gatti, 1999a).

Teenage pregnancy is not unique to the people of Brazil. Teenage motherhood is a global problem. The number of teenage pregnancies in Brazil is similar to most other Central and South American nations. The birthrate in South America varies between a low of 56 per 1,000 teens (girls between

15 and 19 years of age) in Chile to a high of 101 per 1,000 in Venezuela. In Central America the teen pregnancy rate varies from a low of 91 per 1,000 in Panama to a high of 149 per 1,000 in Nicaragua (Gatti, 1999b).

Brazil's birthrate of 72 per 1,000 is better understood in relationship to other countries around the world. In North America, the teen birthrate is 60 per 1,000 teenage girls. Around the world, teen birthrates vary between a low of 29 per 1,000 in Europe, and 58 per 1,000 in Asia, to a high of 130 per 1,000 in Africa.

To better understand teen pregnancy in Brazil, it helps to know that Brazil was a Portuguese colony from 1500 to 1822, and Portuguese is still the official language of Brazil. Descendants of the Portuguese and other Europeans make up approximately 54% of the population. Those of African-European and European–Native American ancestry make up approximately 39%. The remaining 7% are African–Native American, Asian, and Native Americans (Skidmore, 1999).

Before 1960, most people lived in rural areas, especially in the northeast. By 1997, an estimated 80% of Brazil's population, approximately 130 million people, lived in urban areas.

The capital, located near the center of the country, is Brasília. The largest city in Brazil is São Paulo. Probably, its most famous city is the former capital, Rio de Janeiro, which is the second largest city (Hudson, 1998).

The government is a struggling democracy. However, the military retains the right to "preserve the state of Brazil." In the past, this has meant a military coup d'état—a process made easier because many of the military leaders were trained in the tactics of insurrection at the School of the Americas at Fort Benning, Georgia (Page, 1995).

Brazil has a rapidly growing economy. As the 21st century begins, it has the largest economy in Latin America. It is also the most industrialized country in South America. In 1990, Brazil's gross domestic product (GDP) (The GDP measures the value of all goods and services produced in a country; it is calculated by adding personal spending, government spending, investment, and net exports—exports minus imports) reached $438.8 billion (U.S. dollars). By 1997 the GDP had almost doubled at $820.4 billion, or approximately $5,000 per person (Hudson, 1998). The *real* is the Brazilian form of currency. About 8% of the country's income is from farming, forestry, and fishing. Industry accounts for 35%, and the service sector accounts for 57% of the country's income.

Despite the economic growth, the gap between the rich and the poor is one of the largest in the world. In 1995, 20% of the wealthiest people in Brazil controlled 64% of the wealth, whereas the poorest 20% of the people shared 2.2% of the wealth (Hudson, 1998).

Brazil, like other developing countries, is in many ways crippled under heavy foreign debt. Owing to corruption within Brazil, Brazil is perpetually faced with financial disaster and runaway inflation (Haber, 1997).

Defense spending in 1998 was 3.1% of government expenditures, which was a decrease from 4% when the country was under the military government. Military service is compulsory. Men between the ages of 18 and 45 are required to serve from 12 to 18 months in the military.

Life expectancy rose from 57 years in 1960 to an average of 64 years in 1998. The average life span for men was 59 years, and for women, 69.6 years. Women living 7 years longer than men means women make up a majority of Brazil's elderly.

There was a 40% drop in infant mortality between 1970 (95 deaths per 1,000) and 1998 (37 deaths per 1,000).

Similar to many developing countries, parasitic diseases, gastric ailments, and malnutrition still threaten the poor and the young. Tropical diseases continue to take a toll, particularly in the poor regions of Brazil, as they do in many of the developing countries. These tropical diseases include malaria, yellow fever, Chagas' disease, hookworm, and schistosomiasis (Page, 1995).

Roman Catholicism is the principal religion in the country, with 72% of the population. Another 22% identify themselves as members of Protestant churches. Traditional African beliefs brought by slaves and blended with Catholicism have created Afro-Brazilian cults such as Macumba, Candomblé, and Umbanda (Page, 1995).

The official connection with the Roman Catholic Church ended in the late 19th century. However, the Catholic Church continues to influence affairs of state. Traditionally the Catholic Church has been a conservative force. More recently a "liberation theology" has developed among some of the Catholic clergy. This religious philosophy tends to support equal justice for the poor and disadvantaged (Hudson, 1998).

The last major educational reform in Brazil was in 1998. This legislation provides for a primary education of eight years, which is compulsory and free for children between 7 and 14 years of age. Secondary education is an additional four years. Postsecondary education may take the form of continued training for employment or higher education. However, low federal spending for education has left schools underfunded in poor areas. Almost all children attend school between 7 and 14 years of age. However, only about 50% attend secondary school. Some 57% of secondary school students are female. Thus, there is a great deal of variation between the educational experience and opportunity of urban and rural children and children in different social and economic classes (Hudson, 1998).

In 1950, about 50% of the population over 15 years of age were considered literate. Because of a literacy campaign that began in 1971, the 1998 level of literacy was 83%. The highest rate of illiteracy, which is about 40%, is found in the rural, poor northeastern region (Hudson, 1998).

INTRODUCTION

The story of teenage pregnancy in Brazil must be told from two different perspectives. One story is that of teenage girls from the growing middle and upper class, typically girls of European descent. The other story is that of poor adolescent girls, typically rural American Indian and girls of African descent who live in northeastern Brazil. For the most part, teenage girls from these two groups who become pregnant have vastly different experiences. As well, most likely, their future and the future of their child will also be worlds apart from that of middle-class teen moms and their babies.

The consequences of adolescent girls becoming pregnant in Brazil are well documented. If a young mother has to leave school, as 40% of Brazilian teenage girls do who become pregnant, to get married or to work, she will miss important educational opportunities that could benefit her and her child (Buckley, 2000).

Teenage pregnancy in Brazil is also associated with higher rates of maternal morbidity and mortality as well as greater risks for clandestine abortion, delivery complications, and low-birth-weight infants (Gupta & Leite, 1999).

While fertility rates in Brazil have declined a great deal since the 1970s (total fertility rates dropped from 5.8 to 2.5 lifetime births per woman between 1970 and 1996), much of the decline was among women in the middle of their reproductive years. Among 15- to 19-year-old girls, the total fertility rate has increased. This increase is especially acute in the northeast region of Brazil (Buckley, 2000). By 1998, 25.27% of all live births were to girls between 15 and 19 years of age. In 1985, it was 12%. Girls between 10 and 14 accounted for 1.23% of live births. The number of births among girls aged 10 through 19 rose from 565,000 in 1993 to 698,000 in 1998, the latest year for which statistics were available. For 14.3% of these older teenage girls, it was their second child (Osava, 1998a).

Teenage pregnancy in Brazil occurs in a context where religion, culture, class, family planning, and television play a major role, either reducing teenage pregnancy or causing it to increase. While some blame adolescent girls, others are asking questions: What kind of message does *Carnaval*, the annual feast of Brazilian sensual indulgence, send to teenagers? How does Brazil's well-earned reputation for its laid-back ideas on sexual freedom affect teens? What is the impact of easy access to pornography? Does television nudity make a difference? What is the affect on teenagers when TV stars who are not married become pregnant? These are questions being debated among politicians, social workers, and health officials in Brazil (Buckley, 2000). However, there is no debate and general alarm among the public about the astonishing increase in single teenage mothers that have one and sometimes two children.

Vignette

Teresa

Teresa was a child herself when she gave birth at 14 years of age. She said she and her boyfriend, who was a year older, used condoms, although they sometimes forgot. Being a petite girl, when she held her one-year-old son, she looked more like his sister than his mother.

Teresa was afraid to tell her parents about the pregnancy, but after the "shock wore off," her parents were resolute. Abortion was not acceptable for their first grandchild.

Teresa lives with her father, a business executive, and her mother, a teacher. Her boyfriend, who lives nearby, is also from a middle-class family. He attends school and helps with their son.

Teresa is also attending school. The private school she attends is affiliated with the Methodist Church. The school accommodates both the mother/ student and her baby. The school also allowed her to study and take exams at home before and after the delivery of the baby. Now she takes her son to a day-care center at the school. At specific times, she leaves her classes to take care of her child.

Teresa's experience is more common among the middle class. It is the exception among the poor. Among all teen moms, 80% drop out of school, and most never return.

For the poor adolescent girl, early pregnancy contributes to greater impoverishment, child abandonment, and domestic violence. A percentage of teenage pregnancies among the poor are due to rape.

Carmen

Carmen was 12 when she began having sex with her boyfriend. She said she knew more about how to have sex than she did about not having a baby. Within six months, she was pregnant. She had her second child at 15. She became involved with an older married man whom she thought was going to marry her. She said both children were an accident. She said, after her first child, she never thought she would get pregnant again.

Carmen lives with her mother and two younger brothers in a small, cramped two-room apartment in one of Rio de Janeiro's largest and most impoverished slums. Her mother works at a hotel on the beach as a house cleaner.

She said she wished she had not left school after the birth of her first child, but she said it was impossible to go to school and take care of her baby. She had no one at home who could care for the baby while she was in school.

Carmen still has hope that things will be better for her and her children. When her second child is a little older, she hopes to enroll in a government program designed to help teenage mothers earn their high school diplomas. The program will pay her about $75 a month. The father of her second child helps some, but she has no source of income or job prospects.

Overview of Teen Pregnancy

Teenagers and preteenagers in Brazil gave birth to 900,000 babies in 1997, accounting for 26.5% of all live births in the country. Between 1993 and 1997, the number of births in public hospitals and clinics fell from 2.9 million to 2.7 million, but the percentage among adolescent girls increased from 22.3 to 26.5. These numbers were reported by the National Health System, which keeps tracks of about 80% of all births in Brazil. By 1999, 50% of teenage girls who became pregnant in Brazil had their first child by the time they were 16 (Osava, 1998c).

There may be no consensus as to the cause of the increase in the number of adolescent pregnancies, but health officials and social workers agree that teenagers today are much more sophisticated sexually than ever before. In the early 1990s, most teens said their first sexual experience came at age 15 or 16.

By 1996, however, over 20% of girls in urban settings were reporting that they had their first sexual experience between 10 and 14 years of age. With the increase in the number of preteens and young teens becoming sexually active, social workers and counselors point out that providing effective contraceptive education to 10-, 11- and 12-year-old girls and boys is extremely difficult. They typically do not have the discipline needed for most contraceptive methods to work (to avoid pregnancy).

"Most of the questions that children and teenagers asked in the past," said Albertina Duarte, an expert on adolescent sexuality, "were, 'How was I born? At what age can I start a relationship?' Today the children ask: 'How do I know I'm giving the girl pleasure?' " (Buckley, 2000, p. A13).

Teenage Sexuality

Brazil, the Dominican Republic, and Guatemala are the Latin American countries that report the earliest sexual initiation of girls without the use of contraceptives, according to a UNICEF (United Nation Children's Fund) report (Osava, 1998c). Even though 72% of sexually active adolescent girls reported in 1996 that they had used contraceptives, a major increase from the rate 10 years earlier (55%), teen pregnancy has risen dramatically and its social impact is a major concern.

In part, the phenomenon of both boys and girls becoming sexually active at a younger age is worldwide. Table 1.1 compares the number of Brazil's sexually active teenage males with the number of sexually active male teens from other countries around the world.

Table 1.1
Percentage of Adolescent Males Ages 10 to 19 Who Are
Sexually Active

Country	% Sexually Active	Partners per Year
Brazil	61	2.6
Kenya	54	1.6
Tanzania	37	2.5
Thailand	29	3.8

Source: Data from Alan Guttmacher Institute, 1998.

Births to Teens in the Northeastern and Southeastern Regions

Having children at an early age is traditional among indigenous and rural people of Brazil. However, since the 1970s an increasing number of adolescent girls who live in urban areas, whether they are upper class or poor, have been choosing to delay pregnancy for a longer period of time than adolescent girls living in the rural regions of the country. Most often, urban girls want to continue school or seek employment.

The 45.5 million people in northeastern Brazil represent 29% of the country's population and 46% of all rural residents. The average head of a household in the northeastern region earns half as much as his or her counterpart in the southeastern region (Gupta & Leite, 1999). This is one of Brazil's poorest regions, exhibiting some of the lowest socioeconomic indicators: The infant mortality rate is nearly twice the national average (74 infant deaths per 1,000 live births, compared with 39 per 1,000 nationally). This region continues to have the highest birthrates in Brazil. At the same time, women of the northeast have also had the fastest decline in births per woman over the last 10 years, dropping 40%. Births per woman have dropped from 5.2 lifetime births per woman in 1986 to 3.1 per woman in 1996 (Gupta & Leite, 1999).

The nonwhite population is larger in the northeast than in the rest of the country: Some three-quarters of adolescents in the northeast are nonwhite, compared with just over half in the southeast. This substantial socioeconomic inequality between races in Brazil may be an important factor associated with access to reproductive health care for adolescents. In the northeast, for instance, 51% of the girls reported that their last birth was unplanned. This was an increase of 40% since 1986. In 1998, nearly 17% of all female adolescents had given birth in the northeast, compared with 12% in the southeast (Page, 1995).

The Correlation between Education and Fertility

One of the most consistent findings of analyses of fertility behavior in developing countries, including Brazil, is a strong correlation between the level of a woman's education and the number of children she births.

In the northeastern region, education has also been observed to be one of the most effective ways to reduce the number of children born to each woman. In this region, it was found that 54% of young illiterate women become mothers in their teens. Among girls with at least three years of schooling, 29% become teen moms. Of girls with nine or more years of education, only 4% become teen moms (Gupta & Leite, 1999).

HISTORY AND SOCIAL CONTEXT

Many of the social problems that the people of Brazil grapple with today began in the past. After the Portuguese took possession of what is now Brazil, the colony developed a colonial culture (where a few ruled the many) and forged a prosperous plantation economy. This past has left a small and wealthy elite, descendants of the European settlers, who still control the government and most of the resources and land. This past continues to hinder Brazil's transition from an agrarian society to a modern, urban, industrial society (Skidmore, 1999).

The human suffering that has resulted from this cultural, social, and economic transition runs the gamut. There are millions of landless rural workers. The nation's prisons are dangerously overcrowded. Discrimination and racism are pervasive. Poverty is destroying families, and generations of children of the rural and urban poor are being lost. Domestic violence and men murdering their wives occur far too often. Almost a million babies a year are born to teenagers. And there are thousands of abandoned and runaway children living in the streets of Brazil's largest cities (Gutierrez, 1998).

In situations where there are overwhelming social needs, teen pregnancy prevention programs vie for the attention and the limited resources available for children and adolescent programming. Because of these needs, there has been little government support or resources made available for prevention programs aimed at reducing teen pregnancy.

Most political leaders realize that teen pregnancy prevention programs are needed, and they realize that teenage pregnancy contributes to other family and children problems and to the number of street children in Brazil. However, other problems are also being neglected.

Thousands of unaccompanied children wander the streets of Brazil's cities during the day and sleep in the alleys, in the doorways of churches, and in the slums through the night. These are children who have fled poverty, physical or sexual abuse, or were abandoned. Among these children, approximately 26% left home to avoid domestic violence, 25% left because of constant fighting, and 20% left to earn a living (Osava, 1998c).

There are children as young as six years of age trying to live on the street. The street is a violent world where the police assault the children, steal what the children have stolen, and even kill them. Street children also meet with beatings and death threats from vigilante groups that call their violent attacks on street children "social cleansing" (Brennan, 1999).

Street children often find it necessary to steal, but most want to work, and most do work. However, all too often, the work they find is dangerous and low paying, and they may work up to 60 hours a week. Others, both boys and girls, become involved in prostitution.

Drug use is also out of control among the street children. One study reported that 90% of the homeless children in six of Brazil's largest cities have used drugs, and 48% use them daily.

The most commonly abused drug is glue. The vapors of the glue are "sniffed" (inhaled) to get high. Glue does a great deal of damage to the cortex of the brain and other internal organs. Adult drug dealers buy glue in large quantities and break it down into small packets that they sell to the street children (Gutierrez, 1998).

For many street children life is not only horrible but often short. Murder has become the primary cause of death among children 10 to 14 years of age. Of the 359 children 10 to 14 years old that died in São Paulo in 1998, 17.3% were victims of homicide, and 17% were victims of traffic accidents.

One of the saddest examples of police murdering street children was the "Candelaria massacre." On July 23, 1993, while street children slept on the steps of the Candelaria cathedral, a death squad that targeted street children, most of them military police officers, killed eight street children and wounded several others. Some, but not all, of the military police involved were convicted and sent to prison (Brennan, 1999).

There is also domestic violence. In Brazil, the greatest risk of violence that women and children face is not in the streets but in the home. Child abuse, child sexual abuse, and husbands murdering wives and girlfriends is all too common in Brazil. According to a study conducted by the National Human Rights Movement (MNDH), over 66% of men accused of murdering a woman in 1995 and 1996 were husbands or companions of the victim. It is still possible in Brazil for a man to kill his allegedly unfaithful wife and be found *not* guilty on the basis of the "honor defense." Particularly in Brazil's interior, the honor defense may be successful in as many as 80% of the cases in which it is used (Osava, 1998c).

Statistics on other types of domestic violence are typically unreliable and generally underestimated. Nevertheless, the women's divisions of police precincts—a successful initiative that began in 1990—logged 220,000 complaints of domestic violence in 1999.

Domestic violence is not expected to subside. Brazil's judicial system lacks laws designed to deal with domestic violence. It is not that laws have not been proposed; to date, the laws have not had enough support from members of Congress to become law.

Children fare no better than their mothers. A 1998 study reported that 64% of Brazil's children who experience physical abuse were harmed by parents or other relatives. In cases of sexual abuse, 75% of the children were sexually abused by parents or other relatives (Linhares, 1995).

Poverty also impacts the teenager population. Teenage girls from impoverished families with little education disproportionately become teenage moms. There are 10 times more births among poor adolescent than upper-class teens. Among young illiterate women, 54% became mothers in their teens. About 29% of those with three years of school were teen moms. Only 4% of those with nine or more years of education were teen moms (Osava, 1998b).

TEEN PREGNANCY TODAY

Political Views and Public Policies

The Brazilian government has continually failed to develop formal population control policies, and it has not implemented a national family planning program. Toward the end of the 20th century certain family planning–related services were incorporated into Brazil's maternal and child health program, but no formal family planning agency was established at the national level by the government. Even so, in 1996, more than two-thirds of adolescents in the northeastern region who were using a form of birth control relied on the private sector for family planning services (Gupta & Leite, 1999).

The government efforts and hopes for reducing teenage pregnancy and sexually transmitted diseases among teens are concentrated on promoting the use of contraceptives. Television commercials urge teens to use condoms. Neighborhood clinics distribute free birth-control pills, condoms, and other contraceptive devices. At the local level, numerous cities have also created programs to reduce the number of pregnancies and cases of sexually transmitted diseases among teens. These efforts have had some impact. Among sexually experienced adolescents, the pill is the most prevalent method of contraception (27%), followed by the condom (10%).

Despite these relatively high levels of contraceptive use, an unmet demand for family planning services persists. Data collected in 1996 suggest that over 50% of all teenage births were unplanned.

Abortion is an option for some pregnant teenagers. While abortion is illegal in Brazil except in cases of rape or when the pregnancy endangers the life of the woman, clandestine abortions are believed to be widespread, especially among young and low-income women. In fact, abortion is as common in Brazil as in nations where abortion is legal (see Table 1.2).

Table 1.2
**Annual Number of Abortions per
1,000 Girls Ages 15 through 19**

United States	36
Dominican Republic	36
Brazil	*32*
Colombia	26
Peru	23
Britain	19
Japan	6

Source: Data from Singh & Darroch, 2000.

Over the years, Brazil has done little to improve reproductive health services, despite being a signator of the United Nations' Conference on Population and Development held in Cairo in 1994, which passed a resolution that stated reproductive health services are a fundamental right for women (Osava, 1998a).

Social Views, Customs, and Practices

Two social customs clearly contribute to teenage pregnancy: the *ficar* and the influence of the *parentela*.

Ficar

One phenomenon students struggle with is the *ficar*, a long-standing custom among Brazil's adolescents. Typically used as a verb, in Portuguese the word means "to stay." The *ficar* is a time-honored dating tradition. It involves staying with someone for one or two days. Traditionally, it involves hugging and kissing but no sexual relations. Today, students and counselors say, these quickie relationships often include more than hugging and kissing; they often include sexual activity.

A *ficar* can start anywhere—at a party, between classes, on the street. Some surveys estimate that 66% of students have participated in a *ficar*. Some students report being involved in several *ficars* a year.

For the most part, boys control the *ficars*. If a girl wants the young man to wear a condom and he says no, too often the girl gives in (Buckley, 2000).

Parentela

The *parentela* (a kinship system) is another social custom that supports early childbearing by reducing the possibility of abortion and adoption outside the extended family. Historically Brazilian society has been patriarchal, with a strong tradition of male social dominance. While male dominance has been weakened by the expansion of urban employment opportunities for women, immigration, feminism, and the decline of the rural sector, the male-headed family (the *parentela*) is still the crucial social unit. The *parentela*, a kind of kinship system, involves close family and distant relatives, godparents and godchildren, and even family servants. *Parentelas* are generally stronger among the middle and upper classes (Page, 1995).

THE FUTURE OF TEEN PREGNANCY

There is a steady rise in the number of informal partnerships documented in Latin America and the Caribbean by UN population scientists. Fewer parents are raising their children within the institution of marriage. Since the 1980s, the number of adult women who are remaining outside the formal institution of marriage has continued to increase.

CONCLUSION

The 21st century finds Brazilian teenagers sexually active at an unprecedented level. Similar to other South American countries, social change has caused social upheaval for the large population of rural and urban poor. Although the debate over the best approach to reducing teen births and to pay for such programs continues, little else is being done by the government because teen pregnancy has a low priority.

In spite of the fact that little is being done by the government, Brazilian policymakers do agree that to reduce the number of pregnancies among teenage girls it is necessary to better understand the reproductive attitudes, behaviors, and interaction that takes place between teenage girls and boys. With this information, it may be possible to develop educational programs that are culturally appropriate and designed to reduce teenage sexual activity and childbearing.

Education and job opportunities for girls and women are also essential components for reducing the number of teenage pregnancies in Brazil. It is a tried and tested approach. And in some regions and urban areas Brazilian women are finding new opportunities. These opportunities are effectively delaying teenage childbearing. At the dawn of the new millennium, Brazilian women already have a statistical advantage over males. Girls and young women are staying in school longer and getting a better education than males. Women are also living five to seven years longer. However, men continue to dominate in the family, in the community, and in the government.

Teenage pregnancy is predominantly a problem among poor rural and urban families who are of Native American or African descent. It also pretty much ensures that these teenage mothers will drop out of school, probably have health problems (either the mother or the child), work at menial jobs or turn to prostitution, have several other children, and remain poor for the rest of their lives. Their children will probably fare no better.

REFERENCES

Alan Guttmacher Institute. (1998). *Into a new world: Young women's sexual and reproductive lives.* New York: Author.

Brennan, D. (1999, September 14). Law: What they need is a lawyer. *The Independent*, p. 14.

Buckley, S. (2000, January 13). Brazil soberly examines soaring teen birthrate. *Washington Post Foreign Service*, p. A13.

Gatti, D. (1999a, April 14). Children—Latin American: Child exploitation cuts across class divisions. *Inter Press Service English News Wire.*

Gatti, D. (1999b, September 2). Population—Latin America: UNFPA highlights new trends. *Inter Press Service English News Wire.*

Gupta, N., & Leite, C. (1999). Adolescent fertility behavior: Trends and determinants in northeastern Brazil. *International Family Planning Perspectives, 25*(3), 125–130.

Gutierrez, E. (1998, July 14). Children—Venezuela: "Glue sniffers" at the core of a dilemma. *Inter Press Service English News Wire.* (Montevideo)

Haber, S. (1997). *How Latin America fell behind: Essays on the economic histories of Brazil and Mexico, 1800–1914.* Stanford: Stanford University Press.

Hudson, R.A. (Ed.). (1998). *Brazil, a country study.* Washington, DC: Library of Congress, Federal Research Division.

Linhares, L. (1995, July 17). Violence against women in Brazil. Telephone interview. Human Rights Watch, 350 Fifth Avenue, 34th Floor, New York, NY.

Osava, M. (1998a, February 23. Population—health: Increase in teenaged mothers in Brazil. *Inter Press Service English News Wire* (Rio de Janeiro).

Osava, M. (1998b, July 23). Rights—Brazil: Home—not always so sweet for women and children. *Inter Press Service English News Wire.*

Osava, M. (1998c, August 5). Population—Brazil: 900,000 babies born to teenagers every year. *Inter Press Service English News Wire* (Rio de Janeiro).

Page, J.A. (1995). *The Brazilians.* New York: Addison-Wesley.

Singh, S., & Darroch, J.E. (2000). Adolescent pregnancy and childbearing: Levels and trends in developed countries. *Family Planning Perspectives, 32*(1), 14–23.

Skidmore, T.E. (1999). *Brazil: Five centuries of change.* New York: Oxford University Press.

2

CANADA

Mary E. Dillon

PROFILE OF CANADA

Canadian climate is similar to that of the northern United States. Yet it varies from region to region. Owing to its northern location, Canada has a generally cool to cold climate. Canada is a water-rich nation with 9% of the earth's renewable fresh water. Canada is the world's second largest country, only being surpassed by the Russian Federation. It is the largest in the Western Hemisphere. The 1997 population was slightly more than 30 million, with men outnumbering women until the age of 60 and older. The current life expectancy in Canada is 75 years for males and 81 for females. The country's leading cause of death is cancer, followed by diseases of the heart and cerebrovascular diseases.

In 1996, almost 19 million Canadian citizens spoke English, whereas over 6.5 million spoke French. Over 100,000 Canadians spoke both of these languages. All other languages spoken were significantly lower, with Chinese being the most common nonofficial language. In 1991, 45.7% of Canadians were Roman Catholic, and 36.2% were Protestant.

The country's political system has elements from both Britain and the United States. However, it is first a constitutional monarchy, with Elizabeth II, of the United Kingdom, as queen. She appoints a governor general to represent her with the recommendation of Canada's prime minister. This prime minister is the leader of the majority party in the House of Commons. Parliament consists of the Senate, with 104 members appointed by the governor general, and a House of Commons, with 295 members elected by the people.

INTRODUCTION

Many Canadians resent living in the shadow of an economic juggernaut such as the United States. Yet in terms of health care and social services, U.S. citizens live in the shadow of the kinder, gentler Canada. The more "human-friendly" Canadian health care and social services system produces better results in teenage pregnancy rates and outcomes than their neighbor to the south, the United States. Examining the differences between these very prosperous countries can help one better understand the impact of different policies, attitudes, and approaches to teen pregnancy worldwide.

Vignette

One of the legacies of the highly sexed 1970s era, which included an unprecedented explosion in club culture, was sexually transmitted diseases. Despite those hard lessons and years of education emphasizing abstinence or safer sex and condom use, many youth engaged in risky, unprotected sex into the 1990s.

Today "Candy stores" (nightclubs) for teens are busiest at night. One example is Toronto at night when "Candyland" comes to life, with pickup lines, vinyl miniskirts, and eager hands that grab all they can. Candyland attracts the beautiful, the bountiful, and the desperate. In the nightclub atmosphere of billowing fog, deafening music, and sweat-slathered, boozed-up bodies, everything is for sale.

The thousands who hit dozens of Toronto clubs every weekend are not there simply to listen to loud music. And although many will deny it, meeting men or women, and the quest for the "score," is the engine that drives the nightclub scene.

One young man stated, "I worry about HIV/AIDS [human immuno-deficiency virus/acquired immunodeficiency syndrome] during the day, but at night after a few drinks I forget or I'm not prepared." This cavalier attitude about unsafe sex among young adults is obvious and frightening. A few years ago, the average age in North America of initial infection rate from HIV was 32 years old. However, that rate fell to 23 years of age by the end of the 20th century.

In spite of these statistics, four modest-looking girls from a remote Manitoba province showed up on Toronto's night scene. They were dressed in cotton shirts and looked more naive than sleazy. They wanted to experience the nightlife in the Great White North city of Toronto. The mystery fades for the group from Manitoba. As night turns into early morning, they begin to attract a crowd of gyrating, admiring men.

One of the four is Anita Glemaud, a 16-year-old who lives in Manitoba with her parents. While making friends, she is taken by this "free-spirit" attitude of the club dwellers that she never experienced in her community. To Anita, this weekend away from her parents was an experience she could only imagine.

At one club, Anita started dancing with a man she had met a couple hours earlier. He knew the girl from rural Manitoba had come to the big city for a good time. He was enjoying the girl who was willingly coming on to his advances. He was swinging her around the floor, never separating his lips from her face. Sexual urges, according to Anita, directed her to a motel room with this man from the "big city." Anita figured that she would have a one-night stand and never see him again. Thus Anita rationalized, "People will tell you they just want to dance, but we all have urges. And if you feel like it's the right thing, the right chemistry, I say, 'Why not go for it?' "

Unfortunately, for 16-year-old Anita, she learned a couple of months later that she was pregnant. She wanted an abortion but felt torn between her religious upbringing and the reality she faced. Anita was afraid that she and her baby would be HIV-positive. Unbeknownst to her family, Anita opted for an abortion. Whether the child was HIV-positive or not, she would never know. To this date, Anita takes periodic blood tests to check her HIV status.

Overview of Teen Pregnancy

Wadhera and Millar (1997) found Canada's adolescent pregnancy rates somewhere in the middle of 13 comparable countries: Japan and all the Scandinavian countries had lower rates. Iceland, England and Wales, and New Zealand were slightly higher but comparable to Canada. Hungary and Czechoslovakia were significantly higher. The United States and Russia topped the list in the developed countries of the world.

There are fewer teenage pregnancies and a lower rate of teen pregnancies now than in 1974. The teenage pregnancy rate in Canada was at its highest in 1974 (54 per 1,000), then declined until reaching its lowest point in 1987 (41.1 per 1000). The rate then rose gradually until it hit 48.1 in 1992 and has been fluctuating since then. The rate in 1995 was 47 pregnancies per 1,000 for women aged 15 to 19. Just over half of teen pregnancies in Canada resulted in live births in 1994, compared to about two-thirds in 1974. About 19% of teenage women who gave birth in 1994 were married, compared to 75% in 1974 (Wadhera & Millar, 1997).

In 1996, Canada had 21,597 live births to mothers aged 15 to 19 years of age. This is a rate of 22.1 births per 1,000 girls aged 15 to 19 years (Health Canada, 1999). Additionally, 227 babies were born to mothers aged 10 to 14 years of age. Over the past two decades, there has been a decline in the live-birth rate for teens aged 15 to 19 years; these live-birth rates range from 35.6 per 1,000 in 1974 to 22.1 per 1,000 in 1996. With the

Figure 2.1
Teen Pregnancy Outcomes per 1,000 Girls Ages 15 to 19: Canada, 1974–1998

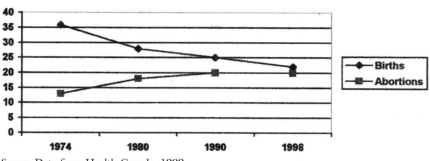

Source: Data from Health Canada, 1999.

exception of the 1987–1992 period, the rate of live births to women aged 15 to 19 years has been declining since 1974. Interestingly, during this same period, the number of induced abortions in this age group has increased and continues to rise. This may somewhat explain the noticeable decline in the number of live births. Figure 2.1 shows the Canadian rate of live births to teenage mothers from 1974 until 1998. The available time trend in rates of induced abortions in this age group is also included.

In comparing trends in birthrate between the United States and Canada, the United States rate is much higher at 54.4 per 1,000 teens. Rates of abortion in Canada are 21.2 per 1,000 compared to 29.2 per 1,000 in the United States. Teenage pregnancy in Canada is 45.4 per 1,000 versus 83.6 per 1,000 in the United States (Health Canada, 1999).

This increase in the abortion rate may suggest a failure to provide accessible, effective contraception for teenagers. Future efforts to prevent teen pregnancies must be accompanied by accurate tracking of all pregnancies and their outcomes in this particularly vulnerable age group. It is of utmost importance to Canadians to address the issue of teen pregnancy openly and to explore contraceptive availability and the risk factors that lead to sexually transmitted diseases (STDs) and HIV/AIDS infection.

The proportion of Canadian teenagers aged 15 to 19 who had sexual intercourse between 1990 and 1996 dropped by 12% for females to 51%, and it dropped 14% for males to 43% (Health Canada, 1999).

Canadian Health Care System

Canada's health care system is predominantly publicly funded and privately delivered. "Medicare" is a system of 10 provincial and two territorial health insurance plans interlocking to provide access to universal, comprehensive coverage for medically necessary hospital and inpatient/outpatient physician services. These services are provided to pregnant or parenting teen mothers in the same way they are provided to all women and mothers.

Private practitioners, who are providing the services, are generally paid on a fee-for-service basis, submitting their claims to the provincial health insurance plan. Canadians present a physician with the health insurance card issued to all eligible residents of a province. Citizens do not pay directly for insured hospital and physician services. They are not even required to fill out forms for these services. There are no deductibles, copayments, or dollar limits on coverage for insured services. This is particularly important to adolescents. This system provides adolescents with access to professional and confidential health care, consultation, and support. Canadians view health care as a basic right and highly value their system.

Provinces and territories also provide public coverage for other health services outside the framework of the national insurance. The elderly, children, and those on welfare are eligible under this plan. These supplementary health benefits often include prescription drugs, dental and vision care, assistive devices/equipment, and services of certain allied health professionals like chiropractors and podiatrists. Despite this, Canadians generally pay out of pocket for noninsured health benefits. Private insurance may be obtained to offset some portion of supplementary health services.

Health care is financed primarily through taxation. Provincial and federal, personal, and corporate taxes are used. In 1996, 9.5% of the gross domestic product was spent on health expenditures. This was down from a peak level in 1992 of 10.2% (Canada's Health System, 1998).

In 1984, the Parliament of Canada passed the Canada Health Act, which stipulates the criteria a provincial health insurance plan must meet in order to qualify for full federal transfer payments. The government recognizes a number of principles that are important to Canadians. These include:

- *Public administration.* A provincial health insurance must be operated nonprofit by a public authority accountable to the provincial government.
- *Comprehensiveness.* A plan must insure all medically necessary hospital and physician services.
- *Universality.* A plan must entitle 100% of the eligible residents to insured services.
- *Accessibility.* It must uniformly provide reasonable access to hospital and physicians without barriers, discrimination, and no additional charges for insured services.
- *Portability.* Residents are entitled to coverage when they move to another province or travel within the country or abroad. Limits are set on coverage for services outside of Canada.

Canada's health care system may be a reason why their teen pregnancy rate is lower than their neighbor to the south. Although no health care plan is perfect, it is easy to see why most Canadians highly value their system.

Teenage Pregnancy and Poverty in Canada

There is evidence that many Canadian teens who become parents are already economically and educationally disadvantaged before having children. Early childbearing often compounds these early disadvantages and makes it more difficult for young parents to keep pace with their peers who do not become parents in their teenage years. Adolescent mothers are less likely to complete their education and more likely to have limited career and economic opportunities (Health Canada, 1999).

Cost of Teen Pregnancy

Teen pregnancy creates a myriad of health complications for the girl and her baby. Individual Canadians, and society at large, pay a significant price for teenage sexual and reproductive health problems. For the adolescent, this includes the emotional cost of loss, pain, and disappointment; the economic costs of lost wages and benefits; and the financial cost of purchasing drugs and other uninsured treatments. Societal costs include the direct cost of health services, the cost of benefits paid to those who could have remained healthy and independent, the sick days that could have been avoided, and the loss of productivity of teens who are emotionally or physically distressed. Although care and support for those affected are essential, prevention clearly is preferable and cost-effective. A few examples illustrate this point (the figures below are in Canadian dollars):

- The average length of stay for a premature baby with complications is about 45 days. The cost of hospital care for these babies is about $650 to $700 per day (Health Canada, 1999).
- The total economic burden associated with the HIV/AIDS epidemic to date amounts to $36.3 billion ($6.4 billion in direct costs and $29.9 billion in indirect costs) (Health Canada, 1999).
- For every $1 spent on early detection and treatment of chlamydia and gonorrhea, it is estimated that $12 could be saved in associated costs.
- For every $1 spent on preventing teenage pregnancy, $10 could be saved on the cost of abortion services and short- and long-term costs of income maintenance.

In a country such as Canada, where the overall population is among the healthiest in the world, when compared to western Europe they still have high levels of teenage sexual and reproductive health problems. Prevention of these problems and effective care and support for the teens affected must be a priority when addressing policy issues.

The following are just a few of the issues that must addressed:

Sexually Transmitted Diseases. Over 33,000 cases of chlamydia and 4,000 cases of gonorrhea were reported in Canada in 1997. These were reported mostly by teenagers. Reported rates of chlamydia in adolescent girls were nine times the national rate. Untreated sexually transmitted diseases are estimated to account for 20% of all cases of infertility.

HIV/AIDS. Since the beginning of the epidemic to December 31, 1998, a total of 16,236 AIDS cases and 11,534 deaths due to AIDS had been reported in Canada. Heterosexual contact accounted for 6.2% of those HIV infected between 1985 and 1994; however, heterosexual contact in 1998 was responsible for 16% of new HIV cases.

Heterosexual contact is nearly three times more likely to lead to infection today than it was five to ten years ago. Overall, HIV infection among women is increasing, raising concerns about transmission to infants. Another significant trend is the increase of HIV among injection drug users. Injection drug use is a more common method of transmitting the virus for women than for men.

Historically, men have had a higher incidence of AIDS than women. However, for nearly a decade, the proportion of AIDS cases among women has been increasing. The same is true for HIV-positive test reports. In 1997, women accounted for 14% of annual AIDS diagnoses in Canada, up from 4% in 1990. In the first six months of 1998, 20% of HIV-positive test reports were among women, nearly double the rate of the period from 1985 to 1994 (Campbell, 1999).

Low-Birth-Weight Babies. Between 1985 and 1995, the number of babies born weighing less than 500 grams increased in number from 4.3 to 8.8 per 10,000. Low-birth-weight babies are more common among the youngest and oldest mothers than among those aged 25 to 34 (Health Canada, 1999). In urban Canada, the incidence of low-birth-weight babies and the infant mortality rate are relatively high in the lowest-income neighborhoods.

Canada's Most "At Risk" for Teenage Pregnancy

The social and economic consequences of teenage births are as important as the health implications. Previous studies suggest that teenage motherhood may result in a loss of educational and occupational opportunities and increase the likelihood of diminished socioeconomic status. Children living in poverty often do not see a future for themselves or a way out of their predicament. They have a tendency to model what they see at home, and if that means living in poverty, giving birth may seem like a rational option.

Although all Canadians are potentially at risk for some form of sexual or reproductive health problem, certain groups face particular challenges that limit their opportunities to achieve sexual and reproductive health. Those who have less power, who experience economic hardship, who have less access to information and services, and who live in marginalized circumstances tend to be most affected.

Perhaps the greatest challenge with sexual and reproductive health is the strong emotional response the topic elicits. Many people, especially adolescents, feel discomfort and embarrassment when dealing with a subject as value-laden and private as sexuality and sexual choices. As a result, finding a balance between differing views and sensitivities when developing public policies and initiatives has often proven to be difficult.

Although there is a growing understanding of the importance of comprehensive, integrated, and multisectoral efforts needed to prevent teen pregnancy, the policies, programs, and services in Canada do not yet reflect this understanding. Access to sexual and reproductive health services are not equally available to all who need them. Some Canadians have little or no access to key services owing to their socioeconomic status, age, abilities, geographic location, language, culture, or sexual orientation.

At the same time, sexual and reproductive health services are particularly vulnerable to reductions in health funding that can be made at all levels of government. This is at least partly due to a lack of knowledge among decision makers and the public about the consequences of teen pregnancies, low birth weight, sexually transmitted disease, and other related problems that impact Canadian society as a whole.

HISTORY AND SOCIAL CONTEXT

Up until the 1950s, the issue in Canada was not the age of the young mother-to-be. The issue was the girl's state of matrimony: Was she married? Historically, the fear was about her being an unwed mother and her child being identified on his or her birth certificate as a "bastard child."

Canada is also a sparsely populated country, outside of its major cities. This was particularly true when most of western Canada was considered a frontier. Life was hard in the west, and women tended to die young, often during childbirth. Females also tended to marry younger on the frontier.

The frontier mentality, British tradition, and American influences shape the public policy and response to teen pregnancy in Canada. When a young girl could not marry, there were the homes for unwed mothers. The number of out-of-wedlock births was viewed as a key indicator of social decay up until the 1970s. Slowly as girls began to postpone marriage until their late teens, the health issue around becoming pregnant too young was the focus of counselors and health officials. Sexuality education in all grades stresses health-related issues.

TEEN PREGNANCY TODAY

Political Views and Public Policies

The use of contraceptives appears to be declining in Canada. This should be a major concern for policymakers. Indeed, Canada now has one of the lowest levels of contraceptive use among all industrialized countries (see Table 2.1).

Table 2.1
Percentage Distribution of Respondents, by Current Contraceptive Use,
According to Sex

Status	1984 CFS Women (N=5,315)	1995 GSS	
		Women (N=3,220)	Men (N=3,449)
Using Reversible Method	35.6	32.1	35.1
Pill	19.2	16.9	9.1
Condom	6.2	9.5	22.4
IUD	5.7	2.6	1.3
Diaphragm	1.2	0.3	0.1
Foam	0.5	0.3	0.3
Rhythm	1.6	0.8	0.6
Withdrawal	0.8	0.5	0.1
Other	0.4	1.2	1.2
Using Nonreversible Methods	39.9	40.4	31.4
Female sterilization (tubal ligation)	24.2	17.3	10.6
Male sterilization (vasectomy)	8.7	10.6	13.1
Sterilized for medical reasons	7.0	12.5	7.7
Other	24.6	27.5	33.8
Pregnant	3.8	2.4	4.0
Using no contraceptive method	20.8	25.1	29.8
Total	100.1	100.0	99.7

Note: All percentages are weighted; all numbers are unweighted.

Source: Data from Canadian Fertility Survey (CFS), 1984; General Social Survey (GSS), 1995.

Prevalence of contraceptive use is even lower than in the United States. This may be surprising, given that Canada's universal health care system provides Canadians with free access to medical services, including contraceptive prescriptions and sterilization procedures.

Why Canada Lowered the Age of Consent

In 1987, the Canadian Parliament lowered the age of consent for heterosexual intercourse from 18 to 14 years of age. "Children are vulnerable to the advances of adults whether they are teens or not," says Kari Simpson, executive director of the Citizens Research Institute in Langley, British Columbia. "Continually lowering the age of consent makes them even more so. Why did they lower the age to 14? One excuse was that a girl could 'look older than she is.' Recently an 11-year-old girl gave birth. The 20-year-old father's defense, 'She looked much older.' "

Young girls impregnated by older men is a phenomenon noted by Canadian health care workers. Junior high school girls who become mothers are typically seven years younger on average than the men who father the child, whereas senior high girls are typically four years younger.

Men aged 20 to 29 fathered over 10,000 babies in 1994 by girls aged 15 to 19, compared to approximately 4,400 fathered by boys 19 or under. The father's average age was 22.6 where the mother's age was under 19 years of age. "Young girls," suggests Jim Sclater, Vancouver-based vice-president of public policy at Focus on the Family, "may be thinking it would be safer to have their first experience with an older, more experienced man—to say nothing of the interest of the older man involved" (Champion, 1996, p. 32). Others have pointed out that these teen girls "tend to have low self-esteem, and they may have lacked a loving father growing up; the girls could be seeking a strong father figure" (Champion, 1996, p. 32). Under these circumstances, males are then in a position to take advantage of their vulnerable partners. As moral and social barriers to personal freedom were dismantled, "predators were given easier access to the most vulnerable in our society" (Champion, 1996, p. 32). The age of consent in the United States ranges from 14 in Hawaii and Pennsylvania to 18 in other states; it is 16 in more than half of American states.

Contraceptive Use among Teens

Contraceptive use in Canada is unique. The decline in contraceptive use over the last decade has left Canada's overall contraceptive prevalence among the lowest in the industrialized world and the rate of sterilization among the highest. The rate of nonreversible methods of sterilization, such as tubal ligation, for women in Canada in 1995 was 40.4 per 1,000. These changes in contraceptive behavior complicate efforts to plan for social and health needs, particularly policy decisions focusing on reducing infections with STDs.

In 1984, 36% of women of childbearing age were using reversible contraceptive methods, such as the pill, intrauterine devices (IUDs), and condoms. Some 40% were protected by nonreversible methods such as tubal ligation.

Nearly 21% of nonpregnant women in their childbearing years did not practice contraception in 1984. The level of overall contraceptive practice (including nonreversible methods such as tubal ligation) in Canada in 1984, some 39.9 per 1,000, was among the highest in the world, and use of sterilization for contraception was also at one of the highest levels among industrialized countries (Campbell, 1999). Women's contraceptive practices in 1995 were similar to those in 1984. In both years, reliance on reversible methods, such as the pill, IUDs, and condoms, was more common than use of nonreversible methods such as tubal ligation. However, overall contraceptive practice has changed somewhat in Canada since 1984. For women of reproductive age, the proportion using reversible methods declined from 35.6 per 1,000 in 1984 to 32 in 1995. The percentage of women using nonreversible methods remained virtually unchanged.

Levels of voluntary sterilization remain high in Canada when compared with other developed countries. However, the proportion of women who were not using any contraceptive method increased from 21% to 25%. Overall contraceptive prevalence (including tubal ligation and vasectomy but excluding noncontraceptive sterilization) declined from 69% to 60%. Among all reversible methods, the pill and condom remained the most popular choices among women. While use of the pill as a reversible method of birth control declined from 19% to 17% between 1984 and 1995, condom use increased from 6% to 10%. The use of all other reversible methods declined somewhat during this time period. Use of the IUD went from 6% to 3%. Levels of sterilization remained similar, but the type of sterilization changed dramatically: There was a substantial decline in tubal ligation (from 24% to 17%) and an increase in vasectomy and in sterilization for medical reasons. Moreover, although vasectomy is on the increase, sterilization was generally lower among men than among women (31% versus 40%) (Campbell, 1999).

Social Views, Customs, and Practices

An important aspect of sexual and reproductive health in Canada is its ongoing commitment to gender equality. Canada's Federal Plan for Gender Equality reflects the commitment to the United Nations Platform for Action arising from the 1995 Beijing Fourth World Conference on Women and the 1994 Cairo International Conference on Population and Development. The Canadian plan includes an objective to improve women's physical and psychological well-being by addressing the broad socioeconomic factors that affect women's health, as well as sexual and reproductive health problems such as teen pregnancy, childbirth, and the overmedicalization of reproduction.

In Canada, the importance of gender sensitivity should also be recognized. Sexual and reproductive health is clearly important both for women and men. Yet the past and current emphasis on reproductive health is disproportionately focused on women. Sadly, teen pregnancy is most often seen as a problem for young women, not for young men, with most of the onus for preventing pregnancy falling on the girl. As well, gender sensitivity is too often taken to mean sensitivity to women's issues. To be successful, policies and initiatives to improve sexual and reproductive health should recognize and respond to the issues, needs, and responsibilities of both women and men, girls and boys. The challenge for Canadians is to recognize the differences, and the similarities, between males and females and to develop suitable interventions to respond appropriately.

THE FUTURE OF TEEN PREGNANCY

Canada's teenage pregnancy rate is lower than that of its neighbor, the United States. Yet the Canadian teen pregnancy rate is much higher than that of Germany and France and about the same as that of England. However, before the problems of adolescent pregnancy in Canada can be fully addressed, the characteristics and problems specific to Canadian teens must be identified. Too much of what is known about teen pregnancy in Canada is extrapolated from studies conducted in the United States. This approach has led to a public perception that the rate of teen pregnancy in Canada is similar. Even more problematic, it is assumed that teen girls in Canada who become pregnant are responding to the same conditions and circumstances that contributed to girls in the United States becoming pregnant.

Adolescent pregnancy prevention programs and sexuality education both at the school level and at the community prevention level need to focus on preventing STDs and other health-related issues.

CONCLUSION

Today's adolescents are the next generation of parents, workers, and leaders. To fill these roles to the best of their ability, they need the guidance, education, and support of their families and their communities and the attention of a government committed to their development.

Individual Canadians, and society at large, pay a significant price for the treatment of sexual and reproductive health problems that arise from a lack of adolescent education about contraception and sexuality.

Comprehensive, universal sexuality education programs should cover more than biological facts. They need to provide young people with practical information and skills to help them learn how to develop mature relationships, manage sexual relationships, and exercise the assertiveness skills necessary to negotiate contraceptive use.

The Canadian government, along with other appropriate institutions and even the media, has a role to play in improving an adolescent girl's ability to protect herself against unwanted pregnancies, STDs, and HIV/AIDS. Additionally, a renewed effort is needed in Canada to educate and motivate males of all ages to cooperate in the use of contraceptives to prevent unwanted pregnancies and condoms to prevent the spread of sexually transmitted diseases.

Two issues of particular note are these:

- Canada's teen pregnancy rates are higher than in many other developed countries.
- Teen pregnancy is almost five times more common in the lowest-income neighborhoods of Canada compared to the highest-income neighborhoods.

REFERENCES

Campbell, J.M. (1999). Environmental scan of sexual and reproductive health in the Atlantic provinces. Health Promotion and Programs Branch. Health Canada, April. Retrieved August 3, 2000, from the World Wide Web: http://www.hc-sc.gc.ca.

Canadian Fertility Survey (CFS). (1984). Social Science Data Centre, Queens University Libraries, Kingston, Canada.

Canada's Health System. (1998). Health System and Policy Division. Retrieved July 15, 2000, from the World Wide Web: http://www.hc-sc.gc.ca/datapcb/dataesa/E-sys.htm.

Champion, C. (1996, July 15). Rethinking teenage motherhood: The main culprits are older men, and a low age-of-consent law, not inept boyfriends. *Alberta Report/Western Report, 23*, 32.

General Social Survey (GSS). (1995). Ottawa: Industry, Science, and Technology.

Health Canada. (1999). Health Protection Branch, Laboratory Centre for Disease Control. Bureau of Reproductive and Child Health, LCDC. Retrieved August 3, 2000, from the World Wide Web: http://www.hc-sc.gc.ca/english/index.htm.

Martin, K., & Wu, Zheng. (2000). Contraceptive use in Canada: 1984–1994. *Family Planning Perspectives 32*(2): 65–73.

Wadhera, S., & Millar, W.J. (1997). *Teenage pregnancies, 1974 to 1994.* Health Reports (Statistics Canada, Catalogue 82–003-XPB), Winter, *9*(3).

3

EGYPT

Andrew L. Cherry

PROFILE OF EGYPT

Egypt is one of the oldest civilizations in human history. Considered the cradle of ancient civilization, Egyptian settlements have been found that are 8,000 years old. The Nile River was an essential element in the development of Egyptian civilization and to Egyptian life today.

Egypt is situated in northeastern Africa and south of the Mediterranean Sea. It covers 385,229 square miles (997,739 square kilometers). However, only 10% of the land is inhabited—the rest is desert. Inhabited areas are to be found in the Nile River Valley and delta, around desert oases, and along the Suez Canal. Egyptian deserts include the Libyan Desert in the west, the Arabian Desert in the east, and the Nubian Desert in the south. The capital of Egypt, and its largest city, is Cairo.

There were an estimated 66,050,004 people living in Egypt in 1998. Some 45% live in urban areas. Almost 99% live within the Nile Valley and delta. The Nile Valley and delta make up less than 4% of Egypt's total land area, which makes the Nile Valley and delta one of the world's most densely populated areas.

Islam is the official religion. Almost 90% of all Egyptians practice Islam. Arabic is the official language. French and English are common second languages among the educated.

Education is free and compulsory, but only 51% of adults can read. Al Azhar University at Cairo, founded in A.D. 970, is the world's oldest continually operating institution of higher learning.

Egypt's trading, financial, and manufacturing sectors are socialized. Private business, agriculture, real estate, and some manufacturing are also closely regulated.

About 40% of all employees work in agriculture. Egypt is one of the world's leading producers of long-staple (long-fiber) cotton. Manufacturing, construction, and mining employ another 22% of the labor force. The basic unit of currency is the Egyptian pound (approximately 3.64 Egyptian pounds equals U.S. $1, in the year 2000).

Under the 1971 Egyptian constitution, the head of state is the president and is elected to a six-year term. A 444-member People's Assembly, elected for a five-year term, has legislative authority. The constitution calls for at least 50% of the members to be representatives of the worker and farmer groups. It also requires that some members be women.

The gross domestic product (GDP) in U.S. dollars was $45.08 billion, or $867 per person per year in 1988, the last year accurate data were available. The Egyptian economy experienced sluggish growth after the mid-1980s and into the 1990s.

The extended family is central to Egyptian life and includes parents, grandparents, uncles, aunts, nephews, nieces, and cousins. The significance of the extended family makes marriage very important. Marriage can help maintain and build relationships between family members and between families. As such, by custom, Egyptians are allowed to marry cousins (Jehl, 1997).

Arranged marriages are still common, although by the end of the 20th century, the better-educated, urban younger were tending to choose their partners. Choice is not as common in the rural areas. Not only are marriages arranged in rural areas, but a new bride is subordinate to both her husband and her mother-in-law. Her status will not improve until she has a child, preferably a boy (Jehl, 1997).

In Egypt, a Muslim man can have up to four wives if he can provide for them and treat them fairly and well. Egyptians tend to indulge their children. Among the poorer and less educated Egyptians, a large family is still considered a blessing from God.

By law, Egyptian women are financially independent. In other legal matters such as inheritance and witnessing, however, a woman counts as "half a man," which severely limits a woman's legal rights. Egyptian women keep their own name when they marry (Digges, 1999).

As Egyptian adolescents enter the 21st century they are the largest group of adolescents (13 million) in Egypt's history. Their numbers will have a major impact on Egyptian society. Yet these adolescents face many obstacles in their efforts to develop their identity, obtain an education, and perhaps raise a family of their own (Digges, 1999).

Though access to an education has improved, there are still major differences found among regions and among people of different socioeconomic status (SES). Adolescents in rural upper Egypt have a school "never attended" rate 10 times higher than the national average. Adolescents from families of the lowest SES are 4.6 times more likely not to attend school than those of the highest SES group (Digges, 1999).

While the rate for girls dropping out of school declined in the 1990s, girls continue to be three times more likely than boys to drop out of school. In Egypt, where poverty is greatest, school nonattendance and failure to complete school are the highest. Boys in poor areas are at risk for not completing school. However, the most disadvantaged groups are the girls whose families are of the low and middle SES; girls who live in rural and urban areas in upper Egypt; and girls who live in rural areas in lower Egypt. A lack of educational opportunity for adolescent girls gives them few options but to seek status and a place in a family by bearing children—often at an early age (Digges, 1999).

In Egypt, 33% of all adolescents work; one in every two boys and one in every six girls are working. Nearly 50% of them work seven hours or more a day. Nearly a third of the adolescents are involved in work that is defined under Egyptian law as hazardous. However, labor laws to protect adolescent workers are limited because they do not protect or regulate children working in agriculture. Poor children working in the cotton fields of Egypt rather than attending school is a major concern. However, poor families depend on the income from their children who work the fields and could not survive without it (Digges, 1999).

The leisure activity of choice among Egyptian adolescents is watching television. They spend much of their free time watching television. Visiting relatives is also an important leisure activity, even though twice as many girls as boys report visiting as a leisure activity. Almost 60% of boys are active in sports outside of school. Yet only 5% of girls are involved in sports outside of school. Girls have limited access to clubs and are discouraged by their parents from participating in sports and from visiting with friends in "uncontrolled" situations (Digges, 1999).

A major problem among Egyptian adolescents is nutrition; they do not get enough iron. Nearly 50% suffer from anemia, reflecting a serious public health problem (a problem that is also widespread throughout the world). Add to this the rate of parasitic infections (57%), which varies widely depending on access to public sewerage, clean water, and the availability of a separate room for cooking. In general, Egyptian adolescents from a low SES group are more likely to be anemic, stunted, underweight, and suffering from parasites (Zanaty, 1996). There is an obvious need for better nutrition, greater access to clean water, and better hygiene—especially in rural areas.

Gender roles continue to change in Egypt for both boys and girls. At times, these role changes occur faster than attitudes. The gap between what is perceived as socially "right" and what is "reality" fuels the conflict over the change in the role of Egyptian women and girls.

Both boys and girls clearly prefer segregated gender roles, but they have come to believe decision making should be shared. Many more adolescent girls than boys, however, think decisions concerning contraceptives, health care, and the wife working outside the home should be as much their decision as their husbands'.

Notwithstanding the changes that have occurred in Egyptian society, many attitudes about family issues have not really changed. In a national survey of Egyptian adolescents in 1998, both boys and girls agreed that a wife should get her husband's permission for everything she does (girls, 89%; boys, 91%). They agreed that the husband should know about pregnancies, childbirth, and any birth complications (girls, 89%; boys, 93%). And most adolescents agree that the wife should keep trying to have a male baby even if she is satisfied with her present number of children (girls, 81%; boys, 80%) (Digges, 1999).

Both girls and boys strongly believe that the two sexes have different roles in life. They also agree that males have a greater value and more authority than females. Even so, girls, young wives, and women are insisting that they have a greater role in decisions that affect their lives (Digges, 1999).

The number of adolescent girls who marry each year began to fall in the 1990s. Yet despite the decline it is still high in rural upper Egypt. The median age of first pregnancy is 17.6 years of age, which indicates that 50% of adolescents become pregnant before they turn 18. One of the reasons for the young age at first pregnancy is that less than 16% of married adolescent girls use contraceptives. Typically, contraceptive use begins only after the first birth, which most often occurs in the first year of marriage (Digges, 1999).

INTRODUCTION

In Egypt, in other North Africa countries, and in Arab countries, teenage pregnancy is common. However, in almost all cases, the teen mom is married.

In Egypt, as in many other developing countries, most girls marry in their teens. Then, because of societal pressures to prove their womanhood and to increase their status, many girls become pregnant soon after marriage. Yet few of these married adolescents know about or understand the concept of reproductive health (Sallam, 1999).

Traditionally, Egyptian men have preferred that their wife (almost always an adolescent) have a child as soon after marriage as possible. Hence, at least 50% of adolescent girls who marry are pregnant for the first time within four months of being married. Consequently, very high rates of stillbirth and infant death are found among married adolescent girls. Typically there are about 45 stillbirths per 1,000 live births and 74 infant deaths per 1,000 live births, compared to young Egyptian women in their twenties, who experience fewer than 65 infant deaths per 1,000 live births (Sahar, 1999).

Egyptian men believe that children are an investment and that they will provide security in old age. Husbands generally prefer more children than do their wives (Sallam, 1999).

Vignette

Manar married when she was 14 and gave birth to her first child, a girl and a preemie, just after she turned 15 years of age. Her baby girl was born 10 weeks early and had to spend eight weeks in the neonatal unit of the hospital. Because she was a preemie, the baby had several other health problems including a breathing problem that constantly worried Manar. The thought that her baby might catch a cold or the flu was a constant source of anxiety. The child had to take diuretics and caffeine to ease her rapid breathing. "I remember thanking God every day that she did not have any other major problems like HIV [human immunodeficiency virus]."

Over the next five years Manar gave birth to two more children and had two miscarriages. She was always exhausted from the daily routine of child care, housework, and helping her husband in the fields.

She did not want more children, but she was afraid to use contraceptives because of all the negative rumors she had heard. Besides, in her family, frequent pregnancies were a natural part of life.

One day, while riding on a local bus, she heard a recorded message asking her to think before having another child and inviting women to attend a community meeting on how family planning could help them. Manar went to the meeting with her sister and found many of her friends and neighbors there. Respected community leaders and doctors were there to answer questions about the safety and effectiveness of different contraceptive methods. The next morning, Manar visited a family planning clinic near her home to learn what contraceptive method would be best for her.

Overview of Teen Pregnancy

Most adolescent Egyptian girls believe that the ideal age for marriage for females is about 20 years old. At this age, young women are viewed as "sensible and mature," and they can better "withstand the burden of pregnancy." However, most girls still do not reach this ideal age before marrying. A significant number of Egyptian girls continue to marry at a young age, given that the mean age at first pregnancy in 1999 was 17.6 years for adolescent wives. These adolescents (80%) also believe that the best place to have a child is in a government hospital. Actual delivery of Egyptian children is split about 50% between a government hospital and at home (Qayed & Waszak, 1999).

Contraception

Almost all older adolescent girls in Egypt are familiar with "family planning," and most have a positive attitude about contraception. However, knowledge of specific methods varies by SES group. For instance, 53% of adolescent girls and younger women are familiar with injectables as compared to 21% of older women. Also, 92% of all adolescent females and women know about "intrauterine devices" (IUDs), compared to 79% of males (Qayed & Waszak, 1999).

Among adolescent wives, the use of contraception increases as the number of children increases. In one study, 15% of those with one child were using contraception, compared with 79% of those with four or more children (Qayed & Waszak, 1999).

Adolescent wives were more likely to be using the IUD. Older women were more likely to be using the pill. Researchers found that some of the reasons women do not use contraception include being an adolescent wife, being illiterate, having an illiterate mother, having neither radio nor television in the home, and having a previous pregnancy resulting in a stillbirth or miscarriage (Sallam, 1999). Women in small families (three or fewer children) were more likely to have begun using contraception after the birth of their first or second child than were women in large families with four or more children (Ragheb & Guirgis, 1999).

The majority, over 90%, of Egyptian women have used contraception at some point in their lives, and at any given time, 80% will be using a contraception method. The IUD continues to be the most popular method. The sex of the living children in a family influences a woman's contraception use. Women were more likely to use modern contraceptive methods when they had boys or both boys and girls than when they had only girls (Ragheb & Guirgis, 1999).

Abortion

In Egypt, abortion is illegal for reasons other than saving the mother's life. A woman who receives an illegal (often an unsafe) abortion and the abortion provider can be prosecuted by both legal and religious authorities. Generally, *unsafe abortions* are defined as the termination of an unwanted pregnancy either by a person lacking the necessary skills or in an environment lacking minimal medical standards, or both. Unsafe abortions are a major global health problem. In Egypt, where access to abortion is limited by law, many women resort to an unsafe practice to end unwanted pregnancy, and in many cases they suffer complications that require emergency care (Alan Guttmacher Institute, 2000).

Although there are no government statistics on the number of abortions performed annually in Egypt, in studies of females being admitted to Egyptian hospitals, 19%—or one in five females—were admitted for treatment of an induced or spontaneous abortion. Some 86% of the pregnancies were terminated at 12 weeks. At least 14% percent of the women admitted were suffering from excessive blood loss, and 5% had one or more infections. Based on these numbers, the abortion rate in Egypt is estimated to be somewhere around 15 abortions per 100 pregnancies.

Treatment for complications from unsafe abortion requires a substantial proportion of Egyptian health care resources (Huntington, Nawar, Hassan, Youssef, & Abdel-Tawab, 1998). Others have argued that stillbirths and miscarriages are more common among adolescent and teenage mothers and can be mistaken for abortions, falsely increasing abortion estimates.

HISTORY AND SOCIAL CONTEXT

In the early 1970s, there was little hope that family planning would work in Egypt. The average family had eight children. Any suggestion that population growth was a problem brought protest from religious and political leaders. In 1970, only about 8% of women used any kind of contraceptive.

Despite the protest, the population exceeded the country's resources. Unemployment and pollution were out of control, whereas education, health, and housing fell gravely short of the need.

With outside support from the U.S. Agency for International Development (USAID) during the 1970s, the Egyptian population began to stabilize (Table 3.1). Early research and services showed that there was significant demand for family planning. Predictions that projected the consequences of unrestrained population growth on unemployment, education, health, and housing dramatically changed the minds of Egypt's political leadership. Contraceptive use also increased among adolescent wives and young married women from 24% in 1980 to 30% in 1984 and 48% in 1991 (USAID, 2000).

There are clear differences in the way boys and girls are raised in Egypt. Because girls typically rank lower than boys in the family, girls often receive less food and medical care. Girls are often overburdened by household chores and caring for young and elderly family members (Ragheb & Guirgis, 1999). These disparities are tragic for many girls.

The difference in treatment begins with decisions about breast-feeding. While Egyptian mothers are as likely to breast-feed their sons as their daughters, the average time most mothers breast-feed their sons is significantly longer than the time they breast-feed their daughters. The proportion of mothers who stopped breast-feeding because they become pregnant or wanted to work was greater among mothers of girls.

Sons typically receive a greater share of protein-rich foods such as milk,

Table 3.1
**Average Number of Children
per Egyptian Family**

1970	8 Children
1980	5.3 Children
1990	4.1 Children

Source: Data from (USAID, 2000).

eggs, and chicken than do their sisters. This provides more iron in the boy's diet. Favored treatment was greater for sons in large families than in small families, regardless of the mother's education (Ragheb & Guirgis, 1999).

There is even evidence of a difference between health care for sons and daughters. Mothers with less education tend to take their sons to private physicians for medical care more often than they take their daughters. In one study, the average number of doctor visits was 1.6 per year for boys versus 0.9 per year for girls. The better educated the mother, the more likely that her daughter will be attending school (Ragheb & Guirgis, 1999).

The practice of female circumcision continues to be widespread in Egypt. The practice is deeply rooted in a tradition shared with countries of the Nile Valley and other parts of Africa. In Egypt, the procedure usually takes place before or just as a girl reaches puberty. Female genital mutilation (FGM) typically involves removing all or part of the clitoris and parts of the labia minora. FGM continues to be practiced because many believe that it will moderate female sexuality and make girls more feminine and marriageable. It is also sanctioned by religion (El-Gibaly, Ibrahim, Mensch, & Clark, 1999). In a 1999 survey of adolescents, at least 70% of girls thought that FGM was necessary for marriage, compared to 90% of boys (Digges, 1999).

Interestingly, nearly all the adolescent girls who participated in the survey had been circumcised. Of these, 11% of the women in both groups experienced difficulties, such as excessive bleeding, severe pain, and fear. Nevertheless, 77% of adolescent girls agreed that "it is important for a girl to be circumcised." And over 65% of the girls said they would have their daughters circumcised (Qayed & Waszak, 1999).

FGM is illegal in Egypt, yet it is widespread, although concealed. FGM can lead to genital infection, infertility, and death in childbirth. It has been shown that FGM can make vaginal intercourse painful because of scarring (Qayed & Waszak, 1999).

Based on the Egyptian Demographic Health Survey in 1995, of those who were ever married, 50% of the FGM operations were done by a physician (Digges, 1999). The remainder were performed by a nurse or midwife (*daya*) in less-educated families (Ragheb & Guirgis, 1999).

While the 1995 Egyptian Demographic and Health Survey found that

97% of ever-married older women were circumcised, it was also found that approximately 84% of girls were, or eventually would be, circumcised. In one study of three groups of girls, it was found that while about 35% of girls aged 16 to 19 had undergone the procedure before age 10, about 30% of girls aged 13 to 15 and 27% of girls aged 10 to 12 had undergone circumcision (El-Gibaly et al., 1999).

Education is important in decisions about female circumcision; daughters of mothers who have attended secondary school or higher are significantly less likely to be circumcised than other girls. Girls who live in urban areas of lower Egypt and the cities of Cairo and Alexandria are significantly less likely to be circumcised than girls residing in rural upper Egypt. Over half of all circumcisions in the mid-1990s were performed by a physician (El-Gibaly et al., 1999).

Although a 1959 law banned female circumcision, it was ignored until 1997 when the Egyptian Supreme Court upheld the minister's ban as well as the 1959 law criminalizing all female circumcision in Egypt (El-Gibaly et al., 1999). Even so, Egyptian newspapers carry story after story of prosecutors charging surgeons with negligence when prepubescent girls die while being circumcised (Asik, 1998).

TEEN PREGNANCY TODAY

Political Views and Public Policies

Urfi

Among adolescents, the *Urfi*, or undocumented marriage, is becoming more popular. The high cost of the marriage ceremony forces young couples to wait several years before they are married, all the while maintaining a platonic relationship. Egyptian society frowns on sex before marriage. The *Urfi* marriage is a way for teens to deal with their predicament.

Urfi is a marriage conducted by a Muslim cleric in the presence of two witnesses, but it is not officially registered and is not financially binding on the husband or the wife. However, before recent legislation, this marital arrangement had many disadvantages for the wives. If the husband chose to leave his wife without divorcing her and even to marry another, the wife from the *Urfi* marriage had no legal right to seek a divorce since the *Urfi* marriage was considered illegal under the old status law. This left the wife with one of two choices: She could remarry and risk being accused of polyandry, punishable by seven years in prison, or she could stay single for the rest of her life (Gubash, 2000).

The Divorce Law

In Egyptian society before the new divorce law took effect in the year 2000, a man could divorce his wife by simply telling her "I divorce you" three times. Yet it could take years for a woman to divorce her husband, if ever. The amended law allows an Egyptian woman, for the first time, to divorce her husband without first getting the husband's permission.

The new law is based on an Islamic practice called *Khul*, which is described in Islamic religious texts. Under this law, a woman can apply for a divorce in court. There is a three-month waiting period to give families time to try to reconcile the marriage. If the couple cannot reconcile their differences, the judge will then grant a divorce. The wife must repay the husband his original dowry, and she waives her right to alimony. A father is still required to pay child support.

While many women's rights advocates contend the new law does not go far enough, they agree that it is slightly more equitable than the old law. It also recognizes undocumented or *Urfi* marriages. Even so, some advocates point out that the Islamic religious texts also say that once a woman decides she no longer wants to live with her husband and she returns her dowry, she is divorced (Gubash, 2000).

Social Views, Customs, and Practices

Unwed and Pregnant

In Egypt and other societies in which female chastity at marriage is of paramount importance, an unmarried pregnant adolescent girl will often commit suicide or may be murdered by family members. In some cases, she might be relegated to a life of prostitution. Most Near Eastern societies and some segments of European society place great value on female chastity at marriage (Gordon, 1991).

In a society like that of Egypt, which demands virginity at marriage and especially where proof of chastity is required on the wedding night, sexually abused girls or girls who were a victim of incest may be unmarriageable or may be rejected by their husbands (the spoiled-goods syndrome). Adolescent girls and women who are raped may not be marriageable or may be driven out of the family if already married (Gordon, 1991). Even if the wife is not rejected by the husband, because of the psychological trauma, she may avoid sexual relations; or because of culturally induced psychological trauma to the husband, he may be unwilling or unable to engage in sexual relations with her (Hammel & Friou, 1996).

Unintended Pregnancy

Even though more than half the married women in Egypt use some method of birth control, unplanned pregnancies are a major concern for many adolescent wives. For instance, in one study, 62% of wives who report an unplanned pregnancy say they became pregnant while using a contraceptive method.

Unintended pregnancies can also mean health and financial problems. Studies have shown that children born as the result of an unintended pregnancy often are low-birth-weight babies, have less educational opportunity, and may suffer from parental neglect (Kader & Maklouf, 1999).

Attitudes about unintended pregnancies typically differ between Egyptian wives and their husbands. Although the majority of adolescent wives had a negative view of an unintended pregnancy, almost 50% said their husbands would be happy about the pregnancy. The main reason the wives gave for their husbands' happiness was "his fondness for children" (Kader & Maklouf, 1999). Couples who did not want another child pointed out the expense of child rearing, the infant's demand for time and attention, health problems for the mother and unborn child, and too many children of the same sex (Kader & Maklouf, 1999).

Especially among adolescent wives, an unintended pregnancy affected their ability to look after their own health, was a financial burden, added household duties, reduced personal time, and reduced the time they had to spend socially or with their other children. In general, their quality of life is reduced because of the extra time that the unplanned child required (Kader & Maklouf, 1999).

THE FUTURE OF TEEN PREGNANCY

Various traditional, institutional, and political barriers and myths about sexuality make it difficult to change health policies for adolescents in Egypt. Many Egyptians believe that providing family planning services to adolescents will promote promiscuity. Consequently, little is known about how adolescents acquire information on sexuality and reproductive health (Qayed & Waszak, 1999).

Egyptian adolescents and teenagers need accurate information to enable them to make responsible decisions about childbearing. Programs should reach out to adolescents and youth in their own environment—schools, recreation centers, and work sites (Qayed & Waszak, 1999).

Adolescents need to be educated about the health benefits to the mother and child when pregnancy is delayed until age 20 or older. They need information about contraceptive methods available to them and how and where to obtain them. Because cultural taboos may discourage frank discussions about sexual issues, adolescent girls and boys need to receive education and information to improve their communication skills on family planning and reproductive health issues. Policymakers and health providers should target adolescent boys with family planning information since they will be the primary decision makers in the home (FHI, 1999). Policymakers should promote education for girls (Ragheb & Guirgis, 1999).

Public and private organizations need to extend health insurance coverage to all families in order to narrow the gender gap in health treatment for girls from poor families (Ragheb & Guirgis, 1999).

Since gender equity is more probable in small families, health providers and policymakers need to promote family planning as a means to encourage gender equity (Ragheb & Guirgis, 1999).

Family planning messages need to emphasize women's perceptions that having control over their childbearing experiences gives them more time to devote to their families and their homes (FHI, 1999).

Nearly two-thirds of Egyptian women reporting an unplanned pregnancy said they became pregnant while using a contraceptive method, including oral contraceptives and intrauterine devices. Because these methods are highly effective, at least some of the failures are likely due to the way they were used. Health workers need to offer better education and more contraceptive counseling to help Egyptian women understand how to use contraceptives correctly (Kader & Maklouf, 1999).

More than one-third of women who experience an unintended pregnancy said they tried to terminate their pregnancy through abortion. Because abortion is illegal in Egypt, many women seek clandestine or unsafe abortion. Women need information on the risks of unsafe abortion, and physicians need training in treating abortion complications (Kader & Maklouf, 1999).

Thirty-eight percent of women were using no contraceptive method at all, although they did not want to become pregnant, because they wanted a "rest" from contraception. The reasons given for the "rest" were because they did not believe they could become pregnant or they feared side effects. Providers and women's advocates should educate women about the importance of correct and consistent use of contraception, as well as provide basic information about fertility and menstrual cycles (Kader & Maklouf, 1999).

Recently television advertising about family planning services in both the public and private sectors was increased and improved. Television is a powerful medium in Egypt, reaching 95% of women on a daily basis (USAID, 2000).

New contraceptive methods such as the injectable Depo-Provera and the Norplant implant provide new and more varied choices to adolescent wives. Education and information about these modern methods needs to be distributed vigorously (USAID, 2000).

In July 1997, President Hosni Mubarak said: "My primary concern for Egypt is the population increase. . . . If we do not deal with this we will be like a country that abandons its people" (USAID, 2000).

CONCLUSION

Adolescent and teen pregnancy in Egypt is a concern because of the young age at which wedded adolescent girls give birth to their first child and the number of times they will become pregnant during their lifetimes. About

50% of adolescents who give birth for the first time are younger than 17.5 years of age. The medical consequences of young girls giving birth have been shown to be far riskier than when young women age 20 give birth.

Few girls in Egypt become pregnant before marriage. If an unmarried girl does become pregnant and the father does not marry her quickly, the consequences can be, and often are, disastrous for her.

The pressure to marry young is offset by the costs of formal marital arrangements and weddings. Alternatives such as the *Urfi* allow young couples to marry. And with the new divorce law in Egypt, the *Urfi* is a better option for young wives than it was in the past.

Egypt is a developing country that continues to struggle with tradition that has yet to be reconciled with the reality of a modern world. Life in the 21st century will require smaller families and mothers who delay birth until they are in their late teens or early twenties.

Smaller families will also reduce the pressure on parents to have a male child, and this should increase the value placed on girls in Egyptian families. Ultimately, as pregnancy is postponed and family size is reduced, the quality of life for Egyptian adolescent mothers and their families will be improved.

REFERENCES

Alan Guttmacher Institute. (2000). *Termination of unwanted pregnancies common in Egypt according to first large-scale study of treatment of abortion complications in the country.* New York: Author.

Asik, Z. (1998, July 29). Egypt girl dies during circumcision, surgeons charged. 09: 00:42 +0300 (WET). Retrieved August 10, 2000, from the World Wide Web: http://www.infobeat.com/stories/cgi/story.cgi?id=2555159496−891.

Digges, D. (1999). Adolescence in profile: The country's first national survey of a critical demographic group indicates some gains in education but ongoing, endemic poverty. Egypt: *The Cairo Times*, (3) 5. Retrieved August 2, 2000, from the World Wide Web: http://www.cairotimes.com/.

El-Gibaly, O., Ibrahim, B.L., Mensch, B.S., & Clark, W. (1999). The decline of female circumcision in Egypt: Evidence and interpretation. Policy Research Division, Working Paper no. 132. New York: Population Council. *Population Briefs*, 6(1).

FHI. (1999). *Egypt: The impact of family planning on the lives of Egyptian women.* Retrieved August 8, 2000, from the World Wide Web: http://www.fhi.org.

Gordon, D. (1991). Female circumcision and genital operations in Egypt and the Sudan: A dilemma for medical anthropology. *Medical Anthropology Quarterly,* 5, 3–14.

Gubash, C. (2000). New divorce law has Egypt astir. *MSNBC, International News.* Retrieved August 3, 2000, from the World Wide Web: http://archive.msnbc.com/aboutmsnbc.asp.

Hammel, E.A., & Friou, D. (1996). *Anthropology and demography: Marriage, liaison or encounter?* Retrieved August 18, 2000, from the World Wide Web: http://demog.berkeley.edu/~gene/brown.94.rev.2.html.

Huntington, D., Nawar, L., Hassan, E.O., Youssef, H., & Abdel-Tawab, N. (1998). The post abortion caseload in Egyptian hospitals: A descriptive study. *International Family Planning Perspectives, 24*(1), 25–31.

Jehl, D. (1997, September 25). King cotton exacts tragic toll from Egypt's young. *New York Times.*

Kader, F.A., & Maklouf, H. (1999). *Egypt: The social and behavioral outcomes of unintended pregnancy.* Family Health International. Retrieved August 8, 2000, from the World Wide Web: http://www.fhi.org.

Knodel, J., Chamratrithiron, A., & Devabalya, N. (1987). *Thailand's reproductive revolution: Rapid fertility decline in a Third-World setting.* Madison: University of Wisconsin Press.

Qayed, M., & Waszak, C. (1999). *Reproductive health among adolescents and youth in Assiut governorate, Egypt.* Family Health International. Retrieved August 8, 2000, from the World Wide Web: http://www.fhi.org.

Ragheb, S., & Guirgis, W. (1999). *Egypt: Family size and gender equity in childrearing.* Family Health International. Retrieved August 8, 2000, from the World Wide Web: http://www.fhi.org.

Sahar, E. (1999). *Transitions to adulthood: A national survey of adolescents in Egypt.* Cairo, Egypt: The Population Council, Regional Office for West Asia and North Africa.

Sallam, S.A. (1999). *Reproductive health of adolescent married women in squatter areas in Alexandria.* Family Health International. Retrieved August 8, 2000, from the World Wide Web: http://www.fhi.org.

Schlegel, A., & Herbert, B. (1991). *Adolescence: An anthropological inquiry.* New York: Free Press.

USAID. (2000). *Breaking Egypt's contraceptive "plateau."* U.S. Agency for International Development. Washington, DC: Author. Retrieved August 8, 2000, from the World Wide Web: http://www.usaid.gov/regions/ane/newpages/perspectives/egypt/fmplng.htm.

Zanaty, F. (1996). *Egypt demographic and health survey—1995.* Culverton, MD: Macro International.

To learn more about circumcision in Egypt, contact the Egyptian National NGO Taskforce against FGM, NCPD, Cairo; phone: (20 2) 350 0757, 378 2659; fax: (20 2) 378 2643; Mail: Mail@main.ncpd.org.eg.

4

ENGLAND

Jennifer Bluth and Douglas Rugh

PROFILE OF ENGLAND

The population of England in the year 2000 was 59,511,464 (July 2000 estimate). The population density was about 1,100 people per square mile (about 430 people per square kilometer). This makes the United Kingdom a country with one of the highest population densities in the world. Seventy-five percent of the people live in urban areas. Only 25% of the land is arable (land that can be cultivated) (Central Intelligence Agency, 2000).

Most English people are descended from early Celtic, Iberian peoples, and Nordic and French invaders. In the year 200, the United Kingdom was composed of England and regional assemblies with varying degrees of power in Scotland, Wales, and Northern Ireland. The country of England occupies the entire island east of Wales and south of Scotland. The chief port is London. Its total area is 50,363 square miles (130,439 square kilometers), including the Isles of Scilly, the Isle of Wight, and the Isle of Man.

The gross domestic product (GDP) per capita in England (a measure of individual buying power) was estimated in 1999 to be $21,800 (in U.S. currency) per person per year. An estimated 17% of the population have incomes below the poverty line. Unemployment is typically about 6% (1999 estimate).

Life expectancy at birth in England is consistent with the best of the developed nations. For the total population it is 77.66 years. For males it is 74.97 years, and for females it is an impressive 80.49 years (2000 estimate). Using a definition of literacy that includes all English citizens ages

15 and over who have completed five or more years of schooling, the literacy rate in the United Kingdom is 99% (1978 estimate) for the total population (Central Intelligence Agency, 2000).

School attendance is compulsory from ages 5 through 16, and elementary and secondary schools are primarily organized and maintained by public funds. The oldest of England's many institutions of higher education are the Universities of Oxford and Cambridge.

English law originated in the customs of the Anglo-Saxons and the Normans. England's basic legal documents, including the Magna Carta and the Bill of Rights, with their emphasis on the legal rights of the individual, have influenced the entire English-speaking world. The Church of England, a Protestant Episcopal denomination, is the state church and the church of nearly 60% of the population. Catholics, other Protestant denominations, Muslims, and Jews make up the remainder.

England is a constitutional monarchy made up of the House of Commons and the House of Lords. The monarchy and the House of Lords have been ceremonial institutions with little or no real authority in modern times. The country is divided into 30 nonmetropolitan counties, six metropolitan counties, and Greater London (established in 1965 as a separate administrative entity) (Central Intelligence Agency, 2000).

It is also important to remember when comparing the United Kingdom to other countries that the age of universal suffrage, the legal age for being considered an adult, is 18 years of age, not 21 as in the United States.

INTRODUCTION

In England, the issue of teenage pregnancy is a major concern, not only for teenagers but for society at all levels. England is faced with the highest adolescent pregnancy rate in western Europe. The English Department of Health has done extensive research on the prevalence of teenage pregnancy and has compiled data on social, emotional, and financial concerns, which all have a direct impact on the teenager's experiences that either promote teen pregnancy or reduce the risk of teen sexual activity and unwanted pregnancy.

According to a report by the Department of Health (1999), "In England, there are nearly 90,000 conceptions a year to teenagers; around 7,700 to girls under 16 and 2,200 to girls aged 14 or under. Roughly, three-fifths of conceptions—56,000—result in live births" (p. 6). Many of these teenage mothers drop out of school, have extreme difficulty securing employment, and end up as single parents "living-on-the-dole." It is important to address this issue openly, to explore the factors that lead to the high prevalence rates of teenage pregnancy, and to begin to think collectively about strategies and solutions to this social phenomenon.

Vignette

Margaret is a 14-year-old girl who has been dating a 19-year-old boy for several months. The two met at school. Their friendship became more intimate and resulted in their becoming involved sexually. The couple did not use contraception regularly; like most teenagers, they just did not think it would happen to them. However, after missing her period, Margaret went to a doctor, who confirmed she was pregnant. She found the visit to the doctor to be stressful and very uncomfortable. The doctor did not take the time to listen to Margaret's concerns and seemed to chastise her for getting herself in this situation.

Margaret attempted to seek support from her boyfriend and her parents; however, both were telling her not to continue with the pregnancy. They talked about how a baby would stop her from fulfilling her dreams of going to college and pursuing a profession. They also were very disappointed in her and felt a great deal of embarrassment. In many ways, it seemed that her family felt responsible for her predicament. They had tremendous difficulty sharing these thoughts with her and instead could only express anger. As a result, Margaret felt isolated. After a month of being convinced to end the pregnancy, Margaret decided otherwise. She wanted to go through with the pregnancy and not give her baby up for adoption. She decided she wanted to raise the baby.

During the first year of caring for the baby, the relationship with her boyfriend started to become strained and distant. He spent most of his time outside the apartment, and Margaret discovered that he was spending nights with another girl. Margaret left that apartment to move back in with her parents. Margaret is now 16 years old and is caring for her daughter. She is working at a fast-food restaurant and has secured day care for her child. Margaret still has hopes of someday fulfilling her educational dreams. She knows that realistically her goals will be delayed until her child is older.

Margaret is one of many who become pregnant at an early age in England. In fact, many young girls become pregnant and face similar adversity while attempting to seek professional supportive guidance. What is important is for teenagers to be able to speak openly with medical professionals, family members, and others without being judged. Many young girls do not accept the challenge of single parenthood with as much dedication and self-assurance as Margaret. Many become depressed and feel isolated. In addition, many make choices that are not congruent with their value systems and make decisions because of a feeling of being pressured or out of fear of being abandoned by loved ones. It is essential for girls like Margaret to know there are people who will help and there are people who care.

Overview of Teen Pregnancy

Many factors in England place the adolescent at risk for becoming an adolescent parent. These factors include economic status, absence of adult role models, lack of education, lack of job opportunities, and low self-esteem, to name a few. In addition to the risk factors that lead to teen pregnancies, teenagers are also at risk of contracting sexually transmitted diseases and of contracting HIV (human immunodeficiency virus). Furthermore, they are at risk of engaging in other types of high-risk behaviors, such as abusing alcohol and drugs, which not only harm the teenager but also harm the developing fetus. In order to implement programs to help girls in need, it is important to explore factors that contribute to high-risk behaviors and to understand factors that influence adolescent sexual activity.

Teenage Sexual Activity

The Department of Health's Consultation Report (1999) makes several good points about teen pregnancy, including economic barriers, lack of social support systems, lack of education about sex and preventive measures, and personal decisions regarding their relationships and pregnancy. While affluent areas in England have high rates of teenage pregnancy, it is the poorer areas that have the highest rates of teenage pregnancy. This is especially true for teenagers who are in foster care and who are not in school. Furthermore, teenage parents are more likely to live in poverty and be unemployed. Because of a lack of education and caring support from adults, these girls are often trapped in this cycle (Wellings, Field, Johnson, & Wadsworth, 1994).

Although in England less than 33% of teens are sexually active before they are 16, half of those who are sexually active use no contraception the first time they engage in intercourse. In hindsight, most girls wish they had waited. However, for a significant group of these girls, sex is forced or unwanted. In 1999, just over 15,000 girls under 18 years of age opted for abortion. In England, at the beginning of the 21st century, 90% of all teenage mothers have their babies outside marriage (Wellings et al., 1994).

HISTORY AND SOCIAL CONTEXT

Throughout its history and until recently, England had a homogenous population made up of Anglo-Saxons and Normans. Government and social institutions developed to meet the needs of the Englishman (not Englishwomen). Historically Anglo-Saxon societies were characterized by strong kinship groups, feuds, customary law, and a system of money compensations (wergeld) for death, personal injury, and theft. England has a long history of citizen's rights, beginning with the Magna Carta confirmed by Edward I with his seal in 1297.

After a long history of struggle between the supremacy of the King of England and his English subjects, the common Englishman gained rights unprecedented in western Europe. During the 1600s through the middle of the 1900s, England was a world colonial power. After World War II, English colonies began demanding and receiving their independence. In addition to the colonies becoming independent countries, indigenous people living in the English colonies (who had been in the service of England) migrated to England instead of remaining in their own country. In modern England, three primary groups make up the repatriated colonist: Bangladeshis, African Caribbean, and Pakistanis. These groups bring different customs and practices to England. They have different values and handle family and personal problems in different ways. This diversity has been difficult for public officials who plan social services. They have been slow to respond to differences in need and to provide social services that meet the needs of this ever-growing diverse country of immigrants.

Efforts to attend to the serious problems faced by teenagers who are at risk of unwanted pregnancy are hampered by the lack of recognition of the diversity of modern England by politicians and public officials. For example, in England, there are no comprehensive statistics on either live births or abortions by ethnic group. The mother's ethnic group is not recorded if the pregnancy is aborted or during the birth registration. Information is collected on the mother's country of birth, but this does not identify her specific ethnicity. Although official surveys recognize three ethnic minorities whose teenage girls are at great risk of becoming teen parents, there is no way of identifying the extent of teen pregnancy by ethnic group: Bangladeshis, African Caribbean, and Pakistanis.

This lack of identification can hinder understanding of the teen pregnancy problem because for these groups the tradition of early childbirth within marriage has a common history. A 1994 survey of Pakistani and Bangladeshi women in their twenties who had given birth in their teens found that over 90% were or had been married, compared with 55% for Englishwomen (nationals) (*Health Education Authority*, 1994). Surveys have also reported that Pakistani and Bangladeshi women are least likely of all ethnic groups to have had sex before the age of 16 (Wellings et al., 1994). In addition, the relationship between low socioeconomic status and early pregnancies appears to be strong for these ethnic minority groups. For example, 41% of African Caribbean, 82% of Pakistani, and 84% of Bangladeshi people have incomes less than half the national average compared with 28% of English nationals (Policy Studies Institute, 1997). Some individuals in the ethnic minority groups are at risk, especially if they are excluded from school or are in a foster care situation. Other advocates point out that sexual health services were typically not designed in a way that would reach specific ethnic minority groups (Department of Health, 1999).

There are several risk factors that contribute to repeat teenage births. As stated in previous sections, poverty tends to contribute greatly to teenagers becoming pregnant, often more than once. According to the Office of National Statistics (1997) Longitudinal Study, the risk of becoming a teenage mother is almost 10 times higher for a girl whose family's income comes from unskilled manual labor than for a girl whose family's income derives from working in a profession. Furthermore, teenagers who live in social housing are three times more likely than their peers living in owner occupied housing to become a mother (Botting, Rosato, & Wood, 1998).

A second factor that often leads to repeated teen pregnancy is institutional care. One survey showed that 25% of the adolescent girls in foster homes had a child by the age of 16. One explanation is an absence of support from natural or biological parents (Biehal, et al., 1992). A third contributing factor for teenagers are those teens whose parents were themselves teenage mothers. In this instance, environmental influences affect the likelihood of teenagers becoming pregnant. A fourth factor is education. The Department of Education noted that in a 1958 UK birth cohort study, low educational achievement was a risk factor for teenage parenthood (Kiernan, 1995). A fifth factor contributing to teen pregnancy is the presence of mental health problems consisting of behavioral disorders. The Department of Education found in 1991 that of 55 hospitalized adolescent teenagers with conduct disorder, 33% became pregnant before the age of 17 (Zoccolillo & Rogers, 1991). Furthermore, those teenagers who had been in trouble with the law were also at greater risk of becoming teenage parents. "It has been estimated that 25 percent of the 11,000 prisoners in Young Offenders Institutions are fathers" (HMIP, 1997, p. 18).

Several medical and social complications result from teenage pregnancy. These medical complications are serious for the teenager and place the fetus at risk as well. Several medical concerns associated with teenage pregnancy are low birth weight, often caused by smoking; birth defects, often caused by the use of alcohol; poor prenatal care; increased feelings of stress, which may result from being unemployed or from family conflict; and increased depression due to feelings of isolation and loneliness. "For many, any kind of conventional ante-natal planning is an impossibility, as they face huge problems of family conflict, likely change of care or fostering arrangements, relationship stress or breakdown, and problems with education, housing and money" (Department of Health, 1999, p. 23).

TEEN PREGNANCY TODAY

Political Views and Public Policies

English politicians reacted with alarm to the high teen birthrates in the year 2000. As a result, Tony Blair, the prime minister of Great Britain, announced a new initiative to deal with Britain's poor record on preventing teenage pregnancies. England's rate is the highest in western Europe and is only exceeded among developed countries by the United States and Russia. When the new initiative was announced, Public Health Minister Tessa Jowell said, "We need to dispel the ignorance which surrounds sex, to combat the low expectations of those young girls who think with a child on benefit [a term meaning welfare or government supported] is the best they can hope for, and to unravel the mixed messages with which children are bombarded—where they are surrounded by sexual imagery without reference to the responsibilities associated with sexual activity." "Just as importantly, we need to ensure that boys are made aware that fatherhood is not a one-night stand, but a long-term responsibility" (BBC NEWS, 1999).

Sexuality and relationship education is important for prevention programs to work. Young girls and boys need the opportunity to learn about relationships and sexuality so that they do not succumb to peer pressure. Furthermore, more education needs to take place in the home. Parents are encouraged to sit down with their children and discuss issues of sex openly. Additional education and prevention work also needs to take place in schools. Specific measures that are suggested include "new guidance for schools on sex and relationships education which helps young people deal with the pressures to have sex too young, and encourages them to use contraception if they do have sex" (Department of Health, 1999, p. 9).

Furthermore, offering support in the schools through peer mentoring programs is an additional way of offering support to those teenagers at risk. In addition, "new school inspection and better training for teachers to bolster the new guidance" are needed. With regard to parents, assistance in the form of "information campaigns" needs to be developed in order to provide support to parents in helping them educate their children. Furthermore, the report discusses the need for "new health service standards for effective and responsible contraceptive advice and treatment for young people" as well as "clear and credible guidance for health professionals on the prescription, supply and administration of contraceptives to under 16-year-olds," "including a duty to counsel them when they seek advice on contraception." Last, it is important to target young men with information about the consequences of teen pregnancy and the emotional and financial responsibilities that go along with it (Department of Education, 1999, p. 9).

Social Views, Customs, and Practices

There is also great concern among the public about the high rate of teen pregnancy, unwed births, and the number of teens who contract sexually transmitted diseases. Before World War II, little thought was given to teen pregnancy, and for the most part, unwanted pregnancy was handled using "homes for unwed mothers" and adoption. Today, however, everyone in England knows of a teenage girl who has given birth to a child out of wedlock. While out-of-wedlock births to teenagers are socially unacceptable in England, because 90% of teenage girls are not married when giving birth, it has been necessary for the public and public social services to accept the reality of the phenomenon.

Another reason for the need to accept teenage sexual activity is the high rate of sexually transmitted diseases among British teens. The use of contraception-blocking devices (e.g., condoms) among British teenagers is dangerously low. By not using condoms, teenagers not only are at risk of becoming pregnant but are at risk of contracting a sexually transmitted disease. In fact, between a third and a half of sexually active teenagers do not use contraception at first intercourse, a higher proportion than in other western European countries. A sexually active teenager who does not use contraception has a 90% chance of conceiving during the first year of sexual activity and of contracting a sexually transmitted infection.

Sexually active teenagers who do not use contraception often report being embarrassed about using or discussing contraception with their partner. In this type of teen culture, it is important to empower teen girls with the skills to negotiate both the extent of the sexual encounter and the use of contraception. Because of the lack of public awareness among teens in England, teenagers are also confused about where they can get contraceptive advice or treatment. They are confused about whether it is legal for them to do so and how to use the information available (Department of Education, 1999).

In a single act of unprotected sex with an infected partner, teenage girls in England have a 1% chance of acquiring HIV, a 30% risk of getting genital herpes, and a 50% chance of contracting gonorrhea. Chlamydia affects teenage girls more than any other age group. It is the leading cause of ectopic pregnancy and can lead to infertility. It can cause discharge and pain, but there are usually no symptoms, so the sufferer may never know they are infected. Diagnoses of chlamydia in genito urinary medicine clinics for 16- to 19-year-olds rose by around 53% between 1995 and 1997 (PHLS, 1999).

Despite the laws protecting the privacy of young girls seeking contraceptive devices and contraceptives, especially those who are 16 and older, many young girls do not choose contraceptive measures as a way to prevent pregnancy or disease. Many young girls dislike using contraception or do not think they are at risk, that it would happen to them. They were afraid of discussing the issue with parents or doctors and are not educated in school about how to use contraception effectively. When teenagers are asked, they want a doctor "who is approachable, who will not judge them, and they need to know that anything they say will be treated in confidence" (BBC NEWS, 2000). The laws help protect young girls by ensuring confidentiality between doctor and patient and providing contraception without parental permission. It is vital that teenage girls be able to explore their concerns in a supportive and confidential way.

Teen Abortion

The Department of Health (1999) has compiled some statistics regarding the prevalence of teen abortion. According to the findings, slightly more than half of those teenagers, who are 16 years old and younger, terminate their pregnancy. According to the report, this statistic has changed little since the 1970s. For those teenagers who are in their twenties, over one-third of conceptions end in abortions, and this figure is rising. Furthermore, it was noted that one in ten 16- to 19-year-olds who have had an abortion have also had one earlier, and 2% have had both an abortion and a birth. Pregnant teenagers are also one and one-half times more likely than women in their twenties to have an abortion at 13 weeks or later. There has been research into the factors that influence a teenager's decision to have an abortion. One author reports that a greater influence seems to be young women's perceptions of their future prospects. Those who have higher education aspirations are more likely to have abortions than their peers, and students tend to have more abortions than non-students (Moore et al., 1996).

THE FUTURE OF TEEN PREGNANCY

There are several strategies that have been found to be effective in reducing and maintaining low teen pregnancy rates. First, it is important that sexual education be redesigned to eliminate the ignorance that surrounds sex for too many British youth. This will require a fact-based component of a national sexual education curriculum. Second, it is important that teenagers have access to contraception and that they are educated about how to use contraception and the importance of using it. Third, programs need to be developed to help teenage parents, especially help to teach parents how to talk with their children about sex, relationships, and prevention. This is important so that teenagers do not feel isolated and that they feel a sense of structure in terms of being parented. Finally, it is important that Public Health Minister Tessa Jowell keep her promise made in the year 2000 to develop new prevention and parenting programs (not disciplinary programs) for boys who are at risk of becoming or are teen fathers.

CONCLUSION

Margaret, the young girl in the vignette, is an example of one of many girls who became pregnant in the 1990s in England. The adversity faced by Margaret while attempting to raise her child is being faced by 90,000 new teenage moms each year in England.

Yet there are many factors in Great Britain that increase the risk of adolescent girls like Margaret becoming pregnant and becoming single mothers. While affluent areas in England have high rates of teenage pregnancy, it is the poorer areas that have the highest rates of teen pregnancy. The Department of Health's Consultation Report (1999) makes several salient points about teen pregnancy. It identifies economic barriers, lack of social support systems, lack of education about sex and preventive measures, and skills needed for decision making regarding relationships and unwanted pregnancy.

More difficult to deal with than teen programming is the attitude of the political and social establishment. The trend in England is to view teen pregnancy as a "personal responsibility" issue. Based on this paradigm and the logical programming that follows, it will be difficult for English social service providers to use the more pragmatic models that have succeeded in other western European nations. A paradigm of personal responsibility will result in programs that attempt to scare teens into celibacy. They will continue to use poorly developed sexual education curriculums and blame teenage girls and boys for adolescent pregnancy.

Although in 2000 Tony Blair acknowledged the British government's responsibility for the high number of teen pregnancies, sadly his answer was to increase government pressure on preteens and teens to fear sex before the age of 16 and to punish girls and boys for their sexual behavior if the girl becomes pregnant. This approach may help politicians with the voting public in England, but such programming will not decrease teen pregnancy in England and will not improve opportunities for girls or their children.

REFERENCES

BBC NEWS. (1999). *Boys face teen pregnancy crackdown.* Retrieved June 14, 1999, from the World Wide Web: www.bbc.newsonline.

BBC NEWS. (2000). *Women GPs "reduce teenage pregnancies."* Retrieved March 24, 2000, from the World Wide Web: www.bbc.newsonline.

Biehal, N., et al. (1992). *Prepared for living? A survey of young people leaving the care of local authorities.* London: National Children's Bureau.

Botting, B., Rosato, M., & Wood, R. (1998). Teenage mothers and the health of their children. *Population Trends, 93* (Autumn).

Central Intelligence Agency. (2000). *The world factbook: United Kingdom.* Washington, DC: Author. Retrieved October 14, 2000, from the World Wide Web: http://www.odci.gov/cia/publications/factbook/.

Department of Health. (1999). New arrangements for 16 and 17 year olds living in and leaving care. Consultation Paper. London: Author.

Health Education Authority analysis of health education and lifestyle survey. (1994). London: Department of Health.

HMIP. (1997). Thematic Review of Young Prisoners by HM Chief Inspector of Prisons for England and Wales. London: Her Majesty's Inspectorate of Prisons.

Kiernan, K. (1995). *Transition to parenthood: Young mothers, young fathers—associ-*

ated factors and later life experiences. Welfare State Programme, Discussion paper WSP/113, LSE.

Moore, K.A., Miller, B.C., Sugland B.W., Morrison, D.R., Glei, D.A., & Blumenthal, C. (1996). *Adolescent sexual behaviour, pregnancy, and parenthood: A review of research and interventions.* Washington, DC: Child Trends.

Office of National Statistics (ONS). (1997). Analysis of birth statistics series, FMI: London, England.

Policy Studies Institute (PSI). (1997). Fourth National *Survey of Ethnic Minorities.* London, England.

Public Health Laboratory Service (PHLS). (1999). Data from PHLS Communicable Disease Centre. London, England.

Wellings, K., Field J., Johnson, A.M., & Wadsworth, J. (1994). *Sexual behaviour in Britain: The national study of sexual attitudes and lifestyles.* London: Penguin Press.

Zoccolillo, M., & Rogers, K. (1991). Characteristics and outcome of hospitalized adolescent girls with conduct disorder. *Journal of the American Academy of Child Adolescent Psychiatry* (electronic version).

5

FRANCE

Louis B. Antoine

PROFILE OF FRANCE

If Charlemagne had had his way, France would have remained an immense theocratic empire, a Holy Roman Catholic Empire, as stipulated in his capitulary of year 802. For a brief time, it seemed that his dream would materialize. Bishops, abbots, abbesses, and counts swore allegiance to the emperor. Vassals of the king went to battle to win over territories in exchange for titles of nobility. Cousins, brothers, husbands, and wives went to war with each other and wrestled land from neighboring England. The conflicts continued for almost a century in a protracted war that came to be known as the Hundred Years War. France, which started out as a mere inkblot on the map of western Europe, became a huge empire with territories in Africa, the Caribbean, and remote islands in the middle of the Pacific. By the time Louis XIV—a.k.a. Le Roi Soleil—inherited the throne, he was ruling over an empire so immense that "the sun would never set on it" (Wagner, 1989).

Then Robespierre came along. He led the takeover of La Bastille and signaled the beginning of the French Revolution. Intellectuals tapped into the pent-up anger of the Third Estate against the oppressive feudal system. It was like a brushfire that would spread over places as far away as the Caribbean where slavery was in full force. The principles of *liberté, egalité, fraternité* were worth fighting for and dying for. A reign of terror followed. Heads rolled under the guillotine, transforming La Seine River into a stream of blood. Not even the inventor of this barbaric machine would be spared.

The aristocrats recaptured the reins of power. However, the government became more secular, and the seeds of rebelliousness were irreversibly sown in the conscience of the French people.

In 1968, after almost two centuries, two world wars, and ten years after presidential democracy was firmly established in the former monarchy, a group of disenchanted youths launched a new kind of revolution. From the amphitheaters of the Sorbonne to campuses across the nation, citizens would demonstrate. Workers would join in and demand full participation in the management of the factories. The youth wanted to take down the Victorian walls of hypocrisy firmly engrained into the sexual mores of the era. The words of the philosopher Epicure were echoed: "Seize the day." France and the rest of the world would never be the same again (Wagner, 1989).

Today, the population of France is estimated at 59 million inhabitants, with a labor force of 25.4 million. In 1998, the gross domestic product (GDP) was close to $1.32 trillion. France has managed to maintain an inflation rate below 1% and is firmly established among the premier industrialized nations of the world, with a per capita income of $22,600. France spends a significant percentage of its resources to maintain its armed forces. However, France was one of the first nations to sign on the European Community (EC) Maastricht Treaty in 1992 (Central Intelligence Agency, 2000).

With the government overseeing the location of hospitals and maintaining strict bed/population ratio, the French citizenry is free to choose treatment in a number of private or public hospitals. There is one physician for every 334 patients and one hospital per 15,000 people. In 1998, the average amount of money reimbursed by social security per inhabitant for health care was Fr12,270, or $2,250. The percentage of gross national product (GNP) spent on health care in France remains well below that of the United States (9.8 in France and 14.2 in the United States) (Central Intelligence Agency, 2000).

The life expectancy in France has reached 74.76 years for males and 82.71 years for females, creating an expanding geriatric group (20% of the population is over 60). There were 11.38 live births per 1,000 population and 9.17 deaths per 1,000 in 1999. Twenty-six percent of the general population remains under 20 years of age. The infant mortality rate is among the lowest in the world, at 5.62 deaths per 1,000 live births (Central Intelligence Agency, 2000).

Although it has a relatively high unemployment rate by industrialized nation standards (11.5% in 1998), very few Frenchmen live under the poverty level. On the recent United Nations Human Development Report surveying 174 nations (measuring personal income, access to health care, education, and life expectancy), France ranked twelfth behind countries like Canada, Norway, the United States, and Finland. There is one television set for every two inhabitants. In France, the predominant ethnic groups are

Celtic and Latin, with some Teutonic, Slavic, and North African in the minority. The population is 90% Catholic, 2% Protestant, 1% Jewish, and 1% Muslim; 6% claim no religious affiliation. Education is readily available to all, and the literacy rate, which is defined as the percentage of the population 15 years old and over that can read and write, is 99%.

INTRODUCTION

Through the years, many unique factors in French culture have shaped the French adolescence experience. Sociocultural constructs balance adolescent need for self-expression and growth, on the one hand, and the need of society to control adolescent behavior, on the other hand. The following explores this process within France, focusing on the complex set of interrelated facets of the French adolescent experience and teen pregnancy.

French adolescents, like adolescents in other developed nations, cannot escape the pressure of fulfilling the expectations of an often-demanding society. Postwar parents have been overly protective of children, giving them confusing messages about moving away from the comfort of the home. Living in a time of mass communication, it has been almost impossible for youth to resist the relentless marketing campaigns using "sex-based adds" to sell products.

The stresses of modern France can be demonstrated by surveying the suicide rate and running away from home; both are measures of relative discontent. While the rate of young people committing teenage suicide in France remains relatively low, the numbers remain a cause for concern. In France the rate of suicide increased from 7 per 100,000 in 1970 to 13 per 100,000 in 1999 (Aubry & Kouchner, 1999). This is comparable to the United States where there was also an increase among young people (5 through 19 years of age) from 5.9 in 1970 to 12 (estimated) in 1999 (U.S. Census Bureau, 1999). In France nearly 4% of French youth between 11 and 19 years of age have had one episode of running away (Toulemon & de Guibert-Lantoine, 1998). Like their male counterparts, teenage girls no longer trust their environment to provide them with a secure future.

Pregnancy brings extensive hormonal and dynamic physiological changes that stress the coping strategies of the pregnant teen to the limits. While the majority of teenagers are trying to master developmental tasks such as a physical sense of self, adjustment to increased cognitive demands at school, and vocational choices, the teenage girl becomes forced to mobilize all of her resources to manage her pregnancy. At great risk to both herself and her child, the pregnant French teen faces an accelerated course of physical maturity with little or no preparation.

However, few other developed countries offer teen moms the supportive institutions necessary to meet the challenges like the French. This support is expressed in the adoption of policies tailored exclusively for the youth.

For example, the government has implemented a nationally mandated sexual education program that starts when students reach 13 (Berne & Huberman, 1999). Parents' religious affiliation or political beliefs are not allowed to get in the way of sex education. Often the government has been willing to take daring and controversial positions. Recently, French policymakers announced a new policy enabling nurses to offer emergency contraception in France's high schools (Bishop, 1999).

French social scientists and policymakers have come to realize that teenagers in France, regardless of their religious background, will often disregard societal values and conventional taboos to undertake one of the most sacred and taunting tasks in a woman's life. The policymakers in France therefore have adopted a pragmatic approach to teenage pregnancy. The government perceives the fact as a public health concern rather than as a religious debate.

The value of delaying sexual activity is promoted in the media. One clear pragmatic message broadcast a few years ago was: "If you do have sex, you need to protect yourself" (Toulemon & de Guibert-Lantoine, 1998). It is also clear that the French media in news stories and articles, although accepting the reality of teenage sex, clearly discourages unintended pregnancy.

Current indicators show that French teenagers are responding to this approach. Adolescents are using both birth control methods and abortion. France has about 10,000 schoolgirl pregnancies each year, of which 6,700 end in abortion. Just over 3% of French girls between 15 and 18 years of age who have sex get pregnant. Increasingly, French teenagers are choosing to abstain from sexual activities. In France, as in most European nations, teenage girls are having sex at an older age. The average age of first sexual encounter is now over 15.8 years (Toulemon & Leridon, 1998).

The number of teenage pregnancies and the reaction to this phenomenon vary from one country to the next. For most industrialized nations, keeping this response free of political and religious biases has been a real tour de force. France has avoided blaming the increased number of childhood and teenage pregnancies on the disintegration of the family. Instead, France and other European nations have opted to view teenage pregnancy as a public health phenomenon with multiple causes. Consequently, they have established a network of receiving facilities for reducing the impact of teenage pregnancy on the educational and vocational opportunities of the teen mother. This and similar French programs have reduced teen pregnancy, teen abortion, and sexual activity.

Vignette

Marianne recently celebrated her fourteenth birthday. The past couple of years of her life have been full of events. She has seen her parents struggle. Her father started to stay out at night. Then he suddenly disappeared altogether. Two years later, her mother received the divorce documents. Life in the home became miserable. Marianne's mother grew increasingly depressed and irritable. She stopped taking care of her personal appearance and hardly came out of her bedroom. She only spoke to her daughter to make demands that Marianne found unreasonable. Marianne felt under no obligation to listen to a woman that never showed her any affection. During increasingly loud arguments, her mother would remind her that she wanted a son, not a daughter. Marianne had to learn quickly how to take care of herself and looked forward to the day when she could get away from her overbearing mother.

Marianne soon lost interest in school and began experimenting with Ecstasy and alcohol. Twice she ran away from home, but the police took her back. Just as Marianne was about to lose all hope, something unexpected happened: Her mother started to go out. Once again, she was visiting her hairdresser. Her outlook on life seemed brighter. Marianne's mother was dating again. One evening she seemed particularly happy. She announced to Marianne that Paul, her boyfriend, was coming for dinner. Marianne had mixed feelings about this sudden change. She had watched her mother struggle through bad times and hoped that her newly found relationship would bring her some happiness. On the other hand, even though their relationship was very bad, she was afraid that her mother would soon abandon her and run off with her new boyfriend, like her father did a few years before. Six months later, Paul and her mother married.

At first, Marianne's mother welcomed the overt display of affection between her new husband and her teenage daughter. She wanted her daughter to accept Paul. Maybe he would be able to make up for the father that she had chased away. She soon realized, however, that she was no match for her daughter, who was developing into a tall and attractive young woman. Her new husband took notice. He became disinterested in the marital bed. Marianne's mother became increasingly suspicious of her husband's attraction to her daughter. Marianne did not do anything to allay her mother's fear and suspicion. In fact, she was infatuated with this charming father figure. For the first time in her life, someone was taking an interest in her and was validating her as an attractive and sensual young woman. Unlike her mother, she started to wear fashionable jeans and provocative tops. Paul soon made it clear to Marianne that his interest was not simply paternal. Marianne found it increasingly difficult to resist the sexual advances of her stepfather. Marianne felt trapped. She was ridden with guilt, blaming herself for the sexual encounters. She often thought about suicide. She often ran away in the middle of the night and hid in an abandoned building nearby.

Two months later, she started to experience nausea and signs of abdominal discomfort. After she missed her period for the second time, Marianne worried that she was pregnant. What would Marianne do? She certainly was not ready to reveal such distressful news to her emotionally unstable mother.

On the one hand, Marianne felt that the situation gave her an opportunity for revenge. On the other hand, she loved her mother and felt a duty to protect her.

Girls like Marianne are prime targets for continuous exploitation, prostitution, drugs and alcohol abuse, and worst of all, illegal, dangerous, and unsupervised self-induced abortions. Many young girls, caught in the web of incest and sexual abuse, choose to go through their ordeal alone. They become entangled in a persistent cycle of unwanted pregnancies, false starts, and rejection from society. Should Marianne decide to go through the appropriate channels, it is hard to imagine that she would be turned away. In fact, Marianne has many options.

In France, there exists a network of receiving facilities waiting to help her and guide her through her ordeal. These include sixty-six Centres d'interruption volontaire de la grossesse, or CIVG (Center for the Voluntary Interruption of Pregnancy) (Aubry, 2000). In addition, France has many units that are more specialized at various hospitals. She can present herself at any public general hospital or a private institution. She might meet initial reluctance because of moralistic considerations, but the physician in charge will have no choice but to initiate the process that will guarantee Marianne a termination of pregnancy if she requests it, thanks to Veil's law, in effect since 1975 (Aubry & Kouchner, 1999).

Before the actual procedure, many steps will be taken on her behalf. First, an anonymous individual statistical bulletin must be created and sent to the regional health inspectors (Direction Régionale des Affaires Sanitaires et Sociales [DRASS]), who will then direct them to the Directorate General of Health and the Institut National de la Statistique et des Études Économiques (L'INSEE). Marianne must wait one week. This waiting period is designed to allow her to contemplate the implications of her decision. Additionally, the physician cannot proceed before acquiring written parental consent. In the event that the pregnancy is the result of an act of violence or sexual abuse, the clinical team will report it to the police. In addition, if her parents refuse to sign consent the team will inform Marianne that an interview with a psychologist or a social worker is obligatory (Uzan, 1999). The counselor ideally will assume a nonjudgmental listening posture in order to help Marianne through the complex psychological conflicts brought on by her pregnancy.

Marianne's case is complicated by the preexistence of deep-rooted family conflicts, the precariousness of her mother's mental health, and the need for secrecy around this incestuous encounter. Should Marianne's mother refuse to give consent, the case will fall under the jurisdiction of the juvenile judge. An appointed ad hoc guardian will be given the power to authorize the procedure. Should the abortion proceed, a case manager from the center will help Marianne transition back to school. The center will arrange for follow-up appointments and will offer Marianne periodic screening for sexually transmitted diseases.

However, Marianne's troubles are far from over. Her mother will have to face her depression and her feelings of guilt for endangering her daughter. Hopefully, the family will continue with counseling until the outlook is improved.

Marianne's story bears many of the characteristics of the dilemma that teenage pregnant girls face in an ever-changing society. The roots of the problem are often buried in a multigenerational set of factors. In her case, she was a victim on many counts. Her immediate family failed to provide her with a safe, caring environment. Early in Marianne's life, she had multiple risks for major emotional difficulty. Fortunately, the community support system was ready to offer the troubled girl a chance to recover from her missteps. However, not every girl will have such opportunities.

Overview of Teen Pregnancy

Condoms have gained in popularity, especially among the younger age group. Condoms are used not only to prevent conception but also to prevent sexually transmitted diseases (STDs). Since physicians in France tend to underreport STDs, the health system has depended on a national sentinel network of laboratories to collect its data. In 1996, these data indicate an incidence rate of chlamydia infection around 110.9 per 100,000 among teenage girls between 15 and 19 years of age, as compared to a rate 2,067 per 100,000 among the same age group in the United States. The figures for gonorrhea show a similar disparity between the rates among teenage girls 15 to 19 of the two countries. The rates stand at 8.2 per 100,000 for France and 758.2 per 100,000 for the United States (Alan Guttmacher Institute, 2000; Panchaud, Singh, Feivelson, & Darroch, 2000).

The percentage of individuals who use contraceptives at their first sexual intercourse has steadily increased. Over 36% of women of childbearing age in France are using oral contraceptives. The majority of contraceptive pills are reimbursable under the governmental social security system. After reaching an adolescent birthrate of 37.4 per 1,000 in 1970, France has managed to decrease the rate to 10.0 per 1,000. Very few other European nations can claim such success (Boonstra, 2000; Singh & Darroch, 2000). The reduction in teen pregnancy did not occur because French schoolgirls have universally adopted abstinence. Although the rate of teenage pregnancy in France remains minuscule as compared to that of the United States, there are still about 10,000 teen pregnancies a year, with close to 70% ending in abortions.

HISTORY AND SOCIAL CONTEXT

The above scenario seems a long way from the beginning of the 20th century when the penal code included harsh punishment for anyone engaged in the practice of contraception or abortion. Incidentally, the two were not always distinguishable under the law. The struggle for the acqui-sition of contraception and abortion rights has been in the center of the women's liberation movement. We will briefly review the history of this struggle.

During the height of the repressive era at the beginning of the 19th century, the fear of forced labor and reclusion did not stop physicians and pharmacists from clandestinely developing contraceptives and performing abortions. For the poor and middle class, the industrial revolution created poverty and misery throughout Europe, making it increasingly difficult to raise large families. During the late 1800s, the women were developing an underground network to obtain contraceptives and abortions. In 1889, 100 years after the French Revolution, Paul Robin created the first center for information and sale of contraceptive products.

The following time line will help the reader understand the changes in French society in relation to women's lives (Aubry, 2000).

1920	Contraception and abortion are forbidden, as is any material propagating such practices.
1923	Importation of contraceptive material is forbidden.
1942	Abortion is declared a state crime punishable by death.
1943	A woman who had an abortion is executed.
1960	French movement for family planning starts.
1967	Neuwirth law abrogates the law of 1920 and authorizes contraception.
1971	*Nouvel Observateur* publishes the manifesto of 343 women who had an abortion and demand that abortion be performed freely.
1974	Contraceptives are now reimbursable by social security.
1975	Simone Veil's law—making "interruption volontaire de la grossesse" (IVG; voluntary interruption of pregnancy) legal and available if requested before the tenth week of pregnancy—is passed.
1987	Marketing of RU486 is begun.
2000	Aubry, the Minister of Employment and Solidarity, and the socialist government of Lionel Jospin propose a bill extending IVG requests from ten to twelve weeks.

TEEN PREGNANCY TODAY

Political Views and Public Policies

While liberal and conservative factions from many industrialized nations continue to debate whether or not access to health care should be consid-ered a basic right for every citizen, France adopted the law of July 29, 1998. This law ensures that no one is excluded from receiving basic rights such as the right to health care, to affordable housing, and to a life of dignity.

Successive governments have continued to maintain a nation built on the principles of the unity and solidarity of all its citizens. They have established a number of priorities designed to guarantee uninterrupted access to health care and reduce the inequalities of care between the different regions of France. The policies in place to provide unimpeded access to voluntary termination of pregnancy and the availability of different methods of contraception are only two examples of a well-planned and -integrated health care system, built to address both the social and health needs of every citizen. The success of this program would not have been possible without the country's high literacy rate and the commitment of all the different state agencies under the leadership of the Ministère de l'Emploi et de la Solidarité, all with one clear motto in mind: "La contraception a vous de choisir la votre" (Contraception: the choice is yours). To implement this program, no resources have been spared (Aubry, 2000).

Social Views, Customs, and Practices

In trying to explain the relative success of the French health system in reducing both unintended pregnancy and abortion, compared to other industrialized nations, one must look at many factors. In the embryonic stage of France as a nation, the ancestors toyed with the idea of establishing a theocracy led by a king under the direct command of God. Successive revolutionary waves shook the conservative foundations of the nation, leaving the Frenchmen *à tort ou à raison* (rightly or wrongly) with the reputation of being a vibrant and rebellious people who would not hesitate to take to the streets when the noble principles of *liberté, egalité, fraternité* (liberty, equality, fraternity) are threatened.

The French people have succeeded in limiting the polarizing influences of extreme religious and political views on matters of health such as abortion rights and teenage pregnancy. Although 90% Catholic, French society has been able to integrate more secular views on how the citizenry should handle social issues such as free union, same-sex or heterosexual marriages, divorce, and termination of pregnancy. Fairly well educated and informed on political issues, the electorate has adequately used its voting power to elect officials who are responsive to individual freedom. When increasing numbers of women began to cross the borders to seek an abortion because of the 10-week limit imposed in France, the Jospin government responded by proposing an extension to 12 weeks. In spite of the inflationary and economic pressure to revamp the system and cut waste, the socialized health system in France is one of the most cost-effective and most user-friendly in the world. Access to health care is regarded as a fundamental right (Aubry, 2000). It also makes economic sense: Every youth restored to normal functioning can be viewed as saving on the future costs to the overall economy.

The importance of innovative approaches to sexual education with a focus on prevention cannot be overemphasized. France was the first country to consider the distribution of a locally produced brand of emergency contraception (ECP), known as NorLevo, in pharmacies without prescription or parental consent. In January 2000, French authorities took the bolder step of granting high school nurses the right to dispense ECPs in both junior and high schools (August, 2000). This measure will undoubtedly be challenged on both legal and ethical grounds. Undoubtedly, this debate will be difficult as the society continues to seek adequate solutions to adolescent pregnancy.

THE FUTURE OF TEEN PREGNANCY

France has played a leadership role in the establishment of the European Union. However, there seem to be several contradictions that have the potential of threatening the foundations of France as a nation. The European Union seems to be promoting the free movement of citizens across the borders of the former nations, whereas members of neofascist groups would like to see immigration from poorer nations and minority groups excluded. The instability of the global market in the post–Cold War era will continue to create disparity and frustration among developing nations, and countries like France will be called upon to lead the world toward a more equitable distribution of resources and debt elimination. In response to these national and international issues, French youth are waiting longer to get married or are not getting married at all. It is becoming increasingly socially acceptable to live in *union*.

These social changes have the potential to bring about serious changes in the social structure of the French nation. To help maintain a replacement population and to develop inheritance laws that protect a child born outside of a traditional marriage, more government interventions are needed.

CONCLUSION

The problem of teenage pregnancy can overwhelm both industrialized and developing countries. However, this problem does not occur in a vacuum. Girls who become pregnant in France have characteristics they share with other girls around the world. Risk factors like family dysfunction, school failure, and low socioeconomic status contribute to teen pregnancy and other adolescent problems in France as in other countries. Taking a purely public health approach to this problem, and providing comprehensive services, for example, like in France and other western European countries, has shown remarkable success. Of course, in countries that are mired in extreme political and religious debates such as the United States, providing free, confidential, and emergency services to prevent or terminate an unintended pregnancy can be extremely difficult. As such, the rates of teen pregnancy in the United States are many times higher than in France. The balance of the health and social needs of the French citizen and the religious influences of the Catholic Church have allowed this Catholic country to lead the world in modern contraception and in strategies that reduce both unintended teen pregnancy and abortion.

Instinctively, most adolescents—at the appropriate time—want to bring healthy children of their own into this world. This in part depends on a mother in good health, knowledgeable of pre- and postnatal care, and physically mature enough to deliver a healthy child. To this end, today in France most teenage girls are delaying sexual activity and are giving birth to their first child in their early twenties. And with the understanding and the support services provided by the best health care system in the world—which both educates and helps adolescents protect themselves and their partners— French youth will continue to have a low unintended teenage birthrate and abortion rate into the 21st century.

REFERENCES

Alan Guttmacher Institute. (2000, February 24). Young adults bear the brunt of sexually transmitted diseases in developed countries. News Release. Retrieved July 25, 2000, from the World Wide Web: http://www.agi-usa.org/pubs/archives/newsrelease32ola.html.

Aubry, M. (2000). Deux ans d'action de lutte contre les exclusions. Retrieved September 24, 2000, from the World Wide Web: http://www.emploi-solidarite.gouv.fr/index.html.

Aubry, M., & Kouchner, B. (1999). L'ivg en France: Propositions pour diminuer les difficultés que rencontrent les femmes. Retrieved July 29, 2000, from the World Wide Web: http://www.gyneweb.fr/sources/contraception/ivg.htm.

August, M. (2000, October 7). French girls may get morning-after pill. *Washington Times*, p. A1.

Berne, L., & Huberman, B. (Eds.). (1999). *European approaches to adolescent sexual behavior and responsibility*. Washington, DC: Advocates for Youth.

Bishop, P. (1999). French pupils get morning-after pill. *Daily Telegraph*. Retrieved September 23, 2000, from the World Wide Web: http://www.elibrary.com.

Boonstra, H. (2000). *Issues & implications—promoting contraceptive use and choice: France's approach to teen pregnancy and abortion*. New York: Alan Guttmacher Institute.

Central Intelligence Agency. (2000). *The world factbook: France*. Washington, DC: Author. Prepared by the Central Intelligence Agency for the use of U.S. government officials. Retrieved July 25, 2000, from the World Wide Web: http://www.odci.gov/cia/publications/factbook/geos/fr.html.

Panchaud, C., & Singh, S., Feivelson, D., & Darroch, J.E. (2000). Sexually transmitted diseases among adolescents in developed countries. *Family Planning Perspectives, 32*(1), 24–32, 45.

Singh, S., & Darroch, J.E. (2000). Adolescent pregnancy and childbearing: Level and trends in developed countries. *Family Planning Perspectives, 32*(1), 14–23.

Toulemon, L., & de Guibert-Lantoine, C. (1998). *Fertility and family surveys in countries of the ECE region. Standard country report, France.* Geneva: United Nations.

Toulemon, L., & Leridon, H. (1998). Contraceptive practices and trends in France. *Family Planning Perspectives, 30*(3), 117–120.

U.S. Census Bureau. (1999). *Statistical abstract of the United States.* Washington, DC: Department of Commerce.

Uzan, M. (1999). Rapport sur la prévention et la prise en charge des grossesses des adolescentes. Hôpital Jean Verdier, Université de Paris XIII.

Wagner, M. (1989). *From Gaul to De Gaulle: An outline of French civilization.* American University Studies. Series IX. History. Vol. 43. New York: Peter Lang Publishing.

6

GERMANY

Andrew L. Cherry

PROFILE OF GERMANY

Germany is a wealthy and highly urbanized country. It is a leading producer of such products as iron and steel, machinery and machine tools, and automobiles. Germans are also known for their love of rich pastries, veal and pork dishes, and various types of sausages and cheeses. German-made beer is considered the best in the world.

Germany is characterized by a high standard of living, generous labor benefits (Germany has a long history of strong labor unions), and comprehensive social welfare benefits. Five of the 10 most prosperous regions in the European Union were in Germany in 1999. Germany has 40 cities with more than 200,000 residents, 12 metropolitan areas with more than 500,000 residents, and a total population of 82,163 million as of 2000.

Most Germans live in the northwest part of the country, especially in North Rhine-Westphalia (Nordrhein-Westfalen). The areas with the smallest populations are in the former East Germany and in the more rural states of Schleswig-Holstein, Lower Saxony (Niedersachsen), and Bavaria. Berlin is the capital and the largest city. Bonn, the capital of what was West Germany, still houses a few government agencies.

The German lifestyle emphasizes recreational, leisure, and physical fitness activities. Many Germans enjoy hiking, camping, skiing, and other outdoor pursuits. Germany has a million property millionaires and 25,000 income millionaires. In 1997, the gross domestic product (GDP) was $2,034,652,100,000. The GDP per capita was $24,792. This can be compared to Brazil, where the GDP per capita was approximately $5,000 per person in the same year (Bureau of European Affairs, 2000).

Germany also had almost 2.7 million people drawing welfare in 1997. When the Germany economy took a down turn, the number on welfare tripled between 1980 and 2000. Social welfare guarantees that the recipient's basic needs are met and that they are somewhat able to participate in the social life of the community. Nevertheless, the experience of 1 million poor children and teenagers in Germany is very different from their peers whose parents are gainfully employed.

Researchers estimate that for each person claiming welfare there are 1.7 Germans who are eligible but do not apply. Some believe it is because collecting welfare would bear a social stigma (Gibson, Penner, Sathiah, Sautter, & Skari, 1998).

INTRODUCTION

Teenage pregnancy in Germany today is of concern but is not viewed as a major social problem. Germany has one of western Europe's lowest teen pregnancy rates. This low rate has *not* occurred because German teenagers are abstaining from sexual relationships; they are as sexually active as ever. However, the number of adolescent girls giving birth has dropped because teenagers have become more responsible when they engage in sexual relationships. This assertion is supported by studies in the late 1990s that show the age of first intercourse was just under 17 years of age as compared to 15 years of age in the mid-1980s (Daruvalla, Kaplar, Labi, Landry, & Penner, 1999).

In the mid-1980s, social and political leaders in Germany, the Netherlands, Finland, and Denmark made the decision that high rates of teenage pregnancy were unacceptable. These countries made strategic policy decisions about the reproductive rights of their adolescents, and some of these policies provided compulsory services, such as "relationship education." Other services such as contraceptives were made more easily accessible to adolescents. Health agencies provided accurate information about adolescent sexual health and ways to reduce teenage pregnancy. The results have been very positive (Handshin, 1999).

In 1980, the adolescent pregnancy rate in West Germany was 43 per 1,000 adolescents. In East Germany, the 1980 pregnancy rate was 65.8 per 1,000 adolescents. This dropped to 14.3 pregnancies per 1,000 among West German adolescents by 1990. It dropped to 40.3 pregnancies among East Germans adolescent girls during the same period (Sing & Darroch, 2000).

In 1970, the adolescent birthrate in West Germany was 43 per 1,000. In East Germany in 1970, the birthrate was 72 per 1,000 adolescents. This dropped to 13.2 births per 1,000 adolescents by 1995 for a united Germany (Sing & Darroch, 2000).

As compared to the United States, the teenage birthrate in Germany is more than 4 times lower. The teenage abortion rate is more than 8 times lower, and Germany's teen AIDS (acquired immunodeficiency syndrome) rate is 11.5 times lower than that among teens in the United States (Berne & Huberman, 1999).

The social planners in Germany and most of western Europe have found an effective approach to adolescent sexuality that both delays adolescent sexual activity and childbirths and reduces sexually transmitted diseases. It is a pragmatic approach, which tends to respect the sexual rights of German adolescents. It is recognition that sexual expression is an essential component in teenage development. Honest, accurate information about sex and access to high-quality reproductive health services have helped empower German adolescent females to express their sexuality in safe and healthy ways. Low adolescent pregnancy, birth, and abortion rates follow as a natural outcome.

German society has undergone many changes since the early 1960s. Television has homogenized popular culture even in the rural areas. However, the greatest changes have probably been experienced by young women. Although society has changed somewhat for males in Germany, the most radical changes have occurred for young women. Most traditional barriers to a woman's career—in particular, barriers to diversified vocational fields and to higher education—have been removed.

Today adolescent girls have choices in Germany. They are not relegated to the traditional family roles of motherhood and child rearing. They also exercise choice in birth control, and this has greatly lowered the birth rate. Large families that were common in the early 20th century were down to an average size of 3.5 members per household at the beginning of the 21st century. In addition, the numbers of single-parent and one-person households are increasing (Bureau of European Affairs, 2000).

Germany does not have large pockets of poverty or great economic disparity, but it has social problems that in some cases are growing. There are substantial numbers of homeless people and persistent problems with crime, violence, alcoholism, and drug abuse.

The crime rates are considerably lower in Germany than in the United States. The possession of guns is controlled. However, nonviolent crimes, such as theft and burglary in urban areas, have increased since the 1970s. Crime is enough of a problem that law and order is typically a political campaign issue.

Between the 1960s and 2000, teenage violence and crime increased. Disruptive behavior and gang membership characterize some urban secondary schools. Neighborhood youth gangs sometimes engage in vandalism, car theft, and other crimes. Some teens joined punk and skinhead groups, which often promoted drug use, violence, and/or racism. By the late 1990s, juvenile crime began to fall, in part, due to the reduced birthrate in the 1970s, reducing the teen population (Doek, 1994).

In the early 1990s, Germany faced its greatest challenge since the end of World War II. There were a large number of immigrants, especially illegal aliens and asylum seekers, who made their way into Germany. During this same period, the East German Communist regime collapsed. Unification of the country was costly in economic and social terms. The problems included tax increases, budget deficits, housing shortages, strikes and demonstrations, unemployment, and rising crime rates.

This period of unfettered social change, economic fluctuation, and the accompanying anxiety resulted in an increase in xenophobia (fear of foreigners). The adults focused on the immigrants as being the cause of their economic problems. The immigrants were competing for housing and other benefits. Teenage gangs attacked the immigrants and set fire to their government-housing shelters. This level of xenophobia peaked in 1992; owing to the reaction of the media in Germany and abroad (it was interpreted as the revival of Nazism), massive counterdemonstrations drew millions of Germans opposed to racism and antiimmigrant violence (Kurthen & Bergmann, 1997).

Of major concern to the government is the rapidly aging and shrinking population. Although this is slowed slightly by a longer life expectancy, the German population continues to shrink and grow older. The average life expectancy for males is 74.7 years (a 2000 to 2010 projection). For women, life expectancy is 80.0 years (a 2000 to 2010 projection). This means that in the future a smaller number of German workers will have to support an ever-increasing number of retired workers. A rising number of retired elderly means that both pension payments and national health expenditures will increase (Bureau of European Affairs, 2000).

The health and social security system in Germany is one of the best in the world. Health, unemployment, and retirement insurance are mandatory for all but the highest wage earners. The services are generous. They are funded by a payroll-withholding plan that requires contributions from workers, employers, and government. The normal retirement age is 65 for both men and women.

The welfare system provides for all widows, orphans, and disabled people. The state provides generous financial assistance and health care, and it subsidizes low-income housing. Consequently, the infant mortality rate is 5 per 1,000 live births. Maternal mortality is 22 per 100,000 live births (Bureau of European Affairs, 2000). These are some of the lowest mortality rates in the world.

Over 99% of German people are literate. In part, this is because education is compulsory for all children between the ages of 6 and 16. The public school system is administered by the states. Primary education is free. After completing this primary education, students may opt for an educational track or vocational training.

School starts with a year of kindergarten and is followed by four years of primary school (*Grundschule*). In the fifth and sixth year of their education, German students are screened to determine their educational future. Those in the advanced track continue at a grammar school (*Gymnasium*) until they are 19. If the student passes the comprehensive academic examination called the *Abitur*, they are admitted to a university. About 17% of all students are admitted to a university. For the remaining students, after the age of 16 there are a variety of vocational schools available (Craig, 1991).

Vignette

Mia H., a 16-year-old student in Berlin, is typical of most of her peers when she says she might want to marry one day "because it's a little girl's dream." She quickly adds that "one day" would be when she is "between 25 and 30." Mia is a sexually active teenager who takes care to avoid pregnancy. She says contraception is necessary. "Not only because of AIDS, which I don't really think about that much, but because I don't want to become a mother at my age."

Mia grew up in a religious family but describes her church's ban on premarital sex as "dumb." "It's important to know the person you're going to be with in a sexual way. If I end up with a guy who does it wrong, it would be very disappointing."

Mia believes, "If you care about your partner deeply, and you know he cares about you, then it's natural to express this love physically." Although many young men share her view on romance, many more than 20 years ago, the idea that sex follows love is still stronger among females.

Mia believes young people in Germany "stand on their own two feet" at an earlier age than in the past. "When I wanted to stay overnight at my boyfriend's house the first time, all my mother said was that she did not want to become a grandmother yet." Mia sees sex as "a matter of trying out and experiencing. And it's fun!"

Mia said German girls are good at negotiating with both themselves and their potential partners on whether they are ready for intercourse. Girls typically talk easily about their expectations and concerns. "Usually boys do not have much to say about sexual relationships," said Mia.

While faithfulness is important, abstinence is not. Mia defines a steady relationship as "one where you can talk with each other and where you do not fool around with anybody else."

Heike S. is a seventeen-year-old single mother of two sons, ages one and two. She lives with her sons in a one-room apartment in a working-class section of Berlin. She receives welfare for her sons. She earns another $400 a month cleaning a neighbor's house. The two amounts total slightly over the rent on her apartment. Inevitably, she is behind with her rent. Her landlord often waits for her at the metro station to ask her for the money.

Heike went back to school after the birth of her first child. She had in-

Table 6.1
Pregnancy, Abortions, and Births per 1,000 Girls Ages 15 to 19

Pregnancy Rate	Abortion Rate	Birthrate
16.1	3.6	12.5

Source: Data from Singh & Darroch, 2000.

tentions of staying in school, but she became pregnant again and did not want to abort her child.

Neither father helps with the support of the children. They are teenagers themselves and are still in school. Heike hopes to marry someday. She also hopes to go to school to learn about computers.

Her mother, who is divorced and unemployed, lives with Heike's three younger siblings several blocks away. Her mother and sister help with babysitting and child care.

Taking care of two toddlers is a full-time job. Heike hopes to go back to school but not until her boys start school. Her future and that of her children are at risk.

Participation in German social life is defined by money. When people do not have it, they are excluded from that society. For the 1 million children and teenagers on welfare in Germany, not being able to keep up with their peers is part of what is called the "spiral of despair."

When their friends go to the movies, children on welfare stay home. Children on welfare do not often go to birthday parties because their parents cannot afford the present. Too often, at school, welfare children cannot go on class trips if extra money is required. If they need tutoring, too often their parents either do not realize the importance of tutoring or cannot help. All too often, children on welfare become discouraged and drop out of school. They often end up as the new unemployed. For these welfare children, poverty is hereditary.

Overview of Teen Pregnancy

Sexually Active

In a survey conducted by the German Federal Agency for Health Education in the late 1990s, 78% of teenage girls and 59% of teenage boys said they wanted "absolute faithfullness" in their relationships. Only 7.5% preferred a "completely open" relationship. This clearly indicates that for the vast majority of German teenagers "sleeping around" is unacceptable behavior (Annie E. Casey Foundation, 1998; Daruvalla et al., 1999) (also see Tables 6.1 and 6.2).

Table 6.2
Birthrates per 1,000 by Age Group

15–17 Years of Age	18–19 Years of Age
4.4	24.5

Source: Data from Singh & Darroch, 2000.

Marrying Later

At the beginning of the 21st century, social scientists would consider most German teenagers to be *serial monogamists*. The majority of German teenagers view sex and marriage as unrelated. They begin their sex life in their late teens, and after one or more sex partners, they may marry. In 1997, for example, women typically married at age 27 years and 10 months, whereas men married at 30 years and four months. During this same year, another 5.25 million Germans were living in union, although unmarried. There is no social division between those who choose to get married and those who do not (Daruvalla et al., 1999).

The Germans, English, and Spaniards are the most liberal, or nontraditional, in their outlook toward children. Some 90% or more of adults from these countries say it is morally acceptable to have a child out of wedlock. In Germany and France, acceptance of out-of-wedlock children is extremely high throughout society, regardless of age of the respondent (Summers, 1999). Acceptance is high because having children is widely perceived as necessary for personal fulfillment. In Germany (49%) and the United States (46%), slightly less than half of those surveyed believe that personal fulfillment involves having children (Gallup Poll, 1997).

HISTORY AND SOCIAL CONTEXT

Germany, because of its central location in Europe, has been a crossroads for many people, ideas, and armies. After World War II, Germany was divided into two countries by the Allies: the Federal Republic of Germany (FRG), also known as West Germany, and the German Democratic Republic (GDR), known as East Germany. The GDR was a member of the Communist block countries between 1945 and 1989.

The people from what was East Germany continue to move into the mainstream of German society. Unification brought greater personal freedom to East Germans, but the market economy also increased competition and a bustling pace of life uncommon in East Germany before unification (Bureau of European Affairs, 2000).

Unification was not good for everyone. Many East German women rightfully worried about how the unification would affect their hard-won gains in East Germany. They were concerned that contraceptives, abortion, child care, maternity leave, and educational opportunities would not be as available to them in the united Germany. They were afraid of losing their right to free contraceptives and an abortion on demand during the first three months of a pregnancy (Fields, 1990).

Teenage pregnancy for older East German girls was not considered a problem if the girl wanted the child and would stay in school. Women were given bonuses and stipends if they kept their babies. Because of East Germany's declining population in the 1970s, women were encouraged to have children and get an education. In this way women could help overcome the need both for replacement population and for skilled labor (McAdams, 1993).

East German women saw their right to an abortion in the context of privacy. Some 25% of all East German pregnancies were aborted before unification (Fields, 1990).

Before unification an estimated 81% of East German women were in the workforce. This was the highest figure in the world in the early 1980s. In many ways, the East German women were the most emancipated women of their day in Europe.

In East Germany before unification, women controlled much of East Germany's schools and health services. The 1 million children in nurseries and kindergartens were entirely in the hands of women. The overwhelming majority of East German teachers in elementary and high schools were women. Moreover, it is estimated that before unification 60% to 70% of the doctors and 80% of the dentists were women (Getler, 1979).

After unification, many large state-owned (Communist) manufacturing companies and agricultural co-ops failed. In the first four years after unification, about three-fourths of the state-owned enterprises went out of business, resulting in high unemployment and disrupting the lives of the majority of East German women. The unified German government continues to invest a great deal of money in the former East Germany to modernize the infrastructure of roads, transport, communications, and housing (Getler, 1979).

TEEN PREGNANCY TODAY

Political Views and Public Policies

Abortion

Abortion is legal in Germany, but a woman seeking an abortion is required to undergo counseling aimed at dissuading her from terminating her pregnancy; then she is required to wait three days after counseling before an abortion may be performed. This abortion law, influenced by what was West Germany, is based on attitudes similar to those who oppose abortion in the United States. East Germany had a different view of abortion: It was a woman's right to decide for herself, no questions asked (Getler, 1979).

Table 6.3
Syphilis per 100,000 Teenagers, 15 to 19 Years Old

Country	Females	Males	Average
Germany	1.1	1.2	1.2
Switzerland	0.5	0.5	0.5
Russia	313.4	112.3	212.9
USA	8.6	4.3	6.5

Source: Panchaud et al., 2000.

Sex Education and Openness

Relationship education is thought to be extremely important to the low teen birthrate in Germany. The openness of sex education with very young children has not led to unwanted pregnancies or to sex at an earlier age, nor has it decreased teenage sexual activity. Sexuality education is comprehensive and targeted to meet the reading and developmental levels of the students, starting at age six (Cizek, 1992).

STDs among Female Adolescents and Young Women

Sexually transmitted diseases (STDs) are disproportionately found among young females in Germany as in almost all of the countries on which data are available. At the same age, young females are infected at higher rates than their male counterparts (see Tables 6.3 and 6.4).

Syphilis, gonorrhea, and chlamydia disproportionately impact young people 15 to 24 years old (Alan Guttmacher Institute, 2000b). Of this group, girls and young women are affected far worse than their male partners. STDs in almost all countries of the world are generally higher among teenage girls and young women than males of the same age (see Tables 6.3 and 6.4) (Panchaud, Singh, Feivelson, & Darroch, 2000).

We speculate that for some teen girls and young women, such as those in Germany, the reason the numbers of STDs are low, although somewhat disproportionate, is because of their high levels of self-confidence in their own sexuality. Consequently, German girls set expectations around intercourse that include condom use. Their ability to make their male partner use a condom during intercourse puts them at less risk than their counterparts in the United States or Russia (see Tables 6.3 and 6.4) (Panchaud et al., 2000).

Social Views, Customs, and Practices

The Role of Religion on Teen Sex

There are a number of conditions that influence the frequency of German adolescent sexual encounters. Religion can be a strong limiting factor. It is

Table 6.4
Gonorrhea per 100,000 Teenagers, 15 to 19 Years Old

Country	Females	Males	Average
Germany	9.3	7.9	8.6
Belgium	1.0	0.3	0.6
Russia	589.2	394.8	492.0
USA	8.6	4.3	6.4

Source: Panchaud et al., 2000.

for Muslim girls in Germany. However, religion can have the opposite effect, as it does on many Roman Catholic girls in Germany.

Roman Catholics are mainly concentrated in the south of Germany, in the Rhineland, and in rural areas. Catholics make up almost 34% of the population. Protestants, largely Lutherans, make up about 35% of the population (Bureau of European Affairs, 2000).

According to a survey by Norbert Kluge (reported in Daruvalla et al., 1999), 36% of Catholic girls surveyed between 14 and 17 years of age had had intercourse more than 50 times. The same was true for only 27% of girls not belonging to any church and for 23% of Protestant girls. Among conservative Catholic families, there was little discussion of sex or sexuality. This left young Catholic girls unprepared for entering their sexual phase of development. The same survey found that more than 25% of the girls surveyed were completely surprised by their first period. Some 39% of the Catholic girls in that group reported being surprised. Of serious concern, 39% of the Catholic girls said they did not use contraceptives the first time they had intercourse (Daruvalla et al., 1999).

THE FUTURE OF TEEN PREGNANCY

Although the rate of teenage pregnancy is low, the number of rapes of teenagers by teenagers has increased in Germany and other European countries. During the 1990s, the number of teenagers charged with serious sex crimes rose across Europe in some countries by over 100%. Part of this increase was the result of teenage girls being more willing to report sex offenses.

Another cause for this increase in teenage rape is that when German and most western European teens meet, they are very assertive in declaring their sexual motives. This leaves little room for flirting. If flirting is involved, a casual meeting can take on a "vulgar and sometimes violent tone" (Daruvalla et al., 1999).

Teen birthrates vary a great deal across Europe. England has the highest rate of teen pregnancy and sexual disease in western Europe. Teenage pregnancies in England are double those in Germany, triple those in France, and six times higher than the number of teen births in the Netherlands (Summers, 1999). The major differences in the characteristics that contribute to teen pregnancy between the nations of western Europe are: (1) ignorance of sexuality (in Germany, sex education starts at age six), (2) the distribution of wealth (England has the greatest inequalities of wealth in the developed world), (3) contraceptives that are free and available to all, (4) confidential and accurate contraceptive counseling, and (5) media that present sexuality, not explicit sex, to increase ratings.

CONCLUSION

The Germans' pragmatic approach to teenage sexual activity, as well as that of other western European countries with low abortion and birthrates, is expressed in the services provided by the country's health agencies. In Germany they promote the "safe sex or no sex" approach (Alan Guttmacher Institute, 2000b). There is a national emphasis on sex education classes that increase knowledge about contraceptives, and contraceptives such as condoms and the pill are strongly promoted. There is support for disease and pregnancy prevention programs. To increase the motivation among young people to delay childbirth, there is a greater emphasis on education and employment opportunities. There is widespread provision of confidential and accessible contraceptive services to adolescents (children between 10 and 19 years of age).

Germany, like all nations, is concerned about the sexual and reproductive lives of its adolescents. The difference is in the way Germany tries to control the sexual behavior of its teens. Unlike the developed countries of England and the United States, teen pregnancy rates, birthrates, and abortion rates are lower because poverty and inequity are less severe in Germany. As well, there are sensitive, confidential, and free contraceptive services. The provision of accurate and frank information about sex and contraception is available to all, including adolescents. "We have a great deal to learn from the experience of our Western European counterparts," says Sara Seims, president of the Alan Guttmacher Institute (Alan Guttmacher Institute, 2000a).

REFERENCES

Alan Guttmacher Institute. (1998). *Into a new world: Young women's sexual and reproductive lives.* Washington, DC: Author. Retrieved July 25, 2000, from the World Wide Web: http://www.agi-usa.org.

Alan Guttmacher Institute. (2000a). *United States and the Russian Federation lead the developed world in teenage pregnancy rates.* Washington, DC: Author. News Release. Retrieved July 25, 2000, from the World Wide Web: http://www.agi-usa.org.

Alan Guttmacher Institute. (2000b, February 24). *Young adults bear the brunt of sexually transmitted diseases in developed countries*. Washington, DC: Author. News Release. Retrieved July 25, 2000, from the World Wide Web: http://www.agi-usa.org.

Annie E. Casey Foundation. (1998). *When teens have sex: Issues and trends*. Baltimore, MD: Author.

Berne, L., & Huberman, B. (Eds.). (1999). *European approaches to adolescent sexual behavior and responsibility*. Washington, DC: Advocates for Youth.

Bureau of European Affairs. (2000, May). *Background notes: Germany*. Washington, DC: U.S. Department of State.

Cizek, B. (1992). Projekt schulische Sexualerziehung (III) [Project on sex education in school (III)]. *Dialog, 8*(1), 4–9.

Craig, G.A. (1991). *The Germans*. New York: New American Library, 1991.

Daruvalla, A., Kaplar, Z., Labi, A., Landry, K., & Penner, M. (1999, August 16). Revels without a cause: Today's cool teenagers in Europe show more mature attitudes to sex than did the '60s "revolutionaries." *Time International, Time,* p. 28.

Doek, J. (1994). The juvenile court: An endangered species? *European Journal on Criminal Policy and Research, 2,* 42–56.

Fields, S. (1990, July 31). Jitters at the reunion. *Washington Times*, p. G1.

Gallup Poll. (1997, November 7). Gallup Poll Special Reports—Global Study of Family Values. Gallup Organization, Princeton, NJ.

Getler, M. (1979, April 24). Emancipation for East German women. *Washington Post* (Foreign Service), p. A13.

Gibson, H., Penner, M., Sathiah, A., Sautter, U., & Skari, T. (1998, December 12). Other Europes: Down and out in the E.U. *Time International, Time,* p. 82.

Handshin, M. (1999, December 14). A teenage tragedy that must be faced. *Adelaide, The Advertiser*, p. 18.

Kurthen, H., & Bergmann, W. (1997). *Antisemitism and xenophobia in Germany after unification*. Oxford, UK: Oxford University Press.

McAdams, A.J. (1993). *Germany divided: From the Wall to reunification*. Princeton, NJ: Princeton University Press.

Panchaud, C., Singh, S., Feivelson, D., & Darroch, J.E. (2000). Sexually transmitted diseases among adolescents in developed countries. *Family Planning Perspectives, 32*(1), 24–32, 45.

Singh, S., & Darroch, J.E. (2000). Adolescent pregnancy and childbearing: Levels and trends in developed countries. *Family Planning Perspectives, 32*(1), 14–23.

Summers, D. (1999, August 16). EU survey shows why Britons are so miserable. *Birmingham Post*, p. 6.

7

INDIA

Douglas Rugh

PROFILE OF INDIA

Union Minister of State for Health and Family Welfare Shri N.T. Shan-mugam said that India touched the 1 billion–population mark on May 11, 2000. He claims that India has reduced the crude birthrate from 40.8 in 1951 to 26.4 in 1998 and halved the infant mortality rate from 146 per 1,000 live births in 1951 to 72 per 1,000 live births in 1998. Life expectancy has risen to 62 years in 1999 from 37 years in 1971 (Lexis-Nexis, 2000).

The people of India represent extreme diversities in language, religion, and socioeconomic class. Hindus account for 83% of the population, and Muslims account for 11% (EIU, 1997). There are also other religions: Christians, Sikhs, Zoroastrians, Buddhists, Jains, and Jews. The total fertility rate in 1992 was 4%. Women make up 48.1% of the population (EIU, 1997). The sex ratio in rural India is 93 women to 100 men. This strong male bias is a result of infanticide, neglect of girls, and male migration to urban areas. In 1992–1993 only 9.2% of the households were female-headed (ESCAP, 1997).

In India, approximately 70% of the population earn their living from agriculture (EIU, 1997). Rural Indian girls and women are extensively involved in agricultural activities. Their roles range from managers to landless laborers. In overall farm production, women's average contribution is estimated at 55% to 66% of the total labor with percentages much higher in certain regions. In the Indian Himalayas, a pair of bullocks work 1,064 hours, a man works 1,212 hours, and a woman works 3,485 hours in a year on a one-hectare farm (Venkateswaran, 1992).

The total adult illiteracy rate in India was 48% in 1995. Women were 62% illiterate, whereas men were 34% (UNDP, 1997). Both male and female literacy rates are substantially lower in rural areas than in urban areas. The difference between rural and urban rates is more pronounced in women. Rural females aged seven years and over are 30.4% literate, whereas the urban female population is 63.9% literate (ESCAP, 1997). These differences are important given that rural population accounts for slightly more than 70% of the total population in India.

Some 42,000 babies are estimated to be born every day in India. Four women die out of every 1,000 live births—approximately 40 women per day. Another way to understand these figures is to consider that every five minutes a woman dies because of a complication attributable to pregnancy or childbirth in India. It is estimated that for each woman who dies, as many as 30 others develop chronic debilitating conditions that seriously affect their quality of life (Lexis-Nexis, 2000).

INTRODUCTION

Nearly 30% of India's population live below the poverty level. In some states the percentage of people living in poverty is as high as 40% to 44%. When exploring adolescent pregnancy in India, it is important to understand the social context in which women find themselves. It is a cruel paradox that when India's prime minister, Indira Gandhi, was arguably the world's most powerful woman, 75% of the country's women were living in villages with little education, few rights, strenuous and poorly paid jobs, and little prospect of anything better.

Problems for Indian women begin at birth. Boys are considered more desirable. Traditionally, sons remain in their parents' house even after marriage. Girls are often seen as a burden, as they not only leave the family when married but also need an adequate dowry. Consequently, girls may be fed less if there is insufficient food, and their education is neglected. Clinics in India advertise pregnancy testing to determine the sex of the fetus. In many instances, abortions are performed if it is a female. Although such practices are now illegal, it is believed they still occur.

Arranged marriages are the norm rather than the exception. A village girl is likely to find herself married while still in her early teens to a man she has never met. She then goes to live in his village, where she is expected not only to perform manual labor, at perhaps half the wages of a man, but also to raise children and keep house. Maintaining a house in India is hard work. It might involve a daily trek of several kilometers to bring back water, as much again to gather firewood, and again to gather fodder for domestic animals. The girl would have no property rights, and domestic violence is common. In many ways, her status is little better than that of a slave.

For the urban, middle-class adolescent girl in cities such as Delhi and Bombay, life is materially more comfortable. She is more likely to be given an education. However, once married she is still expected to be mostly a mother and homemaker. Like her village counterpart, if she fails to provide a son, the consequences can be severe. Daily newspapers describe girls burning to death in kitchen fires. The majority of these cases are either suicide or murder.

A girl faces even greater pressure if she wants to divorce her husband. Few are in a position to do this and will become outcasts from society. Even a girl's own family will turn its back on her, and in India there is no social security net. A marriage in India is a social contract joining two people and their families. It is then the responsibility of the couple to make the marriage work. If the marriage fails, the consequences for the girl are far worse than it is for the man. Given this social environment it is easy to see why divorce rates are low in India.

Vignette

Soon after coming to Bombay, Sarita Wagh was brought to a public hospital. She was battered and bruised. Her back was covered with scabs and open wounds, her face black and blue, her arms swollen, her palms branded with a hot spoon.

Six months earlier, Sarita, who is almost 12 years old, left her village in the Ratnagiri district with a villager who had acted as a broker for her job as a maid. "I did not want to come," she recalled. "Other girls in the village say the life of a domestic worker is horrible."

Sarita's father is dead, and she has not seen her mother in over three years. Her grandmother has been taking care of her, but because of the strong market for domestic workers, she decided to sell Sarita to a brokerage company. These events led to Sarita, who has never been to school, leaving her home. Instead of working in the village (tending cattle, carrying water, washing dishes, cooking, looking after her younger brother), she went to work in Bombay. For Rs300 a day (U.S.$7.90), she labored for a family of four, washing, cleaning, cooking, and feeding the children.

Some weeks after this new life started, the violence began. The madam flew into a rage over a small mistake Sarita had made. Sarita had washed the kitchen floor with the soap ordinarily used in the living area. Sarita was hit that day with a rolling pin. After that, the violence continued. "If neighbors intervened, she would say it is none of your business—she is our servant," says Sarita.

"She beat me with a stick, with slippers; she would punch me, burn me with a hot ladle. At times, her husband would also fling shoes at me. If I cried out, she would stuff my mouth with a piece of cloth. If I asked for food, she would singe my palm with a steaming spoon. She would not let me use the toilet or bathe when I needed to. A neighbor gave me food and I bathed when she was away at work."

Sarita is illiterate. She could not write home. She was not allowed to step out of the small flat in Mahim, north Bombay. The neighbor who gave her food and initially intervened refused to mediate further. "I kept wondering how to escape. I would beg them to stop beating me and asked to be sent home. I was very frightened," recalls Sarita.

One day, she was sent on a rare visit to a nearby shop. The woman shopkeeper saw her condition and called Childline, an emergency hotline for children. Volunteers and the police intervened. Sarita was brought to a hospital.

Sarita's options, even after being rescued, were limited. With luck, a shelter would be located for her. "I want to go back to my village," she said. "But what will I do there? Maybe I'll stay on and look for another job." In many cases, the next job for girls like Sarita Wagh is prostitution, which increases the likelihood of another pregnancy for an adolescent to cope with.

Overview of Teen Pregnancy

Malnutrition

Malnutrition in India has been a major problem throughout the 20th century. Family malnutrition arises from inadequate employment and incomes; seasonal migration, especially among tribal populations; relatively high food prices; geographic and seasonal misdistribution of food; poor social organization; and large family size. Malnutrition is concentrated among women and children for the following reasons. The low status of women in Indian society results in women and girls getting less than their fair share of household food and health care. When a girl finds that she is pregnant, she is likely to consciously eat less in the hopes of keeping the baby small so that delivery might be less painful. This is called "eating down." Uneducated Indian girls hear stories of difficult births in unsanitary conditions and believe that eating causes the baby to grow too big before delivery (Lexis-Nexis, 1999).

Malnourishment and illnesses like fevers, coughs, malaria, scabies, and diarrhea are common. In Maharashtra, almost 1.9 million children below age five years are registered as malnourished under the government's Integrated Child Development Scheme (ICDS). The number represents the proverbial tip of the iceberg. Maharashtra is considered one of India's more "developed" states. A recent analysis of data from the 1992–1993 *National Family Health Survey of India* made known that girls are breast-fed for shorter periods than boys and are less likely to be vaccinated or to receive treatment for diseases such as diarrhea, fever, and acute respiratory infections. Child mortality in the zero- to four-year age group is 43% higher for females (at 42 per 1,000) than for males (29 per 1,000) (Sen, 1994).

The majority of women are not educated. Nutrition and health information beyond folk remedies are unavailable. Widespread malnutrition among children and adolescent mothers is a major barrier to reducing the mortality rates. Because of the girl's low prepregnancy height and weight, a large proportion of mothers are at high risk of maternal mortality. Moreover, an intergenerational cycle begins when a malnourished mother gives birth to a low-birth-weight female child. The girl remains small in stature and pelvic size due to further malnourishment. She then produces malnourished children in the next generation. Unfortunately, malnourishment also lowers cognitive development during school years and subsequently results in continued low rates of educational achievement.

Marriage

Segregated and asymmetrical gender relations are reinforced by Indian social customs. Marriage is seen as an alliance of patrilineal kin groups. In order to maintain group relations, it is acceptable for a young girl to marry a man many years her senior. When two villages wish to become closer partners, it is the norm for girls to move away from her family to live with his. These customs ensure that girls fulfill traditional gender roles. Under this situation, a girl's individual desires are defined in terms of the family's or group's needs (Karkal, 1995).

Early marriage not only denies years of relatively independent growth and development, but it is harmful to a girl's health. In spite of legislation preventing early marriage, urban girls who are married between the ages of 15 and 19 years range from 3% in Goa to 64% in Madhya Pradesh. The percentages for the rural populations range from 35% (Goa) to 73% (Madhya Pradesh) (*National Family Health Survey of India*, 1993). A female should be, at minimum, between the ages of 18 and 20 before she is physically mature enough to bear the burden of pregnancy. Girls married before age 20 are at risk. The physical immaturity of mothers also affects the growth and development of their children and explains the high incidence of maternal mortality and morbidity and low-birth-weight babies seen in India.

The official number of children that women bear has shown a decline, from over 5 in 1971 to about 3.4 by 1992. However, fertility in younger women continues to be high. One explanation for the decline is forced sterilizations and not a change in the girl's situation. Young girls do not consciously decide to have fewer children, and they are still denied development opportunities during their adolescent years (Karkal, 1995).

Child Labor

If you were to go to India and talk to a few girls, this is what you would hear: "I constantly have powder in my nose, my mouth, nails, eyes, everywhere," says Sujata Khobragade, 10, who rolls incense sticks in a Nagpur slum. Chandrabhaga Tidule, 11, of Hasrani village in Latur district, says, "My body aches with constantly squatting to weed and moving on my haunches. The heat is intense. I feel like not going to the fields at all but I have to go every day" (Joshi, 1998, p. 1).

Estimates of the number of child laborers in India vary from 20 million to more than 100 million. The Union Labor Ministry claims only 20 million children less than 14 years of age work. No one knows how many work as rag-pickers, fish cleaners, beggars. According to one study, at least 500,000 children under the age of 15 are sex workers. The Operations Research Group, a nongovernmental organization, places the figure at 44 million in 1983 (Joshi, 1998).

One statistical profile on child labor, commissioned by the International Labor Organization (ILO), calls child workers the "nowhere children." This is a category of India's population that is neither in school nor reported as economically active. Girls who work in homes tend to be the most invisible. However, large numbers of girls also work in factories. For example, of the 45,000 working children in the Sivakasi match industry in Tamil Nadu, approximately 90% are girls under the age of 14. Other industries that depend on child labor include the gem polishing trade in Jaipur, the coir industry in Kerala, the lock-making industry in Aligarh, the brassware industry in Moradabad, and the embroidery industry of Varanasi (Joshi, 1998).

In 1991, India had a child population (from 0 to 14 years old) of 296.9 million, nearly half of them girls. With over 50% of the population living in abject poverty, it is estimated that at least 50% of the child population works either part-time or full-time. Already in poor health, girl laborers face various occupational hazards. Rag-pickers cut themselves on rusted metal and pieces of glass in the garbage. Domestic workers must wash clothes and clean floors daily. Agricultural laborers deal with cuts, heatstrokes, and stomach cramps. Garment and rug workers must survive in cramped, unventilated factories. These children operate unsafe weaving machines. Given the lack of supervision and overall neglect, sexual molestation and violence constantly threaten these children.

HISTORY AND SOCIAL CONTEXT

How did India get to this point? It did not happen overnight. Soon after independence in 1947, the size and growth rate of the population were recognized as potential problems. India was the first independent government in the world to adopt a national family planning program. India officially began to implement this program in 1952. In the rural areas, at the beginning of April 1991 there were 130,978 subcenters, 22,059 primary health centers, and 1,923 community health centers (Zodgekar, 1996). These statistics constitute just one of the indicators that show that the program has succeeded in establishing a sound infrastructure through which family planning facilities and services have increased over time. However, there are doubts about the utilization and quality of the services.

India's national family planning initiative has contributed to increased awareness about family planning, contraceptives, and available medical services. According to Department of Family Planning statistics, the percentage of females either sterilized or fitted with (intrauterine devices) IUDs increased from 10.4% in 1971 to 44.1% in 1991 (Department of Family Welfare, 1990–1991). Most of this increase has been achieved through sterilization alone, and the mean age is women more than 31 years of age. These relatively older couples have, on average, 3.3 living children. This profile has hardly changed over the years. This means that India's family planning has not been very successful in recruiting younger couples, and it has not been able to popularize the use of safer forms of birth control such as condoms (Zodgekar, 1996).

Research on childbearing suggests that solely relying on contraceptives as a means of curbing fertility seldom succeeds. Family planning efforts are more effective when joined with other services like education that simultaneously promote health and welfare. The UN International Conference on Population and Development in Cairo (1994) affirmed the need to focus on women's welfare as the cornerstone of national population policy. This conference recognized that childbearing patterns in a society are inextricably linked with women's status and welfare (Zodgekar, 1996).

TEEN PREGNANCY TODAY

Political Views and Public Policies

The draft population policy produced by the Swaminathan Commission in 1994 accepted the need to progress from the contraceptive target approach toward population reduction goals. The Swaminathan Commission report presented a more sophisticated view of population dynamics and, in particular, of the interrelationship between childbearing patterns and socioeconomic conditions in India. The report explicitly recognized that future reductions in population growth would depend on wide-ranging changes in social and economic conditions of women. In keeping with this view, the new population policy called for changes in women's status, full implementation of the Minimum Needs Program, a renovation of family planning services, more choices and supportive counseling for adolescent girls, a closer link between family planning and health services, and incentives for couples who adopt a smaller family norm. It also called for political commitment to population goals at all levels of the government (Sen, 1994).

It has also been argued that the role of school education as a force for social change may have been oversold. This line of reasoning has a special appeal to many people in positions of influence and power in India, given the predilection of the upper classes in India to dismiss the importance of schooling for the lower order. Formal education, especially for girls, is one of the most neglected social objectives in India. The Indian upper classes have a long record of being extremely suspicious of the value of basic education for the masses. Despite the promise made by the Indian political leaders before Independence to make India fully literate, things have moved with remarkable slowness in this field. Even today, only half the adult Indian population is literate, and two-thirds of the women remain "absolutely illiterate" (Sen, 1994). The upper-class politicians who make up the bulk of the leadership of the major political parties in India—both in office and in opposition—seem to find it perfectly acceptable that a default of this magnitude has been allowed to occur and that it is not being remedied with any speed.

Social Views, Customs, and Practices

In some developing countries like India, adolescent motherhood is closely associated with early marriage leading to early initiation of sexual activity. In Indian society, early motherhood, as well as large family size, is still considered ideal to ensure that an optimum number of children, especially sons, will survive to adulthood to provide old-age security for the parents. Consequently, both ignorance of birth control methods and the desire to compensate for child loss have encouraged couples to have a large number of children. For example, high infant and child mortality rates are common among the poor. Since poor parents desire to have some of their children survive to provide support for them in their old age, they maintain high fertility rates in order to offset high infant and child mortality rates; in other words, they have more children than they actually need for "insurance" purposes (ESCAP, 1997).

Most adolescent girls, being illiterate, are not aware of family planning methods, and even if they are, they do not have easy access to family planning services or fail to utilize them due to inhibitions or pressure to attain motherhood to satisfy their mothers-in-law or husbands. Naturally, the idea of seeking an abortion in the early stages of childbearing is neither approved by the family members nor socially sanctioned. Since the bulk of the deliveries in India, especially in rural areas, take place at home, the risk to the mother's life is high. This risk is compounded by early pregnancy, malnutrition, and inadequate antenatal care.

In order to provide better health and family planning services to adolescents, it is necessary to understand the distribution of adolescent marriages and motherhood and their consequences. Therefore, an attempt has been made in this chapter to examine the magnitude of the problem in terms of marriage and motherhood among adolescent girls and the consequences in terms of child survival and maternal mortality. It may be noted, however, that it is difficult to get information on the incidence of fetal loss and morbidity related to adolescent motherhood, which are also important consequences of early marriage and motherhood.

During the last three decades, India has seen a transition in the age at marriage from the childhood (i.e., a very early age) to the adolescent years. The mean age at marriage has increased from less than 15 years before 1961 to around 18 years in 1981 and is very likely to reach 19 years in 1991. In 1961, there were 4.4 million married women aged 10 to 14. This number declined to 2.6 million in 1981. During this same period, the number of married women in the age group 15 to 19 years increased from 12 to 13 million. This means that there are over 13 million married women under the age of 18, the legal age at marriage. Undoubtedly, then, there has been a decline in the number of child marriages, but adolescents are still marrying at almost the same rate. The Marriage Act of 1978 thus seems to have had no impact on marriage behavior. Therefore, in order to bring about a rise in age at marriage, we need to bring about a congenial social change wherein the parents are able to accommodate modern ideas by engaging their teenage daughters in school or in some economic activity (Pathak & Ram, 1993).

In absolute terms, then, there were 2.2 million adolescent mothers in 1961, increasing to 2.7 million in 1971 and to 3.3 million by 1988. This means that the number of adolescent mothers has increased by 50% during the last 27 years and is likely to increase further due to the population momentum (Sen, 1994). Surprisingly, the share of births occurring to adolescents among all births has also increased from 11% in 1971 to 13% in 1981. This again indicates a slower decline in adolescent fertility as compared to fertility among older women.

With modernization certain social and cultural norms restricting sexual behavior become relaxed and might have led to an increase in marital fertility. It is necessary, therefore, to evolve a strategy to increase the use of family planning methods among married adolescents. According to a 1988 All India Survey of family planning practices, only 8.6% of women in the 15- to 19-year-old age group were using contraception (Pathak & Ram, 1993).

In India, data on infant mortality by age of the mother are generally not available. We know, however, that the infant mortality rate (IMR) is still very high (above 80 per 1,000 births). It appears, then, that over 300,000 children of adolescent mothers (15 to 19 years) die in infancy and, further, that their survival beyond infancy is comparatively lower. A number of studies have shown comparatively higher infant mortality rates for children born to adolescent mothers. At higher levels of infant mortality, children of adolescent mothers experience a 24% higher mortality risk as compared to children of mothers in the 20- to 24-year age group (Sen, 1994).

Child loss among adolescent mothers has far-reaching effects on their future reproductive behavior. By postponing first births beyond the age of 20, not only can a large number of children be saved from dying, but child survival beyond the age of one can be enhanced. Postponement would also allow adolescent girls to become more physically and mentally mature, ensuring their bearing healthier children at a later age.

It is felt that the infant mortality rate (especially its neonatal component) and the maternal mortality rate can be reduced significantly by educating women to use the services of trained nurses at the time of delivery. In this context, the improvement of health services and their utilization becomes very important. The proportion of deliveries attended by untrained persons is negatively related to the availability of nurses and doctors. The less developed states have problems of recruiting trained nurses and doctors to staff several of their Primary Health Centers.

THE FUTURE OF TEEN PREGNANCY

India will enter the 21st century with a supportive policy framework to tackle its immense malnutrition problem and several active programs that could succeed in reducing malnutrition significantly. These include the Public Distribution System (PDS), the ICDS program, the National Mid-day Meals Program (NMMP), and several employment programs providing food for work. However, these programs fall short in meeting the needs of the poorest segments of the population. Their quality and coverage are inadequate.

It is essential therefore that poverty be alleviated and unemployment and underemployment be reduced. In addition, if a smaller family norm is to be accepted in India, there must be social "safety nets" in the face of insecurity, child morbidity, and mortality. The Minimum Needs Program needs to be pursued much more rigorously by the government in order to improve the basic quality of life for the majority of India's population.

It is being increasingly recognized that there is a close association between various aspects of women's status or position in society and demographic patterns of fertility, mortality, and migration. This association is more pronounced with respect to fertility and the social processes associated with it. General improvement in the status of women, accompanying their growing economic, social, and political participation outside the home, has resulted in the need for families to shift some household functions that have traditionally been performed by women to other family members. A review of demographic research around the world clearly indicates that fertility decreases as the status of women improves. While it is difficult to assess accurately the status of women within society and individual households, it is generally agreed that indices relating to educational, health status, and labor force participation are particularly important for studying the association between population and the status of women.

The case of Kerala, the most socially advanced state in India, is particularly worth noting here because of its remarkable success in fertility reduction. Kerala's fertility has now fallen below the "replacement level" to 1.8. This is lower than China's fertility rate of 2.0. There is considerable evidence that Kerala's high level of female education has been particularly influential in bringing about the decline in birthrate (Sen, 1994).

Kerala has favorable features for women's empowerment and agency, including a greater recognition of women's property rights for a substantial and influential part of the community. It is also worth noting that since Kerala's low fertility has been achieved voluntarily, there is no sign of adverse effects such as increased female infant mortality and widespread abortion. Kerala's infant mortality rate per 1,000 births (16 for girls, 17 for boys) is much lower than China's (33 for girls, 28 for boys), even though both regions had similar infant mortality rates around the time of the introduction of the one-child policy in China. Further, while in China the infant mortality rate is lower for males (28) than for females (33), in Kerala the opposite is the case, much in line with what is observed in the more advanced countries (Sen, 1994).

Child rights activists advocate free and compulsory education for all children under 14 as one imperative solution to child labor. If implemented, this would withdraw children from the labor force.

CONCLUSION

It is increasingly recognized that there exists a close association between various aspects of women's status in society and demographic patterns of fertility and the social processes associated with it. Although the debate continues in political circles and among professional human service providers, it has moved from campaigns to stop teen pregnancy to family planning programs that give teenage girls reasons to postpone pregnancy. In order to achieve a greater demographic impact, the image of the family welfare program has to change from a birth control program to a program for improving the people's quality of life. Improving the quality of life means increasing literacy, increasing the status of women, decreasing infant mortality, and reducing the level of poverty. These are prerequisites for India to achieve its stated objectives of reaching replacement-level fertility (Sen, 1994).

REFERENCES

Department of Family Welfare. (1990–1991). Family welfare programme. In *India Year Book* (pp. 257–263). Delhi: Author.

EIU. (1997). *India Nepal: Country profile.* London: Economist Intelligence Unit.

ESCAP. (1997). *Women in India: A country profile.* New York: United Nations.

Joshi, S. (1998). India's "nowhere" girls. *People & the Planet,* (3) (electronic version).

Karkal, M. (1995). Our health: How does it count? In M. Karkal (Ed.), *Our lives our health* (p. 191). World Conference on Women, Beijing '95, August 1995.

Lexis-Nexis. (1999, November 22). Despite health improvements, malnutrition remains a silent emergency in India. M2 Communications Ltd., M2 Presswire.

Lexis-Nexis. (2000, May 11). Indian government national population policy 2000 on Website. M2 Communications Ltd., M2 Presswire.

National Family Health Survey of India. (1993). Bombay: International Institute for Population Sciences.

Pathak, K.B., & Ram, F. (1993, March). Adolescent motherhood: Problems and consequences. *The Journal of Family Welfare, 39*(1), p. 17–23.

Sen, A. (1994). Population policy: Authoritarianism versus co-operation. *Social Change, 24*(3–4), 20–35.

UNDP. (1997). *Human development report.* New York: Oxford University Press.

Venkateswaran, S. (1992). *Living on the edge: Women, environment and development.* New Delhi: Friedrich Ebert Stiftung.

World Bank. (1991). *A World Bank country report: Gender and poverty in India.* Washington, DC: Author.

Zodgekar, A.V. (1996). Family welfare programme and population stabilization strategies in India. *Asia-Pacific Population Journal, 11*(1), 3–24.

8

ISRAEL

Darcy Schiller and Leslie Gomberg

PROFILE OF ISRAEL

In the historic region of Palestine, Israel was formed in 1948 as a Jewish state. Bordered by predominantly Arab countries, Israel has been and continues to be influenced by its Arab neighbors in demography, economic policy, and domestic and foreign relations. Israel's social services, politics, compulsory education, and military service are strongly influenced by Jewish sentiments of Zionism (or national preservation). Some 81% of Israel's population are Jewish. About 36% of the world's Jewish population live in Israel.

Israel is the realization of Zionism, which is a movement that began in the 1890s to unite the Jews of the Diaspora to their historic homeland of Palestine (Ministry of Foreign Affairs, 1985). In 1880, Palestine had a Jewish population of approximately 25,000 people. By 1914, the Jewish population had grown to approximately 85,000 people (Holliday, 1998).

In 1922, the League of Nations gave Britain control of Palestine to aid in the establishment of a Jewish national homeland. Britain's support of Zionism encouraged the immigration of 100,000 Jews between 1919 and 1939 (Ministry of Foreign Affairs, 1985). The Palestinian people, who also consider the region to be their homeland, revolted against the establishment of a Jewish national homeland in Palestine.

In an attempt to pacify both communities, Britain reaffirmed a Jewish national homeland in Palestine but did not consider Palestine, as a whole, to be the Jewish homeland (Holliday, 1998). Britain limited Jewish emigration to Palestine. Even so, emigration routes helped 85,000 Jews to escape the Holocaust.

On May 14, 1948, British control lapsed. David Ben-Gurion declared Israel a state, appointing 13 ministers and himself as prime minister (Ministry of Foreign Affairs, 1985). The establishment of statehood resulted in the mass immigration of 687,000 Jews and a series of Palestinian attacks on Israel. The November 1948 census, the first national census in Israel, recorded 713,000 Jewish and 69,000 Palestinian residents (Ministry of Foreign Affairs, 1985).

The wars continued between the Jewish and Arab nations, resulting in several territorial wars including the Suez Canal Crisis, Six Day War, War of Attrition, Yom Kippur War, and Lebanon War (Scheindlin, 1996; Weiner & Weiner, 1989). Israel gained land but lost more than 12,000 soldiers and 1,796 civilians who served as border patrol guards in those wars (Holliday, 1998; Weiner & Weiner, 1989). Long-standing tensions remain between Jewish Israelis with both Palestinian Israelis and neighboring Arab countries. Internal tensions are most clearly evidenced by the voluntary segregation of Jewish and Palestinian people and the compulsory militia service of only Jewish citizens.

Israel is a country composed of young people and immigrants. As of January 1999, slightly more than 6 million people lived in Israel. Children under 14 represent 29% of the total population, and the elderly (over 65 years) represent 9.9% of the population. Between 1989 and 1998, Jews from around the world, especially from Russia, migrated to Israel. During that period, Israel absorbed 900,000 people, approximately a 15% increase in population (European Social Welfare Information Network, 1999). Annual immigration rates at the beginning of the 21st century are about 55,000 people a year.

Israel is a "deeply divided society" (Ben-Rafael, 1982). The Jews and Palestinians of Israel, by choice, lead segregated and separate lives. Israel is home to 4.782 million Jews and 1.255 million Palestinians. Palestinians are either Muslim or Christian. They believe they are descended from the people who remained in the region after the Israelis were expelled centuries before. The Palestinians, therefore, regard Palestine as their home, unrightfully invaded by Jewish people. The Jews also believe that Palestine is their homeland. They believe that they were unjustly expelled from Israel and that they have a historical right to reclaim their homeland.

Jews and Palestinians live in separate areas, speak different languages, follow different cultural traditions, and attend separate schools. Hebrew and Arabic are both the official languages in Israel, and they are taught in the schools. Because of the choice for separate identities, the Jews choose to speak Hebrew and the Palestinians choose to speak Arabic. Israel's statehood and continued expansion further divide the already segregated Jewish and Palestinian people.

Divisions also exist within the Jewish community. People separate themselves by ethnicity, nationality, and religiosity. Two principal Jewish ethnic groups exist in Israel: the Ashkenazim and Sephardim. These two groups differ in religious rite, political power, economic status, social customs, and Hebrew dialect. Israeli Jews have emigrated and continue to emigrate from more than 100 countries. Diversity is found in cultural practices brought from former homelands (Ministry of Foreign Affairs, 1985). Differences also exist between religious denominations. Orthodox and non-Orthodox Jews are in conflict about religious rites and national politics. Although strict religious observance has declined overall in Israel, the importance of Judaism in social and international political matters is paramount.

Education is compulsory and provided free to children between 5 and 16 years of age. Most students attend school until the age of 18. The state school system includes religious schools (Jewish, Muslim, and Christian) and secular schools (Ministry of Foreign Affairs, 1985). Private schools cater to religious denominations. Before attending college, most young people who are Jewish begin their compulsory military service at age 18. Palestinians are exempt.

Deeply committed to Israel as the Jewish homeland, Jewish Israelis live by the Israel Defense Force (2000) doctrine. The doctrine states the Jewish Israeli's mission is: "To defend the existence, territorial integrity, and sovereignty of the state of Israel. To protect the inhabitants of Israel, and to combat all forms of terrorism that threaten daily life."

The Jewish people view military service with a sense of duty. Highly religious and observant Israeli Jews may have their military tour waived. As an alternative to military service, religious Jews volunteer in indigent neighborhoods or in hospitals. The mandatory time required for service includes three years for men and two years for women. Men are then placed on reserve duty for 45 days annually through their fifty-fifth birthday, and unmarried women are placed on reserve duty for 45 days annually through their fiftieth birthday.

Israel is a multiparty parliamentary republic with legislative, executive, and judicial branches. The legislature—or "Knesset"—is a single-chambered body that passes laws. The citizens elect the Knesset by voting for a political party and the prime minister by a popular vote. The prime minister and cabinet, primarily Knesset members, propose legislation. The judiciary system has both secular and religious courts. Secular courts have jurisdiction over legal and civil matters, whereas religious courts have jurisdiction over marriage, divorce, adoption, alimony, guardianship, and inheritance. Local governments oversee education, social welfare, and the local infrastructure (Ministry of Foreign Affairs, 1985).

Despite the government's focus on economic growth, including privately owned business entrepreneurships, Israel's economy is stagnant. The gross domestic product in 1997 was $91,935,000,000 (European Social Welfare

Information Network, 1999). Many Palestinians depend on Israel for employment opportunities. In 1997, for example, 50% of the Israel Palestinians, compared to 8% of the Israeli Jews, were unemployed in Israel (Rouhana, 1997).

The unemployment rate is at 8.5%. This high rate may be attributed to the immigration of nearly 1 million people from the former Soviet Union in the 1990s. Immigration rates are expected to remain high, at about 55,000 people a year (Ministry of Foreign Affairs, 1985; Rouhana, 1997). New immigrants struggle with assimilation. Because a disproportionate number of these immigrants is elderly, Israel's social service budget is stretched to its limits.

Even with the economic cost of immigration, Israel offers comprehensive social services. The Ministry of Labour and Social Affairs administers social services that are guaranteed by the National Insurance Law of 1954. The law provides old-age pensions, unemployment insurance, disability payments, survivors' benefits, maternity benefits, income maintenance, and child allowances (European Social Welfare Information Network, 1999). All employed people are taxed to pay for the social services (European Social Welfare Information Network, 1999; Ministry of Foreign Affairs, 1985). Based on this single payroll tax, the National Insurance Institute distributes funds among regions according to a need-based capitation formula (European Social Welfare Information Network, 1999; Ministry of Foreign Affairs, 1985).

A national health insurance law passed in 1995 guarantees all Israeli citizens a minimum health care benefits package determined by the Ministry of Health and the newly created National Health Council (Chinitz, 1995; European Social Welfare Information Network, 1999). In the future, these services may need to be limited or reduced due to national financial difficulties in late 1990s.

Women and children are expected to be subservient to men in family life. Physical punishment is viewed as a legitimate punishment for a woman's noncompliance (Rouhana, 1997). Beginning in the 1990s, several agencies in Israel have emerged to assist victims of family violence. In addition, the International Organization Women's League for Israel has made their philanthropic mission to build homes and shelters for the abused women and children of Israel. Although the social service system is combating family violence, this type of family violence continues to grow at an alarming rate.

Few statistics are collected about teenage pregnancy, birth, abortion, and parenthood in Israel. However, researchers claim that teenage pregnancy is very low in Israel. According to the Central Bureau of Statistics (1999), in 1997, 6,690 girls (2% of all girls) between 13 and 19 years of age became pregnant. Teenage pregnancy in Israel does not appear to be a major social problem. The low rate of teenage pregnancy is in part due to the low rate of adolescent premarital sexual activity. An Israeli study in 1995 reported that 28% of adolescent males and 14% of adolescent females in tenth and eleventh grades reported premarital sexual activity. The strength of the family, "family planning education" or sex education, birth control, nationalism, and religion in the lives of Israeli adolescents influence the low rate of sexual activity.

INTRODUCTION

Imagine waking up in terror, wondering if your home is going to be bombed or if your land is going to be the target of another terrorist attack or international war. Imagine wondering if your parents are going to be killed on their way to work or if your child will be murdered on her or his way to school. Given these circumstances, would you want to have a baby and raise a child in this type of environment? Yet this is your homeland, the only homeland you know, one to which you are proud to belong. Your duty as an Israeli is to serve Israel, to help maintain its independence, to enable its economic and social growth, and to live your life, with your "family," the most cherished of all Jewish values.

Under these circumstances, why would a Jewish teenager in Israel have a child out of wedlock? Why would a Jewish Israeli teenager become pregnant, knowing her compulsory 24-month military tour begins when she turns 18 years old? Why would an unmarried Jewish Israeli teenager defame herself and her family by becoming pregnant? This chapter will discuss the Israeli teenager who becomes pregnant, statistics concerning Israeli pregnancies, the division between Israeli Jews and Palestinians, abortion rates, and reasons for the low rate of teen pregnancy in Israel.

Israel is a deeply divided state; the prejudice here between the Jews and Palestinians runs deep and has developed over a long period of time (Shipler, 1985). One cannot understand the plight of the pregnant Israeli teenager without knowing the history of Israel. And one cannot understand the pregnant Palestinian teenager without knowing the oppression with which they live.

Vignette

Ori, a 16-year-old Jewish female, is attractive, popular, and very outgoing. She lives with her parents and two younger brothers. Ori's father is employed as a business manager of one of the more Conservative synagogues in Israel. As a family, they practice Conservative Judaism. Her mother is a full-time housewife. All three children attend school full-time. Ori was in her last year of public school when she became pregnant. The family was very close, but she did not feel comfortable talking about her pregnancy.

Like most adolescents, Ori at 16 is developing her own identity. She had begun secretly dating a boy she had known for several years. He was Palestinian, and she was Israeli. She was quite attracted to him. After they had been dating for several months, Ori decided she was adult enough to engage in sexual intercourse. Birth control is easy for Israeli youth to obtain, and Ori decided to take birth-control pills. Because the pills made her nauseous, she stopped taking them. She and her boyfriend used condoms at first, but he said that sex felt too artificial, inhibiting his pleasure. Consequently, Ori chose to use the rhythm method to avoid pregnancy. Unfortunately, this method failed. When she realized she was pregnant, several things in her life suddenly changed. She knew she could not tell her parents she was pregnant. She knew she could not tell them who the father was because intercultural dating between Israeli and Palestinian youth was prohibited. In addition, she knew her father would be enraged and very hurt that she chose to abandon her religious faith and date a non-Jewish person.

When Ori informed her boyfriend she was pregnant, he proposed marriage. He wanted the child and suggested they live in his quarters. Ori became confused. She knew in her heart that if she bore the child and married this boy, her family would reject her, her new family, and her new child. Like most adolescents, Ori sought the advice of her friends. They provided her with conflicting suggestions. Some said, "Marry your boyfriend"; others said, "Give the baby up for adoption." A few said, "Have the abortion and don't tell anyone." As a result of the conflicting advice, Ori decided to seek out professional help through a social service agency. Once there, Ori was provided with an array of information, including the services available to her, should she choose to have the child. After carefully considering her options, she decided to abort her child, without her parents' knowledge and without their consent.

Because Ori was under 17 years of age, she appeared before a hospital committee to request a legal termination of her pregnancy. The committee approved the abortion. Although her health insurance would cover the cost of the procedure, Ori chose to use a private abortion facility so her parents would not know.

After the abortion, Ori knew that she could no longer see her boyfriend and that she would have to carry this secret with her for the rest of her life. In addition, she knew she could never tell her mother or her father because of the hurt and betrayal they would feel. In silence, Ori was alone to deal with her losses.

Overview of Teen Pregnancy

In 1997, the live-birth rate for girls 19 years of age or younger reached an all-time low of 3.4% ($N = 4,182$) of all births in Israel (Central Bureau of Statistics, 1999). This was a continuation of a decline that started in the 1980s. However, between 1992 and 1998, while Jewish Israeli girls were having fewer babies, Palestinian Israeli girls were having more babies. The

Table 8.1
Live Births of Mothers under 19 Years by Religion

	1992	1993	1994	1995	1996	1997	1998
Jews	1,990	1,918	1,839	1,709	1,609	1,507	1,538
Other	2,650	2,623	2,645	2,737	2,917	2,675	3,027
Total	4,640	4,541	4,484	4,446	4,526	4,182	4,565

Source: Data from Central Bureau of Statistics, 1999.

average number of births during this period to Jewish teens was 1,730 children, and Palestinian teens gave birth to 2,753 children. Table 8.1 displays the number of live births to teenagers 19 years of age or younger, by their religion. The higher Palestinian birthrate may be attributable to the younger age at which Palestinians marry. Teenage pregnancy within marriage is socially acceptable.

However, single parenthood for teenagers is not accepted among the Israeli population. Limited services are available for pregnant Israeli adolescents and adolescent mothers. Israel's child protection agency, Sherut LeMa'an HaYeled, is funded by the Ministry of Labour and Social Affairs. It operates a group home for pregnant girls (J. Zakes-Pack, personal communication, June 19, 2000). This is the only program for pregnant girls in Israel. Although the group home has about 15 beds, it is seldom filled to maximum capacity. The girls seeking help from the home are encouraged to give their children up for adoption. The capacity, utilization, and counseling of this agency represent the cultural attitude toward adolescent pregnancy and parenthood in Israel.

Girls who do not give their children up for adoption may be eligible for welfare assistance. Financial awards, based on the needs of the mother and the number of children in her family, are available through the Ministry of Labour and Social Affairs. This service is available to all mothers in Israel. Because statistics are not available for teenage parenthood, we cannot determine the number of teenagers who raise children or need government assistance.

Teen Abortion

The abortion rate for Israeli girls in 1997 was 37% ($N = 2,508$) (Central Bureau of Statistics, 1999). Although the number of teenage abortions in Israel is low, there is a high percentage of abortions among those who become pregnant.

Abortion is not only condoned for single teens, but it is encouraged (J. Zakes-Pack, personal communication, June 12, 2000). Single teenage par-

Table 8.2
Reasons for Abortions

Danger to Adolescent's Health	Malformed Fetus	Out of Wedlock Pregnancy	Age of Adolescent	Total
91	54	1,914	447	2,506

Source: Data from Central Bureau of Statistics, 1999.

enthood is socially and religiously stigmatized. Unmarried girls are either encouraged to marry, if they have been in a long-term relationship with their boyfriend, or they are advised to have an abortion. If a teenager continues with her pregnancy, it is usually because she is planning to marry or her pregnancy exceeds the 24-week legal limit for an abortion. Parental or guardian consent is not required for a girl to obtain an abortion. Abortions are a medical benefit for females 17 years old or younger or for medical necessity. All other abortions become the financial responsibility of the female seeking the abortion, including teenagers over the age of 17. The "Penal Law of 1977, termination of pregnancy" requires approval by a medical committee for any one of the following reasons:

1. The woman is under marriage age (17) or over 40 years.
2. The pregnancy is a result of relationships prohibited by criminal law, an incestuous relationship, or extramarital relations.
3. The fetus is likely to have a physical or mental defect.
4. Continuance of pregnancy is likely to endanger the woman's life or cause her physical or mental harm.

Table 8.2 shows the number of abortions for female adolescents 19 years or younger, based on the reason for the abortion. Almost 95% of teenage abortions were requested because the female was unmarried or underage.

Abortion among Jewish adolescents is significantly higher than for Palestinian adolescents. Jewish teenagers abort their pregnancies at a ratio of over 6:1 to Palestinian. Abortion is especially encouraged among single Jewish adolescents. Family, religion, and nationalism are seen as important. It is less encouraged among Palestinian adolescents. This trend will be explored further in the following section.

TEENAGE PREGNANCY TODAY

Political Views and Public Policies

Social services are provided and administered by the Israeli government. The government, and the social services it provides, is very much influenced by religion. The May 1999 election brought religious diversity to the Knesset as new political parties were elected, including the United Arab List (a combination of the Democratic Arab Party and representatives of Israel's Islamic Movement); the Shas (the largest religious party representing Sephardic Jewry); the Zionist National Religious Party; and the United Torah Judaism (comprising an Ashkenazi and a Sephardi party) (American Embassy, 1999). Despite the differences in religious beliefs held by the newly elected parties, they support the continuance of religious influence of social services because some beliefs they hold in common. The major religious factions, for example, discourage single teenage pregnancy. In addition, Israeli Palestinian and Jewish relations are under public scrutiny, as numerous countries are supporting Israel's economic development and political growth.

As a result of religious influence in government, the current worldwide publicity, and Israel's newly Westernized growth, teenage pregnancy is not an issue to which Israel draws attention. Social services available now will likely remain in effect, with changes that would only increase the availability of abortion and the promotion of prevention (including easier access to birth control and abortion).

Jewish and Palestinian Adolescents

Although the rate of teenage pregnancy in Israel is low, there are interesting trends and issues that are different for Jewish and Palestinian teenage girls. Palestinian adolescents have a higher rate of pregnancy and births than Jewish Israeli adolescents. Jewish Israeli adolescents have more abortions than Palestinian adolescents.

Jewish Adolescents

Strong family relationships, religion, Zionism, and military duty are factors that likely discourage teen pregnancy and births among Jewish Israeli adolescents. The majority (75%) of Jewish Israeli adolescents report having good family relationships. Compared to American adolescents, Jewish Israeli adolescents hold more conservative sexual attitudes and have stronger family relationships (Seginer & Flum, 1987). For example, over 50% of Jewish Israeli adolescents report accepting parents' authority and wish their future families to be similar to their own families. Friedman (1991) reports that over 50% of Israeli adolescents ask for advice from parents or siblings. Premarital sexual activity and single parenthood are not accepted in Jewish families. For the religious Jewish population, premarital sexual intercourse is considered a violation of their beliefs because sexual intercourse is for the procreation of children. The majority of Jewish Israelis living in Israel are Orthodox or very religious.

Strong nationalistic sentiment and military duty may also serve as deterrents to adolescent pregnancy and birth. Israeli adolescents have unique concerns. Israeli adolescents are concerned not only with typical adolescent concerns but also with unique concerns including national preservation and the destiny of the Jewish people (Friedman, 1991). Within the last decade, Israeli adolescents have become "Westernized." They are more likely to engage in independent and autonomous behaviors than in prior years.

Palestinian Adolescents

Although Palestinian teens give birth more often than Jewish teenagers, the Palestinian teen birthrate is still low compared to that of teens in the United States. However, the difference between the Jew and Palestinian is important when studying factors that contribute to Israeli teenage pregnancy.

The Palestinian female adolescent marries younger than the Jewish Israeli adolescent. In 1997, 4,017 Palestinian girls married at the age of 19 or younger, compared to 2,998 Jewish girls (Central Bureau of Statistics, 1999). The mean age of marriage for Palestinian females in 1997 was 22.1, compared to 25 for Jewish females. Consequently, Palestinian females start their families at a younger age.

Youthful marriages may be influenced by social and economic factors. There is a higher unemployment rate among the Palestinian people. In addition, education for Palestinian girls is not as valued as it is for Jewish girls. This discourages Palestinian girls from continuing school beyond age 16, when compulsory education ends. Additionally, Palestinians are not required to serve in the militia. As a result, Palestinian adolescents have fewer opportunities and less structure in their daily lives as might be provided through employment, education, and military service. Last, the Palestinians do not promote abortion as strongly as the Israeli Jews (Ben-Rafael, 1982). These differences contribute to a higher fertility rate among Israeli Palestinians as compared to Israeli Jews.

Social Views, Customs, and Practices

The low rate of teenage pregnancy in Israel can be explained in part by the high availability of birth-control information and devices/methods, early sexual education, the importance placed on family planning, and cultural and religious values. The National Center of Information, Guidance and Training Sexuality and Social Education—Israel, for example, provides seminars including sexual education, sexual health, sexuality, family life sex education, and family planning. Birth control is both available and easily accessible to Israeli youth. Although birth control is not covered by medical insurance, it is available without parental consent.

Another significant influence is culture. Both Jewish and Palestinian families function under a strict system of patriarchy. If a female adolescent engages in consensual premarital sexual activity and becomes pregnant, she is faced with the severe criticisms and punishments of her father. Single parenthood is not socially accepted in Israel. Most adolescents choose to wait for marriage before having children. Girls who choose to engage in premarital sexual activity use some birth-control method.

THE FUTURE OF TEEN PREGNANCY

Teenage pregnancy is a social issue that will exist regardless of the best prevention efforts. Despite Western influence, the major deterrents to single teenage pregnancy for Israeli adolescents—family, religion, and nationalism—remain high. Therefore, it is likely that the low rate of teenage pregnancy will remain stable in future years.

CONCLUSION

As adolescents develop, they begin to separate from their parents and look for emotional relationships with their peers. For female adolescents, most struggle with being accepted by their peers, being attractive to their male peers, deciding on a career, and/or family planning choices. Jewish Israeli adolescents are faced with additional concerns including a tour of duty in the militia, national preservation, and the destiny of the Jewish people.

Family is an important institution in Israel. The concept of family is respected by both the religious and secular society. Israeli children tend to be close to their families and respect their parents' input about their futures, which includes the family and religious values of marriage before pregnancy.

Although there are many reasons why teenagers become pregnant, including the choice not to use birth control and cases of incest and rape, Israel maintains a low rate of teenage pregnancy. Significant contributing factors to the low rate of teenage pregnancy in Israel include the following:

1. Israeli Jewish and Palestinian family values that prohibit premarital sexual activity;
2. The low number of adolescents engaging in premarital sexual activity;
3. Universal sex education;
4. Education and job opportunities for Jewish teens;
5. Easy access to birth-control materials.

REFERENCES

American Embassy, Tel Aviv. (1999, July). Country commercial guide for Israel: Fiscal Year 2000. Retrieved August 20, 2000, from STAT-USA, on the World Wide Web: www.stat-usa.gov.

Ben-Rafael, E. (1982). The emergence of ethnicity, cultural groups, and social conflict in Israel. Westport, CT: Greenwood Press.

Central Bureau of Statistics. (1999). *Statistical Abstract of Israel*. Retrieved June 9, 2000, from the World Wide Web: http://www.cbs.gov.il/engindex.htm.

Chinitz, D. (1995). Israel's health policy breakthrough: The politics of reform and the reform of politics. *Journal of Health Politics, Policy, and Law, 20*(4), 908–931.

European Social Welfare Information Network. (1999). *The Israeli ESWIN social welfare summary sheet*. Retrieved June 10, 2000, from the World Wide Web: http://www.eswin.net/il/

Friedman, I.A. (1991). Areas of concern and sources of advice for Israeli adolescents. *Adolescence, 26*(104), 967–976.

Handelman, D., & Deshen, S. (1975). *The social anthropology of Israel*. Tel Aviv, Israel: Institute for Social Research.

Holliday, L. (1998). *Children of Israel, children of Palestine: Our own true stories*. New York: Washington Square Press.

Israel Defense Force. (2000). *Doctrine*. Retrieved June 22, 2000, from the World Wide Web: http://www.idf.il/english/history/born9.stm.

Israel Family Planning Association. (2000). *National center of information, guidance, and training sexuality and social education—Israel*. Retrieved June 22, 2000, from the World Wide Web: http://www.geocities.com/Heartland/Oaks/1048/ifpa.html.

Ministry of Foreign Affairs. (1985). *Facts about Israel*. Jerusalem, Israel: Author.

Rouhana, N.N. (1997). *Palestinian citizens in an ethnic Jewish state: Identities in conflict*. New Haven, CT: Yale University Press.

Scheindlin, R.P. (1996). *The chronicles of the Jewish people*. New York: Michael Friedman Publishing Group.

Schiff, Z. (1974). *A history of the Israeli army (1870–1974)* (R. Rothstein, Trans. & Ed.). New York: Simon & Shuster.

Seginer, R., & Flum, H. (1987). Israeli adolescents' self-image profile. *Journal of Youth and Adolescence, 16*(5), 455–472.

Shipler, D.K. (1985). *Arab and Jew. Wounded spirits in a promised land*. New York: Penguin Books.

Weiner, E., & Weiner, A. (1989). *Israel—a precarious sanctuary: War, death, and the Jewish people*. New York: University Press of America.

9

JAPAN

Andrew L. Cherry

PROFILE OF JAPAN

Japan entered the 21st century as the second of the leading developed nations and economic powers of the world. In 1997, exports totaled $411 billion in U.S. dollars. They exported motor vehicles, machinery and equipment, electrical and electronic products, metals, and metal products. Japan's major trading markets are Southeast Asia, 37%; United States, 27%; China, 5%; and western Europe, 15%.

Japan is a beautiful island nation with a rugged mountain range running down the middle of the island like a great spinal column. It is located in the north Pacific near the Asian continent. It is primarily made up of four main islands (Honshû, Hokkaidô, Kyûshû, and Shikoku). Together the islands cover 377, 765 square kilometers (145,856 square miles). This is an area that is slightly smaller than the state of California. Only 17% of the land is inhabitable.

The capital of Japan and its largest city is Tokyo. The population in 1998 was 126.2 million. Less than 10% of the population is foreign born or immigrants. The Japanese call their country Nihon or Nippon, which means "origin of the sun."

Japan is a stable country with a high degree of domestic tranquility. The social indicators are some of the best in the world. The literacy rate is 99%. The infant mortality rate is very low at 4 per 1,000 births. The maternal mortality rate is 8 per 100,000. Life expectancy for males is 77 years and

83 years for females (Department of State Foreign Affairs Network, 2000; Dolan & Worden, 1994).

The people of Japan are ruled by a constitutional monarchy with a parliamentary government. The prime minister is the head of government. The legislative branch of the government is made up of the bicameral Diet (House of Representatives and House of Councillors). The Constitution took effect after World War II on May 3, 1947. The legal age to be an adult in Japan is 20 (Dolan & Worden, 1994).

Japan has a high standard of living and one of the highest per capita gross domestic products (GDPs) of any nation in the world. The GDP in 1998 was $3.797 trillion (U.S. dollars). That works out to a per capita GDP of $38,160 (U.S. dollars). Japan accomplished this level of development with few natural resources. They import most of the raw materials for their manufacturing industry (Department of State Foreign Affairs Network, 2000).

The two primary religions in Japan are Shintoism and Buddhism. Shintoism is the indigenous religion of Japan. It is based on myths, legends, and ritual practices of the early Japanese. Buddhist monks brought Buddhism to Japan in the sixth century. Buddhism has contributed a great deal to the religious and social life of Japan. It has had a tremendous influence on the arts, social institutions, and philosophy (Buckley, 1998).

Neither Buddhism nor Shintoism is the dominant religion in Japan. Most Japanese observe both Shinto and Buddhist rituals. Buddhism is used for funerals and Shintoism for births, marriages, and other occasions. Although Japan is essentially a secular society where religion is not a central factor in daily life, certain religious traditions and practices are very important. These traditions define Japanese society, and most Japanese people affirm some religious affiliation.

All children in Japan are provided a free public school education through junior high school. About 94% of students go on to a three-year senior high school, and almost 90% of these students finish high school. After high school nearly 34% go on to college. Both high schools and universities typically admit students on the basis of competitive entrance exams. Because Japan's most prestigious jobs typically go to graduates of elite universities, the competition to gain entrance into these universities is unrelenting. Because of the limited space in Japanese colleges, many students go abroad for their university education (Sugimoto, 1997).

Many educators believe that Japan's education model is excessively rigid. They make the point that the government-controlled system emphasizes memorization of facts, places little value on creative development, and promotes social conformity over student self-expression. Reformers also want teachers to have increased flexibility in curriculum and classroom procedures (Buckley, 1998; Dolan & Worden, 1994).

For children under school age, the family plays the major role in their education. The mother typically takes the lead in the child's education. Preschool training orientates the child to his or her role in the family and in the greater society. Learning to comply with the requests of parents is still extremely important (Dolan & Worden, 1994; Sugimoto, 1997).

Today, however, children raised in Japan's democratic society find many of the traditional rules and roles provided for them to be too restrictive and unrealistic in a modern world. They are aware of the world around them, and many resist taking on traditional obligations to their parents and extended families. Nevertheless, the behavior of adolescents and teenagers is strongly influenced by tradition. In effect, it took the influence of tradition, modern birth-control methods, the changing attitudes of Japanese women, and new job opportunities for Japanese women and girls to reduce their birthrates to current levels (Jolivet, 1997).

Japan's social welfare system is designed to help citizens maintain their quality of life when they lack adequate means to care for themselves. Public assistance provides a basic income for people unable to earn enough on their own to maintain a minimum standard of living. Citizens are also provided social insurance in the form of health and medical coverage, unemployment compensation, and public pensions. There are also social welfare services to address various special needs of the elderly, the disabled, and children. Like most developed countries, these social programs in Japan are funded by contributions from employers and employees and with government funds (Sugimoto, 1997).

A major social issue facing Japan is the aging of the Japanese people. Increasingly more women are working outside of the home, and fewer elderly are living with their children. This has driven the cost of social welfare up to about 20% of the national budget. This cost will continue to increase as the need of long-term care for the elderly increases (Tolbert, 2000). Providing for the needs of the elderly is going to become increasingly expensive. Subsidized nursing homes, regular health examinations, low-cost medical care, home care, and recreational activities at community centers may not be available to the elderly in the future. The problem is made worse because of the decline in the time-honored tradition of family members taking care of aged relatives. These changes will continue to place more of the burden for care on the government.

The first Japanese contact with the Western world was in 1542. A Portuguese ship blew off course to China and landed on one of the Japanese islands. Not quite 200 years later, during the 17th century, Japan's powerful Samurai became suspicious that Western traders and missionaries had military intentions. In response to the perceived threat, they placed European and other foreigners under progressively tighter restrictions. Eventually, they forced all foreigners to leave Japan, and they barred all contact with the outside world except for severely restricted commercial contacts with the Dutch and Chinese. Japan's isolation lasted for another 200 years. In 1854,

Commodore Matthew Perry of the U.S. Navy forced Japan to open its doors to trade with the West (Reischauer, 1987).

Over the next 100 years, Japan moved from a feudal system to a modern economy. The Japanese people fought three major wars. Over 3 million Japanese died in World War II, including the deaths of those who died from the two atomic bombs dropped on Hiroshima and Nagasaki that ended World War II.

In the half century after World War II, Japan continued its rapid development into a major industrial nation. By the early 1970s, Japan was again a world power—not a military world power but an economic world power. During this period of great prosperity, most Japanese workers were given guaranteed lifetime job security. However, because of the extended recession in Japan in the 1990s, this guarantee could not be fulfilled by many companies and financial institutions (Bureau of East Asian and Pacific Affairs, 1999).

INTRODUCTION

Japanese adolescent girls have the lowest pregnancy rate and birthrate of any girls in the world. Only four girls per 1,000 (between the ages of 15 and 19) give birth in Japan. It is even lower for girls between the ages of 15 and 17. They give birth to 1.1 child per 1,000 girls. This is an amazingly low level of adolescent births when compared to the adolescent girls in the United States who gave birth, in 1999, to 54 children per 1,000. The birthrate in the United States is only surpassed by the teenage birthrate in Armenia, which is 56 births per 1,000 girls of the same age (Singh & Darroch, 2000).

The low adolescent birthrate in Japan is also interesting because Japanese girls have one of the lowest abortion rates in the world. The concern over the rate of abortion, when teen birthrates go down, is associated with the fact that the lower number of teens giving birth may be the result of an increase in the number of teenage girls having abortions. The teen abortion rate in Japan is among the 10 lowest in the world. Even so, the concern about Japanese teenagers using abortion as a way to control births is real. In 1995, around 1.2 million Japanese women had an abortion (Shirk, 1997).

The low birthrate can be attributed to a number of factors; however, it is no coincidence that Japan's young people lead the world in the use of condoms as protection against unwanted pregnancy and disease (Bankole, Singh, & Haas, 1998).

This low birthrate is interesting in light of Japan's declining population. Births at the turn of the 21st century were less than one-third of what they were before 1950. The average couple now raises 1.5 children, which is enough to replace the current population. Consequently, population projections suggest that Japanese women will continue to have a low birthrate, and the country's population will drop from 126 million at the beginning of the 21st century to about 100 million by 2050. This will be a 20% drop in population (United Nations Population Division, 2000).

The probability of a significant decline in population, combined with very low immigration, worries many Japanese policymakers. They are concerned that there will not be enough people of working age to support the growing number of elderly.

However, even with a declining birthrate, working to maintain a low adolescent pregnancy rate is still a good national policy for Japan. Young teenage mothers and their children face too many risks. They are more prone to complications in childbirth. Their infants are at greater health risks, and the birth threatens the future of both the teen mother and her child.

By trying to understand the conditions that come together to reduce teen pregnancy in Japan, it may help us to better understand the phenomenon and determine the best ways to reduce the numbers of adolescents who become pregnant in other countries. The question we will attempt to answer in this chapter is, Why are the numbers of adolescent pregnancy so low in Japan?

Vignette

Yamada was one of the Japanese girls who decided not to go to college in 1998. She found a job as an office worker in Tokyo. Her mother had supported her and her younger brother since their father abandoned them after losing his job during the recession in Japan in the mid-1990s. She felt the need to help her mother. She knew it would have been a major financial burden on her mother if she had gone on to college. Besides, she wanted the things she could buy with a full-time job.

After several months on the job, she became romantically involved with an older man. Shortly thereafter, she became pregnant. The father of her child was married and had children. After talking it over with her mother, she decided to keep the baby. In part, she made the decision to keep the child because of the trips she had made to the Chingogo Temple with her mother over the years. Her mother regularly visited the Temple to ask Mizuko Jizo, the god who watches over the souls of aborted fetuses, to protect the two *mizukos* or "water babies" (the term used for a fetus) her mother had aborted. For Yamada, the child was a "blessing" from god, and she was not going to give up her baby.

For Yamada and her little girl, the future is not as bright as it would be if Yamada were not a single mother. Her baby will be legally discriminated against, and the child's status as an out-of-wedlock birth will be legally recorded. Her child will have fewer inheritance rights than other children. Her daughter will likely be ridiculed and bullied by other children. Her

Table 9.1
Pregnancy, Abortions, and Births per 1,000 Girls Ages
15 to 19

Pregnancy Rate	Abortion Rate	Birthrate
10.1	6.3	3.9

Source: Data from Singh & Darroch, 2000.

daughter could even be turned down for admission at many high schools because of the out-of-wedlock status.

Yamada will also be discriminated against. She had to find another job after she decided to keep her baby because her boss thought there would be trouble between her and the baby's father if she continued to work for the same company. Later, after the baby was born, she was turned down by several possible employers because she was a single mother. As a never-married mother, she will pay a higher income tax than married or divorced women. She also will be required to pay higher day-care fees for her daughter and more for health care than women who were married or divorced.

Knowing all of the consequences, Yamada is still happy about her decision to keep her child. Yamada believes, along with others, that opposition to children born to unwed mothers is changing. Moreover, in a large metropolitan area like Tokyo, she believes she and her baby will not face the level of stigma they would face if they lived in a small village.

Slightly over 1% (approximately 15,000 births per year) of Japanese births are out-of-wedlock births. In contrast, in the United States, around 30% (approximately 1,250,000 births per year) of births are to single mothers.

Overview of Teen Pregnancy

There is no question that Japanese adolescent girls have an extraordinary low birthrate. (Tables 9.1 and 9.2). It has been falling since the mid-1970s (Singh & Darroch, 2000). Since 1970, Japan has experienced a period of great prosperity.

Explaining the Drop in Teen Birthrate

The reduction in Japan's rate of teenage pregnancy occurred because there was a major change in fertility behavior among Japanese women. First noticed by Kingsley Davis in 1963, Davis described the change in women's sexual behavior as a "response to some powerful unknown stimulus." "Within a brief period [Japanese women] quickly postponed marriage, embraced contraception, began sterilization, and utilized abortion" to meet their reproductive goals (Davis, 1963, p. 345). By the year 2000, (40-plus years later), it was clear that the change in behavior was extremely effective and continues to be effective in reducing Japan's fertility rates.

Table 9.3 shows that Japan's teenage birthrate is stable at a very low level

Table 9.2
Birthrates per 1,000, by Age Group

15–17 Years of Age	18–19 Years of Age
1.1	24.5

Source: Data from Singh & Darroch, 2000.

among Japan's teenage girls. As you can see, the drop in teen childbearing rates that began in the 1970s are expected to continue into the next century (Singh & Darroch, 2000).

Conditions That Reduced Teen Pregnancy

The conditions that have coalesced to reduce teen pregnancy in Japan are unique in many ways. On one hand, the teen birthrate is affected by the same conditions that are effectively reducing teen birthrates in most of the developed countries around the world. It is often referred to as the *European model*, which tends to be the model found in the developed countries around the world. On the other hand, the young people of Japan are still controlled by tradition and culture, particularly the role of females in Japanese society.

The traditional and cultural factors related to the role of females in Japanese society were established in the 1400s, and they changed little until after World War II (Sugimoto, 1997). While rapidly losing direct influence on female behavior, traditional expectations continue to be one standard by which girls and women are evaluated. On the positive side, tradition contributes to the Japanese having one of the highest rates of condom use in the world. This is congruent with the fact that most Japanese adolescents and teenagers view childbearing very seriously and in terms of how it will affect their lives and futures.

Teen Crime

The public is more likely to be concerned about teenage crime and controlling unmanageable children than teen pregnancy. In the past, Japan has issued manuals to help educate parents about behavioral management techniques that could be used with children in an effort to reduce behavior problems with teens and teenage crime, mostly property crime.

Serious teenage crimes have always bewildered the Japanese people. The crimes are viewed as being senseless and without motive. These extreme cases have also raised both awareness and alarm. In one case, a 17-year-old boy shocked the public when he hijacked a bus and fatally stabbed an elderly woman. Holding a six-year-old girl at knifepoint, he kept the rest of the women passengers on the bus as hostages for 15 hours. The police had to storm the bus. Later he said he was trying "to show what I can do" (Takada, 2000).

Table 9.3
Japanese Teenage Birthrate, 1970–1995 (births per 1,000)

1970	1975	1980	1990	1995
4.4	4.1	3.6	4.0	3.9

Source: Data from Singh & Darroch, 2000.

Some attribute the increase in teenage crime to an education system that is excessively regulated by the state. These nationally standardized regulations and policies result in little freedom for children, and they increase youth stress levels by placing inordinate importance on how well children do when taking difficult exams. Others ascribe the increase in teenage crime to a lax legal system. The Japanese Parliament takes the view that juvenile crime is a justice problem and continues to toughen juvenile laws, much like other governments around the world. In most cases, those who are 20 or younger and who are arrested for a crime are considered juveniles, and their cases are heard in a family court.

One case that swayed sentiment to stronger juvenile laws was that of a 14-year-old boy who beheaded an 11-year-old playmate and left the severed head in front of the school. He was quoted as saying: "Since I'm only a child, I wouldn't have to go to jail, would I?" (Takada, 2000).

HISTORY AND SOCIAL CONTEXT

The *Iye* or *Ie*

The history of women in Japan is a history where women made few contributions outside of the *iye*—the extended family group. It was not until the passing of the Constitution of 1947 that women were given equal rights to men. The Constitution also established a conjugal basis for the family rather than the *iye* being the basic unit. Prior to the 1947 Constitution, wives were selected by parents or go-betweens.

Traditionally, marriage was used as a way of developing ties with another *iye*. Marriage was not the basis of the *iye*; it was secondary to the *iye*. Family lineage was the glue that held the *iye* together.

In 1947, and for years after the legal change, there was formal and informal opposition to reforming the traditional patriarchal law that perpetuated the *iye*-bound position of women in Japan (Koyama, 1961). Teenage girls, although strongly influenced by modern thought and the materialism around them, still defer to the family. The desire to avoid bringing shame on the family continues to influence the sexual behavior of both male and female children.

Poor Girls Begin Working Outside of the Home

In the earlier 1900s, the world began to change for Japanese girls from poor families. When Japan began industrializing, poor and rural girls who had only been allowed to work on family farms and in the home began working in textile mills. It signaled great changes to come.

The change in the role of women over the next 50 years was slow, but change did take place—even in the face of stiff resistance. The modern Japanese economic system was built on the idea that men were the breadwinners and corporate warriors, and women should work part-time, if at all, and care for the family (Koyama, 1961).

The other major role for women in Japan's history was that of the *geisha*. The word is of Chinese origin and denotes an individual of artistic accomplishments. Geishas were a class of professional women who entertained at professional or social gatherings of men. They sang, danced, recited poetry, and conversed in light conversation with the guests in order to lend an atmosphere of class and merriment to the gathering. Training began at seven years of age. A young girl was contracted with an employer for many years.

After World War II, the selling of daughters became illegal. Consequently, the geisha as a profession has almost died out. At the end of the 20th century, there were still 200 practicing geishas and over 50 *maiko*, adolescent girls in training to become geishas (Steele-Perkins, 2000). Now geishas have more rights, and many are unionized.

Young Women Disillusioned

Today young Japanese women are struggling for happiness. Many are disillusioned with married life. They spend long hours at home alone while their husbands are away at work. They may also be burdened with the demands of older relatives and are finding it increasingly difficult to accept the role of mother and wife based on the competing demands of tradition and a modern world. However, Japanese women are determined to develop a role for themselves that combines motherhood, self-fulfillment, and social usefulness as perceived by the Japanese people. Even so, Japanese culture in many ways still celebrates male dominance and female submissiveness (Miyazaki, 1999).

TEEN PREGNANCY TODAY

Political Views and Public Policies

In the second half of the 20th century, there was a general move toward more individual freedom and diversity in Japan. Even so, Japanese society remains strongly group oriented compared to other cultures. Japanese children learn group consciousness in the family before entering school. Group membership includes the child's class in school, the neighborhood, and the extracurricular clubs during senior high school and college; as an adult, group membership includes the workplace (Sugimoto, 1997).

Children are taught to be wholly committed to the group. They are taught to sacrifice personal gain for the benefit of the group as a whole and to value and maintain harmony within the group. In many ways, the Japanese nation as a whole may be thought of as a group to which one belongs and to which one has obligations. These values and the desire to maintain group inclusion help maintain the low teen birthrate in Japan.

Most groups are organized hierarchically after the structure of the *iye*. Individual members have a designated rank within the group, and individual responsibilities are based on their position. Seniority has traditionally been the main criterion for obtaining a higher rank. The socialization of young people in Japan emphasizes respect and deference to one's seniors.

Birth Control Pills and Viagra

Although the rights of women are protected under the Japanese Constitution, Japanese women continue to face widespread gender bias. An example of this gender bias is the efforts of women's groups who fought for over 40 years before the Health and Welfare Ministry approved low-dosage oral contraceptives instead of the more dangerous medium-dosage pills used in Japan until the year 2000.

Approval was not granted on the merits of the case. Low-dosage birth-control pills had long before been tested in Japan and shown to be 99% effective when used correctly. It was a birth-control method approved by every other country in the United Nations except for North Korea. Approval was granted because the predominantly male committee in charge of deciding whether to approve the pill was embarrassed by a public outcry after they approved the anti-impotence drug Viagra in six months (Gaouette, 1999; Hindell, 1999; Kakuchi, 1999).

Sex Crimes

In Japan, although it is slowly changing, many people blame the victims of sex crimes. There continues to be an unspoken rule that female victims of sex crimes remain silent. Japanese young girls and women who have been sexually assaulted often face similar problems if they go to the authorities. They face being blamed for the sexual assault, and they may face rejection by their husbands, boyfriends, family, and friends—familiar experiences known to sexually abused women around the world. Much like other nations, the Japanese justice system is often unsympathetic and unresponsive to the needs of females who report being sexual assaulted.

The gender bias is also reflected in the way the criminals who commit sex crimes are treated. In one case in 1999, a man followed an American visitor to her apartment, threw her against the door, and tried to molest her. She fought him off, and later the man was arrested. She pressed charges, but police dragged their feet. The prosecutors who took over the case suggested that she drop charges against the man even though he had confessed. The prosecutors pointed out that her male attacker had no prior record and was a source of financial support for his parents. Although she pressed charges, her attacker was given a suspended sentence. Feminists and others claim that, as a general rule, sex crimes in Japan are not dealt with as serious crimes.

One of the reasons young girls and women are reluctant to report sex crimes is because of the stigma attached to being sexually assaulted. Often, these victims of sex crimes are considered dirty or worthless.

In 1998, there were 6,124 rapes and sexual assaults reported in Japan. This is approximately 6 rapes and sexual assaults for every 100,000 people 15 years or older. To put these numbers in perspective, in the United States during a similar period (1997), there were approximately 200 rapes and sexual assaults for every 100,000 people 12 years or older (U.S. Department of Justice, 1998).

Although Japan has a low incidence rate of rapes and sexual assaults, some believe it is because these crimes are underreported. Those in the Japanese justice system say that at least part of the statistical gap is due to a genuinely lower incidence rate (Prideaux, 2000). However, surveys have indicated otherwise.

One survey in 1999 conducted by Makiko Sasagawa (a counselor at St. Marianna Medical Institute near Tokyo) and Takako Konishi (a psychiatrist at Tokyo's Musashino Women's University) found that 80% of the 459 Tokyo women surveyed reported that they had experienced some sort of sexual assault. These assaults ranged from sexually oriented verbal abuse to rape (in Prideaux, 2000).

Of the various forms of sexual assault, molestation of women on commuter trains is probably the most common. In a survey in 1997, almost 80% of the 1,553 women surveyed by Tokyo government employees said they had been inappropriately touched on a train at some point in their lives. The problem is so widespread that subway authorities have considered making some subway cars off-limits to male passengers. Even so, there are few formal complaints by women about commuter train molestation. Most women who are touched inappropriately simply get off and wait for the next train (Prideaux, 2000).

Social Views, Customs, and Practices

Child Abuse on the Rise

In Japan, children's rights are a new concept. Traditionally, parents were considered to have complete authority in the home. Child abuse has never been much of a public issue. However, civic groups are now demanding that the government become more involved. The Japanese Health Ministry did not start keeping records of child abuse cases until 1991. This effort is hampered because the police do not keep statistics on the number of children who die from abuse at the hands of their parents.

The number of cases of child abuse has continued to increase over the years. State-run counseling centers for children reported 5,352 cases of child abuse in 1998. This was a fivefold increase from the numbers reported in 1990. The real number could be as high as 20,000 cases a year because of underreporting and the practice of government officials of counting only cases handled by government-sponsored counseling centers (Macintyre & Hiroko Tashiro, 1999).

Nongovernment surveys have turned up some very high numbers. A poll by Tokyo's Center for Child Abuse Prevention found that 10% of Tokyo mothers confessed to beating or neglecting their preschool children. There are no official numbers, but pediatricians believe that the number of cases in which children are seriously injured or even killed is also on the rise (Macintyre & Hiroko Tashiro, 1999).

Until the mass migration to the large urban centers, most Japanese tended to live in small communities where neighbors and family members were involved in caring for all children. It was obvious to others when a child was being mistreated. With urbanization, the involvement of the extended family in raising children was lost (Koyama, 1961).

Without mothers and mothers-in-law around to offer guidance, young mothers at times use poor judgment. In 1999, a five-month-old baby girl was found crying in a coin locker at a train station. The young parents of the baby had placed the child in the locker so that they could enjoy dinner at a nearby restaurant. When asked why they put the child in the train station locker, the father reportedly told the officers he thought "the locker would be a warm, safe place to park the kid" (Macintyre & Hiroko Tashiro, 1999, p. 35).

Prostitution among High School Girls

The desire for faddish consumer goods among the younger people of Japan disturbs many adults. It is linked with the increase in prostitution among high school girls. Many of these girls use the money to buy the latest clothing fashions, expensive concert tickets, and other desired items (White, 1994). In 1995, there were 5,481 girls arrested for prostitution. During that same period approximately 8% of schoolgirls who were not going on to college were prostituting.

Status of Women

An important long-term social problem that will continue to affect Japanese girls and young women is the general status of women in Japan. Internationally, Japan is known as the largest market for enslaved women in the world (Yayori, 1999). In Tokyo, prostitution is legal as long as a pimp is not involved. A man can legally have sex with a child as long as he or she is over the age of 12 and consents. Furthermore, incest is not a crime unless it is a rape (Reitman, 1996).

Women continue to struggle for equal access to employment and advancement in their chosen career. Toward the end of the 20th century, the attitude that women should stay home and be mothers is more prevalent in Japan than in other developed countries. In spite of underlying resistance, efforts to increase women's opportunities in Japan have enabled more women to succeed in business and other professions (Leblanc & Saskia, 1999).

THE FUTURE OF TEEN PREGNANCY

The preference of Japanese couples for small families is clearly evident. It is a choice that transcends all levels of Japanese society. Certainly, the desire for a small family is a side effect of the emphasis on economic prosperity and the pursuit of materialism at the cost of self-sacrifice for the group and family.

One interesting variation on the small-family theme that is seen in most developed and developing countries is the choice of gender of the only child. In countries such as China and India, where there is pressure to reduce family size, the desire is to have a male child. In Japan, the reverse is true: A large proportion of couples desire a female child because they believe girls will have more options than boys in the future (Women Envision, 1999).

There continues to be a need for teen pregnancy prevention programs in Japan. The numbers of pregnant teens are small but indicate that the continuing need for social services for pregnant teens still exists. About 50% of abortions in Japan were performed on adolescent and teenage girls because the pregnancy was unwanted or mistimed (Cohen, 1997).

Services and programs that will help teenagers develop their sexual lives will also help Japanese women as a group better meet their childbearing goals. Japanese women reported in 1997 that they wanted between 2 and 3 children. Since the mid-1980s, women have been averaging 1.4 births per woman (Breslin, 1997).

Condom use among Japanese young people represents a major change in sexual behavior and has the highest level of use in the world. In Japan, 92% of Japanese couples who use protection use the barrier method provided by male condoms. In contrast, in the United States, male condoms are used by 17% of couples. Roughly 600 million male condoms are purchased annually in Japan, and typically, these condoms are purchased by women, not men.

In the year 2000, concern about the spread of HIV/AIDS (human immunodeficiency virus/acquired immunodeficiency syndrome) throughout Asia, and the level of use of male condoms, the Female Health Company of Chicago received permission to sell female condoms in Japan (Shatz, 2000). These are large condoms compared to male condoms, made specifically for females to use when they want to be sure a condom is used when they are engaged in sexual intercourse.

CONCLUSION

In the second half of the 20th century, cultural forces converged with modern birth-control methods to reduce the Japanese teenage birthrate. Three main forces came together to change the reproductive behavior of these teens:

Tradition. Group identity and individual sacrifice for group gain continue to play major roles. These group standards have resulted in both a high rate of male condom use and a low rate of out-of-wedlock births.

Religion. The lack of religious sanctions against the use of modern birth-control methods has allowed for a quick and permanent change in sexual behavior. Japanese people can best be described as being a *secular society.* For Japanese adolescents and young adults, there have been no insurmountable religious sanctions against using modern birth-control methods to prevent unwanted pregnancy.

Materialism. Individuals and small families are flourishing in Japan's modern economy. Their sense of fulfillment (rather than coming from group affiliation) comes from individual accomplishments; and for many adolescents and their parents, the drive for the latest fashion, toy, or electronic game is almost totally consuming. A variety of government-supported afterschool clubs and activities keep Japanese children occupied in positive and character-building activities after the school day ends.

For the Japanese adolescent, the message is clear: The more children in the family, the less there is to go around: the younger you are when you give birth, the less you have and the less you can do. In this highly organized society, adolescents have heard these messages loud and clear. Adolescent and teenage girls are delaying marriage. They are delaying the birth of their first child. They are opting for birth-control methods that provide them with the means to control their reproductive lives so that they can develop roles for themselves in addition to that of wife and mother.

REFERENCES

Bankole, A., Singh, S., & Haas, T. (1998). Reasons why women have induced abortions: Evidence from 27 countries. *International Family Planning Perspectives, 24*(3), 117–127, 152.

Breslin, M. (1997). Japanese women want more children than their total fertility rate suggests. *Family Planning Perspectives, 29*(6), 291–292.

Buckley, R. (1998). *Japan today* (3rd ed.). Cambridge, England: Cambridge University Press.

Bureau of East Asian and Pacific Affairs. U.S. Department of State. (1999). *Background notes: Japan profile*. Washington, DC: U.S. Department of State.

Cohen, S.A. (1997). *Issues in brief: A response to concerns about population assistance*. New York: Pew Charitable Trusts/Global Stewardship Initiative, Alan Guttmacher Institute.

Davis, K. (1963). The theory of change and response in modern demographic history. *Population Index, 29*(4), 345–356.

Department of State Foreign Affairs Network. (2000). *National Trade Data Bank (NTDB)*. Washington, DC: Author. Retrieved from the World Wide Web: www.stat-usa.gov.

Dolan, R.E., & Worden, R.L. (1994). *Japan: A country study*. Washington, DC: Federal Research Division, Library of Congress.

Gaouette, N. (1999, March 11). Japan's low birthrate slows birth-control pill approval. *Christian Science Monitor*, p. 8.

Hindell, J. (1999, March 4). International: Japan may get the Pill after 40-year debate. *Daily Telegraph*, p. 25.

Jolivet, M. (1997). *The childless society?: The crisis of motherhood*. New York: Routledge Press.

Kakuchi, S. (1999, February 9). Population—Japan: Too quick on Viagra, too slow on the pill. *Inter Press Service English News Wire*.

Koyama, T. (1961). *The changing social position of women in Japan*. Switzerland: UNESCO.

Leblanc, R.M., & Saskia, S. (1999). *Bicycle citizens: The political world of the Japanese housewife*. Berkeley: University of California Press.

Macintyre, D., & Hiroko Tashiro, H. (1999, June 7). Asia: Hearing their cries—the rate of child abuse in Japan has silently skyrocketed, but activists are finally listening. *Time International*, 35 (electronic version).

Miyazaki, T. (1999). Representation of women in Japan's media. *In changing lenses—women's perspectives on media* (electronic version).

Picken, S.D. (1994). *Essentials of Shinto*. Westport, CT: Greenwood Press.

Prideaux, E. (2000, January 14). Sex-crime victims keep quiet in Japan; fearing social stigma and blame, most women fail to report. *Washington Times*, p. A15.

Reischauer, E. (1987). *The Japanese today*. Boston: Harvard University Press.

Reitman, V. (1996). Japan's new growth industry: Schoolgirl prostitution. *Wall Street Journal* (electronic version).

Shatz, M. (2000, May 15). Female condoms perfect fit for Japanese market. *Japan Times* (electronic version).

Shirk, M. (1997, March 18). Temples show Japan's ambivalence toward abortion. *St. Louis Post-Dispatch*, p. 3A.

Singh, S., & Darroch, J.E. (2000). Adolescent pregnancy and childbearing: Levels and trends in developed countries. *Family Planning Perspectives, 32*(1), 14–23.

Steele-Perkins, C. (2000). Japan: Geisha girls. *Mother Jones, 26*, 29.

Sugimoto, Y. (1997). *An introduction to Japanese society*. Cambridge, UK: Cambridge University Press.

Takada, K. (2000, May 22). Japan to give parents manuals on educating kids. *Reuters Press*.

Tolbert, K. (2000, July 9). Japan spending billions for seniors to live at home. *Miami Herald*, p. 9A.

United Nations Population Division. (2000). *Replacement migration: Is it a solution to declining and aging populations?* New York: United Nations.

U.S. Department of Justice. (1998). *Crime statistics: 1997*. Washington, DC: Author.

White, M. (1994). *The material child: Coming of age in Japan and America*. New York: Free Press.

Women Envision. (1999). Preference for baby girls: A two-way deal in Japan. *Women Envision, 76*, 6.

Yayori, M. (1999). *Women in the new Asia*. London: Zed Books.

10

MEXICO

Irene Moreda

PROFILE OF MEXICO

Mexico is a developing nation with a heritage rich in cultures and traditions. As the country begins the 21st century, it is transitioning from an agrarian economy to an industrial economy. This transition has caused widespread economic and cultural displacement. Almost all Mexican families have been impacted by these changes. Parents and children can no longer rely on the "old ways" of doing things in the face of new values, experiences, and choices.

Mexico's current population is approximately 100 million; projections are for the population to increase to 140 million by 2025. It has an annual growth rate of 2.2%, with 36% of its population under 15 years of age.

Despite a gradually lowering birthrate, the actual population is increasing at over 2 million people a year. "This growth, coupled with large-scale migration from rural to urban areas, is straining Mexico's infrastructure and government services. Living conditions have deteriorated significantly for most Mexicans in the last decade. A good part of Mexico's population, more than 20 million people, lives on the edge of survival." Almost 75% of Mexicans live in urban areas (IPPF, 2000).

Inhabited in pre-Columbian times by the Aztecs and Maya, among others, Mexico was conquered by Cortés in 1521 and held by the Spanish until 1821. The Treaty of Guadelupe Hidalgo that ended the Mexican War (1846–1848) awarded all lands north of the Rio Grande to the United States. Mexico City is the capital and the largest city.

The Estados Unidos Mexicanos (United Mexican States) is a federal democratic republic. Mexico's gross domestic product (GDP) is $334.8 billion (in U.S. currency in 1996) or $3,590 (U.S.) per individual. The average annual inflation was 18.53% between 1990 and 1996. Mexico also has a large national debt; it totaled 21% of its GDP in 1994. National spending for health took up 3.17% of all government expenditures, whereas education spending took another 24.19%. The literacy rate in Mexico is 90%, with men having a slightly higher literacy rate (91.8%) than women (87.4%).

Mexico, in its effort to industrialize, has allowed a large number of multinational corporations to establish factories along the United States–Mexico border. These industrial sites are a major source of employment for the Mexican people, but they are also a major source of social problems. The *maquiladora* plants, assembly plants in Mexico (especially those located along the Mexico–U.S. border), are plants where materials and parts are shipped in from, for example, the United States to be assembled and the finished products shipped back to the U.S. market.

The U.S. multinational corporations' *maquiladora* plants have been built and grow rich off the labor of Mexican girls and young women. Today there exist about 4,000 such plants employing almost 1 million workers in Mexico, 80% of which work in plants along the border. Since the *maquiladora* program took hold in the 1970s, girls and young women have provided a majority of the assembly plant workers.

While children can legally be hired when they turn 16, in fact, it is common for girls as young as 12 (with false documents) to be working for some of the largest multinational companies. At age 14, some girls work legally with their parents' permission or with permission obtained from local authorities. Most of the girls will leave the plants before they reach 30. To get and keep their jobs at many plants, the adolescent girls and young women must submit to medical examinations and pregnancy tests to prove that they are not pregnant.

In Tijuana, Juarez, Piedras Negras, Reynosa, and all border towns, the same scene is played out every day. Early in the morning, one can see the girls heading to work through the dirty streets of the city slums. The girls live in little adobe or concrete blockhouses or sometimes in shacks made of shipping pallets, crates, and cardboard—housing that most often lacks running water and electricity. Even so, they somehow manage to wash their faces and neatly comb their hair. Despite the dust and mud, the mostly dark-haired and dark-skinned girls wear bright white blouses. Some walk awkwardly in their high heels, whereas others wear bright lipstick; they all clutch their little purses as they walk along the street or sit or stand on the buses giggling and gossiping.

When they arrive at the factory, the workday begins, usually under the control of Mexican foremen who report to foreign-born supervisors from the United States. The somewhat older men in their twenties or thirties often engage in sexual harassment. In order for many of these female workers to keep their job or to get a pay raise, a transfer, or a promotion, they must fend off demands for sexual favors.

The U.S. corporations have built state-of-the-art manufacturing, assembly, and packing plants in Juarez. Their Mexican partners have created modern industrial parks with huge truck parking facilities, powerful electric lights, and in some cases, beautifully landscaped exteriors. The U.S. and Mexican governments and private industry have constructed superhighways, railroad tracks, terminals, and airports to serve the *maquiladora* zone. U.S. and Mexican customs officials have built new warehouse facilities, trucking, and railroad terminals. And they have hired a small army of officials to ensure that the movement of parts will not be delayed and that parts will arrive at the assembly plant on time. However, among this industrial opulence, the workers continue to live in hovels and to walk down streets that remain unpaved and dusty and turn into rivers of mud and debris during heavy rains.

This scene of adolescent girls going off to work in textile mills has been played out historically since the beginning of the industrial revolution in England. It has been one of the patterns of industrial development in almost every country that is today known as a developed nation. This same pattern continues today. Many developing countries that are struggling to industrialize have started with the textile industry and the cheap labor provided by adolescent girls to develop their industry and improve their economy.

Employers in Mexico often discriminate against pregnant workers. A recent Human Rights Watch report states that factories in the "*Maquiladora* Sector," in the north, demand that women produce urine specimens for pregnancy tests. *Maquiladora* doctors and nurses stand accused of performing physical exams to check for pregnancy; and the girls are required to reveal private information about their menstrual cycles, birth-control practice, and sexual activity. The report stated that pregnancy testing is often a condition of continued employment. However, government officials claim that pregnancy testing does not violate its laws, and Mexican authorities do not believe pregnancy testing has any adverse consequences for their workers (Deen, 1998).

Though education is free and provided by the state at all levels, the average child only goes to school for five years. The schools are overcrowded and rundown and lack supplies. Consequently, many of the children do not go to school; they go to work.

Those who skip school and do not work spend their time sniffing little cans of intoxicants such as the dangerous Resistol (a glue compound). More recently, crack cocaine has become the drug of choice for those who can afford it.

Public safety has all but disintegrated in parts of the northern border states and cities. The drug dealers, police, and even the Mexican Army cooperate in the movement of drugs across the border. Sometimes this uneasy peace between these factions breaks down, and gunfights erupt between rivals. The police routinely shake down workers and rob them of their wages. The bodyguards of the wealthy and the security guards at the factories add to the many bodies of armed men who threaten the safety of citizens.

The people of Mexico are in a struggle to develop their resources, and their major resource is cheap labor. The cheapest labor is that of adolescent girls who live in the slums of Mexican border towns and work for multi-national companies, making goods they will never be able to afford.

INTRODUCTION

According to the Pan American Health Organization (PAHO), poverty greatly increases the risks of pregnancy among Latin American adolescents between the ages of 15 and 19. As well, approximately 70% of these Latin American teens that become pregnant (particularly girls living in rural areas) are the most disadvantaged group in Latin America. Children of teen mothers have poorer nutrition, are less likely to attend school, and show poorer motor skills than children of adult women, according to the PAHO report. In Chile and Mexico, approximately 75% of women who gave birth before the age of 20 are the children of teen mothers themselves (PAHO, 1998).

Vignette

At age 11 years, Maria left her hometown of Torreon, Coahuila, and went to Juárez to look for work. Her family could not afford to keep her. She went to live with her 16-year-old brother and his wife. They lived in an adobe shack in a dusty working-class slum. Maria paid $20 for a false birth certificate and got a job at the factory where her brother's wife worked, at the Electrocomponentes de Mexico. The U.S.-owned *maquiladora* hired the child and paid her about $4 a day to assemble electrical components. However, she actually brought home a little less, since she had to pay for public bus transportation to and from work.

Maria was only a girl, just a child, and she did not adjust easily to 48 hours a week on the assembly line. *Maquiladora* managers often say that it is hard to manage the mostly female workers in the electronics plants because "they're just kids, and of course they want to talk and play." The corporations are quick to discipline these children. Soon after she started, the company suspended Maria for talking.

When Maria ran short of money, she would walk home from work. On her way home one night she was attacked, raped, and left in a ditch. This was her first sexual experience, but it was not the last time she was sexually assaulted.

After working for five years for the same electronics manufacturer, Maria was fired. She was 16 years old. Her employer learned that she was pregnant with her second child. Incidents like these are common in Mexico, where public and private companies routinely discriminate against pregnant employees. Mandatory pregnancy testing is common in companies along the United States–Mexico border. Thousands of export-producing factories, many of them U.S.-owned and supplying American corporations, regularly give pregnancy tests, as a condition of employment, to the adolescent girls and women who typically work for these companies, assembling products from shirts to computer monitors.

Maria's foreman had begun harassing her after she became pregnant with her first child. He warned her that company management would make him fire her if she began to pay more attention to her child than her work. After the company's pregnancy test showed she was pregnant with her second child, Maria was fired for "neglecting her duties."

Her friend Caridad was not so lucky; her child was born on the streets. Maria remembers feeling helpless and so sad that her friend Caridad was having such a hard time. Two nicely dressed men went to Caridad one day and tricked her into signing papers that she did not understand. Later, the two men came back and took Caridad's baby. Caridad had no idea where her baby was taken and never saw her baby again. The illegal deportation, and subsequent adoption, of Mexican babies is a prosperous business.

Overview of Teen Pregnancy

Teenagers in Mexico who become pregnant often find themselves alone and facing a major crisis. In Mexico, contraceptives are often difficult to acquire, especially for the rural or urban poor. In addition, abortion is illegal throughout the nation. These circumstances often lead to sad choices for all involved. Recently an 81-year-old midwife, almost blind, was jailed for a year for performing an abortion on a 16-year-old girl. The girl's father, who found the aborted fetus in a jar under her bed, reported her to the police. The girl and her boyfriend were then removed from their homes and placed under the protective custody of the juvenile authorities for three years (Ross-Fowler, 1998). This is but one example of the emotional and physical costs of teen pregnancy in Mexico.

Contraceptive Use

Contraceptive use has been low among sexually exposed adolescents in Mexico. One recent study of adolescents living in León, Mexico, found that male students scored higher on knowledge of sexuality but that female students had a greater knowledge of contraception. Both males and females among the lower socioeconomic class scored lower on knowledge of sexuality, contraception, and sexually transmitted diseases (STDs) than did those of the middle and upper classes (Huerta-Franco, Díaz de León, & Malacara 1996). An estimated 36.4% of married adolescent girls between the ages of 15 and 19 use some form of contraception (IPPF, 2000). The percentage of women ages 15 to 49 using contraception (all methods) is 65%; and 56% of women ages 15 to 49 use a modern method of contraception. "Contraceptive use among women without education who live in rural areas is under 30%. Among women from urban areas with six or more years of schooling, the contraceptive use exceeds 75%" (IPPF, 2000). Among adolescents, the IPPF report noted that although 68% of adolescents ask for contraceptives, only 29% use them. At the turn of the 21st century, adolescents were giving birth to more than 500,000 children a year in Mexico.

Consequences of Adolescent Pregnancy in Mexico

Adolescent childbearing in Mexico has a wide range of other significant social, health, and economic consequences (Buvinic, 1998; Weil, 1991). The earlier the pregnancy occurs, the more the physical risks escalate for both mothers and children. In addition, most early pregnancies occur within the lower socioeconomic class, where there is poor nutrition and little or no access to prenatal care or postnatal care.

Adolescent childbirth also tends to be unplanned, and the younger the mother is, the less likely she is to be married. Unmarried adolescent mothers face social ostracism at all social levels. They have insufficient family support and no financial support from the government. If a girl becomes pregnant, there is intense pressure for her to marry, even if she thinks that a forced marriage would end up in severe martial conflict and divorce. The consequences of not marrying would limit her prospects of marrying again in the future. In terms of the emotional development of these adolescent mothers, they have only just begun to develop their own identities, only to find themselves defined by a new situation and an irreversible commitment (Buvinic, 1998).

Early childbearing is also associated with low completion rates of secondary education. This makes it difficult for these young parents to function effectively in Mexico's economy and often leads to becoming entrenched in poverty. Employers want available employees to meet work responsibilities; however, the companies do not provide child care or child care leaves.

In addition, early sexual activity without protection tends to lead to increases in STDs and HIV/AIDS (human immunodeficiency virus/acquired immunodeficiency syndrome), which can strain a nation's resources to the breaking point. Since 1983, 365,000 cases of AIDS have been registered in Mexico. Like most Third World countries, Mexico is committed to reducing its population growth and improving its public health (Po, 1997).

The economic well-being of the family is also greatly affected by early pregnancies. In one recent study, 26% of adolescent mothers surveyed lived in conditions of poverty, compared with only 4% of the mothers 20 years and older.

Four years after having their first child, Mexican adolescent child bearers who lived in consensual unions, or alone, were at higher risk of being poor than were those who were married, and mothers who had had their first child with a biological father who was 17 years old or younger were two times more likely to be poor than were mothers who had had their first child with older biological fathers. (Buvinic, 1998, p. 203).

In addition, adolescent motherhood appears to affect the work patterns for poor and nonpoor women differently. Nonpoor adolescent childbearers were less likely than were nonpoor adult childbearers to work in the child's fifth year. Compared to nonpoor adult mothers, poor adolescent mothers worked substantially fewer months per year (-1.69), fewer months in the first five years after becoming adolescent mothers (-10.33), fewer hours per month (-26.86), and fewer days per week (-0.82). Consistent with these findings, nonpoor adolescent childbearers were less likely to head households jointly and provide financial support than were nonpoor adult childbearers. In addition, for poor women, adolescent motherhood "is associated with lower earnings, even after controlling for mothers' educational level. These monthly earnings of adolescent mothers are about 90% lower than those of adult mothers" (Buvinic, 1998, p. 206).

Absent Fathers

Another factor associated with adolescent motherhood is absent fathers. Absent fathers place special demands on the single parent and her nuclear family if they are willing to support her. Further, studies have shown that compared to adult mothers, adolescent mothers tend to take their child to preschool or child-care facilities less often. "In addition, these early child bearers express lower educational expectations for their children than do later child bearers." Studies have also found that the nutritional status of the children of younger mothers is significantly poorer than that of older mothers. Similarly, disadvantages were also found in children's psychosocial development. The children of adolescent childbearers score lower on language-development tests, and their mothers report behavioral problems more frequently (Buvinic, 1998, p. 208).

Religion and Adolescent Pregnancy

Religion in Mexico plays an important role in adolescents' understanding of their sexuality and its consequences. The primary religion is Roman Catholic, which has a general prohibition against modern contraceptive devices. While the Roman Catholic Church in Mexico "is not losing followers to the same degree as in other Latin American countries" (Guatemala is now estimated to be 50% Protestant), there are also small but significant numbers of "Protestants, Jehovah's Witnesses, Mormons, and evangelical groups winning converts" (Corchado, 1999, p. 1A). These evangelical groups also tend to be against modern contraceptive methods, and they exert conservative pressures on the state concerning various forms of contraception. These pressures periodically lead to conflict between church and state priorities regarding family planning.

Recently, the secretary general of Mexico's National Population Council said that the position of the Roman Catholic Church on birth control was "ineffective as a foundation for family planning because it depended too much on dedication, discipline and personal involvement" (Molina y Verdia, 1996). The government's apprehension concerning the position of the church is an acknowledgment of the influence that the church has on limiting the flow of information on birth control and human sexuality.

Low Level of Premarital Sex

This generally conservative social climate has contributed to a low percentage for premarital sex in Mexico, "in keeping with a conservative non-metropolitan society" (Huerta-Franco, Díaz de León, & Malacara, 1996). Studies have shown higher rates of marriage for working adolescents than for students—both males and females. "The indices of sexual activity in unmarried adolescents were higher in workers than in students, and in males compared to females" (Huerta-Franco, Díaz de León, & Malacara, 1996, p. 11).

In female workers, a low level of education could be a consequence rather than a cause of premarital sexual activity, considering that early unprotected sexual activity often results in pregnancy and in dropping out of school. Nonetheless, unmarried female workers had higher rates of pregnancies.

In general, adolescents in Mexico are not sexually active as early as they are in the United States; however, Mexico's teen birthrate continues to rise. In some studies, up to 24% of urban childbirths were initiated without a male partner present in the household, with the proportion higher among adolescent mothers (Buvinic, 1998). Mexico's crude birthrate is 27 births per 1,000 people. The percentage of women ages 15 to 19 giving live births each year is 7% of that number (IPPF, 2000).

A recent MORI de Mexico poll reported that 65% of adolescents in Mexico City know a friend or acquaintance of their own age that is sexually active, and 23% say teenage sex is acceptable. Attitudes among these urban teenagers about the once-taboo issue of premarital sex now mirror those of other industrialized nations (Corchado, 1999).

HISTORY AND SOCIAL CONTEXT

Mexican heritage combines Spanish tradition, Meso-American native traditions, and Catholic traditions. While there are wide variations in class and heritage, Mexico is a traditional society where conservative values prevail (Pick & Palos, 1995). The Mexican child is seen as subservient to his or her family. He or she owes and gives respect to parents and elders and has fewer individual "rights" and privileges and more responsibilities and duties to the family. Daughters, in particular, are held closer to home.

Boys, on the other hand, are allowed greater freedom to engage in activities outside the home. This greater freedom extends to sexual activities, where there are fewer penalties for them than for girls. In addition, machismo encourages sexual prowess and reproduction without promoting responsibility for contraception. Many Mexicans believe that "women must protect themselves against unwanted pregnancies while men seek out sexual liaisons with the reckless notion that a bunch of children validates their masculinity" (Walker, 1995, p. A2). Public and private family planning education has been directly combating this tradition of machismo.

Adolescents are faced with many challenges in Mexico, but one of the most serious challenges is to their family's traditional lifestyles. The early marriage, childbirth, and large families of the past do not fit easily with the demands of growing industrialization and employment. Neither do they fit with the increasing awareness of ecological and population stressors. High birthrates, while they may be prized in traditional agrarian cultures, are often seen as deleterious to the environment and the economy of the industrial state.

TEEN PREGNANCY TODAY

Mexico is a developing nation divided by income and education. While a middle class is developing in the cities, there remains widespread poverty and sharp divisions between the wealthy educated elite and the poor. Not only do 40% of urban dwellers have incomes below the poverty level, but a large percentage of government employees also can be classified as having incomes below the poverty level.

At the same time, many areas of Mexico are experiencing a great industrial boom. Industrialization—along with the promise of work—is drawing many from rural areas to urban areas. This produces a clash of agrarian and urban cultures with many ensuing challenges to the family's traditional way of life and in particular to the role of men and women. In addition, Mexico has recently experienced rampant growth in the illegal drug industry. This has led to large increases in crime and disorder. The poor and the young, of course, are the most vulnerable to these destabilizing forces.

There are no official statistics kept on teen pregnancy by socioeconomic class of the mother, nor are there good studies that show the differences between the three socioeconomic classes in terms of child-rearing customs, child-care challenges, and opportunities available to adolescents. However, wide economic division is but one of the conditions that make it difficult to generalize about the Mexican adolescent experience. Mexico is a nation with large populations in both agrarian and urban settings. The values and customs that children learn in these settings are often quite different. In addition, Mexico's people include many different races and ethnic groups, with customs and values rooted in Spanish tradition and Meso-American native traditions. The adolescents raised in these different worlds receive different kinds of parenting, engage in different sexual and marital customs, and encounter very different economic realities.

Abortion varies from state to state but remains mainly illegal in Mexico. Each state is able to legislate the nature and type of exceptions allowed. Women who induce their own abortions, or who allow others to do so, can receive penalties of six months to five years in prison. This criminalization of abortion "means that only wealthy women have access to safe abortions, while poor women have to resort to clandestine abortions in extremely unsafe conditions" (Ross-Fowler, 1998).

Where abortions are allowed under limited circumstances, public polls indicate that most favor abortion in cases of rape, a damaged fetus, and protecting the health of the mother. Polls have also shown that 31% support abortion in cases where the parents are too poor to take care of the child (Corchado, 1999).

Among Mexican adolescents under the age of 20, over 500,000 become pregnant each year. Of these, 380,000 adolescents give birth; the other 120,000 lose their babies through abortion or medical complications (Education-Mexico, 1999). Between 300,000 and 600,000 women of all ages have clandestine abortions each year. In addition, the government-run National Health System reported that four women die every day in Mexico from maternity-related causes, and 40% of these women die from the consequences of induced abortion.

Political Views and Public Policies

Increasing Population

Mexican officials believe that early sexual activity without contraception leads to adolescent pregnancy and an increased population that increases the strain on Mexico's limited resources. Spokespersons for Mexico's National Population Council recently stated:

Our resources are growing at a slower rate than the population. All these children are going to need housing and health care. They are going to go to school. Then when they become adolescents, they are going to look for jobs. We want them to find good-paying jobs, because a job that is not well-paid is miserable. But if our economy does not grow, we will face inertia. The Population Council's goal is to persuade Mexicans that part of the solution to persistent economic problems is family planning. (Walker, 1995, p. A2)

Health Care

Health care is one of the limited services provided by the government. Yet the need for health care is so great it cannot meet the needs of adults or children. The Center for Reproductive Law and Policy (CRLP) reports:

The Federal Constitution of Mexico guarantees the right to health care. An estimated 10 million people have no access to public health care services. Also, public health institutions lack the resources to provide quality health care, and a focus on increasing capital rather than providing incentives for improved medical care characterizes the health insurance industry. This combination results in inequitable, inadequate coverage, deteriorating services, and more financial restrictions. Although Mexico has strengthened its maternal health care programs, this increase in coverage and services has not expanded to other areas of women's health care. (Ross-Fowler, 1998, p. 3)

Medical Complications

Each year, 650,000 children are born in Mexico with some congenital or hereditary anomaly, ranging from a malformation of the heart to Down syndrome, or from diseases originating in the prenatal period, such as low birth weight or being born prematurely. These figures are becoming a public health problem, which is a crime "against the quality of life" of people and "diminishes the intelligence of the individual," says Gildardo Magana, co-ordinator of the Genetics Clinic in the Department of Medicine at the National Autonomous University of Mexico. Due to genetic anomalies, Mexico has an annual infant mortality rate of 3,800 per 100,000, whereas Brazil has more than 3,100; Chile has 628; Canada has 328; Germany has 654; France has 416; and Russia has 2,900, according to the World Health Organization.

Malformation most frequently occurs in children of low birth weight or those born prematurely—those who do not complete 40 weeks of gestation. In 60% of the cases, the origin of birth defects is unknown, but in the remainder, they are attributed to environmental factors and hereditary problems, explained Magana. "The very poor nutrition of many Mexican mothers, who through ignorance or lack of economic resources" do not follow an adequate diet, also causes the birth of children with defects of their nervous systems, a problem that affects 20 of every 10,000 babies, he affirmed.

The high incidence of teenage pregnancy "is exacerbating the problem, as it is very difficult for women who still don't have a mature reproductive system to give birth to healthy babies," he added (Pilar, 1999).

Social Views, Customs, and Practices

The Family

The nuclear family consists of parents, unmarried children, and occasionally extended family such as grandmothers or other kin. Girls in particular are discouraged from early sexual activity by family supervision and limits. When children marry, they generally leave the parental household and establish a new residence. Often the son or daughter will locate his new home near the parental household (Weil, 1991).

The family's bond is generally strong, held together by "bonds of loyalty, common economic goals, interdependence," and marital union. There are three types of marriage in Mexico: civil, religious, and "free union." Free union and illegitimacy are more frequent in the northern and southern regions of Mexico than in the central region. Both of these are more prevalent among the poor, the rural, and Indian populations (Weil, 1991).

In addition to the nuclear family, ritual kinship exists involving a system of *padrinos* and *compadres*. These kin and friends have a special relationship with the family. "*Padrinos* and *compadres* perform economic and social functions by assisting in child rearing and providing economic help in emergencies. *Compadrinazgo* emphasizes the pattern-value behavior of respect between individuals and represents a model for social interaction at all levels" (Weil, 1991, p. 5).

A sexual division of labor that is especially fixed in rural areas characterizes the family. "The traditional activities of the *mestizo* wife centers in the household, where she is in charge of child rearing and other domestic duties . . . except in times of harvest when she may work in the fields alongside the men" (p. 5). The husband's role includes working outside the home in crafts, agriculture, and commerce in rural areas. In urban areas, the husband may work in manufacturing, business, or the professions. "In some rural areas such as the state of Oaxac, men till the fields while women run the marketplace" (p. 3).

The family is responsible for child rearing and socialization. Because Mexico is a developing country, children are less likely to be influenced by third parties, such as day care or television. Schools have been slow to enter arenas that involve cultural values and behavior patterns traditionally assigned to the family. In Mexico, "the father maintains the power to regulate behavior through physical punishment" (p. 3). Respect and authority are emphasized in parent-child relations. Children are reared to respect and obey their parents. Responsibility to the family is important because an individual's status and security originate in the family. Often the success or disgrace of a member of the family reflects on the father's responsibility for the children. Thus, regardless of age or marital state, a son is under the father's authority as long as he remains in the household. Another example of the recognition of hierarchical powers and duties within the family is the dominance of older brothers over younger ones" (p. 3).

Boys and Girls—The Making of Men and Women

It is also the family's responsibility to socialize children as to accepted sexual roles. Traditionally, "boys were taught to be assertive, brave, honorable, and protective—in short, to manifest all those qualities embodied in 'machismo' " (Weil, 1991, p. 4). *Machismo* is a popular term used to describe attitudes and behaviors that exalt the male over and above all else. Women, on the other hand, are taught to submit to their fathers and later to their husbands, to be pious, and to base their lives in the domestic sphere.

Sexual Roles in Flux

Because of the social and economic changes sweeping over Mexico, sexual roles are in flux. Women are working outside the home more often, especially in urban areas, and bringing home paychecks, which alter their power positions in the family. However, consider that women were not given the right to vote until the mid-1950s. Fifty years ago, they did not have basic civil rights. This position of powerlessness translates into powerlessness in family relationships, where women have difficulty in making their partners share the responsibility for contraception and child care.

THE FUTURE OF TEEN PREGNANCY

The Mexican Constitution recognizes a citizen's right to freely choose the number and timing of children. In 1974, when family planning became a constitutional right, the National Council on Population was created to coordinate family planning efforts. In order to reach its goal of reducing the population growth rate to 1.75%, the government works closely with private organizations (IPPF, 2000).

Today Mexico's family planning initiatives are among the best in Latin America. Even so, government family planning clinics only offer two forms of contraception: the intrauterine device (IUD) and sterilization, arguing that these are the methods of choice for the majority of women. Some women have complained that they have given birth despite using the contraceptives, and others have said that doctors fitted them with an IUD or sterilized them without their consent. In one survey, 25% of the women who were sterilized were not told that the procedure was irreversible. Some 39% of the women who were sterilized claimed not to have signed a consent form (Ross-Fowler, 1998).

These situations will surely change in the future because Mexico has one of the most active and efficient private Family Planning Associations in Latin America. The Fundación Mexicana para la Planeación Familia (Mexfam) provides 8% of the national family planning supplies for the nation. Mexfam, which is active in 32 Mexican states, attempts to reach sectors of the population not served by the national program, particularly such marginal sectors as poor people, young people, and men. They particularly emphasize community health and family planning in rural areas. In addition, they have developed medical centers in the major cities in Mexico, and they take family planning programs for men into factories and the armed forces.

The government associations tend to serve women and the public at large. Private organizations tend to aim at key underserved groups, such as men, rural dwellers, and urban slum dwellers. The use of modern contraceptives varies widely according to educational level, socioeconomic class, and place of residence. Nevertheless, family planning services provided in both rural communities and urban slums cannot meet the need.

The Mexican government recently won a six-year battle with conservative groups that were attempting to prevent the government from providing sex education in state elementary schools. Sexuality education content was added to all teaching manuals to be used with sixth-grade pupils. In addition, Mexfam offers a variety of programs in the schools, including family life education, using films and dialogues with parents, teachers, and youth groups. They also have a youth program called Gente Joven (Young People) that trains youth to be peer counselors and promoters of family life and reproductive health. They focus on topics salient to youth, including dating, peer pressure, teen pregnancy, drug use, and STDs (Fundación Mexicana, 2000). Mexico City schools were chosen for the first of these programs.

CONCLUSION

In an effort to reduce the overwhelming number of adolescents who become pregnant, have abortions, and bear children, Mexican legislators have been persuaded that sex education as a component of the educational curriculum in every elementary school is a major part of the answer. The text they plan to use discusses the value of staggering births and using contraceptives. The material discusses nontraditional families and the fact that fathers and mothers may live separately with their children. It does not present the traditional view of the Mexican family; in fact, the curriculum carries a strong message that the male's machismo role in the family is no longer acceptable. The curriculum makes the point that not only is machismo contrary to equality, but "it is frequently the origin of aggression and violence towards women" (Ejecución del Programa de Acción, 2000).

These are strong words and ideas for this developing nation. They show a strong national commitment and willingness to enter the 21st century facing new challenges and balancing traditions with the needs of its adolescent population.

REFERENCES

Binder, M. (1998). Family background, gender and schooling in Mexico. *Journal of Developmental Studies, 35*(2), 54–61.

Buvinic, M. (1998). The costs of adolescent childbearing: Evidence from Chile, Barbados, Guatemala, and Mexico. *Studies in Family Planning, 29*(2), 201–209.

Corchado, A. (1999, January 17). Many Catholics in Mexico struggling to keep the faith. *Dallas Morning News*, p. 1A.

Deen, T. (1998, December 30). Rights—Mexico: Companies violate rights of pregnant workers. *Inter Press Service English News Wire.*

Education-Mexico: Sex-ed introduced in elementary schools. (1999, August 11). *Inter Press Service English News Wire.*

Ejecución del Programa de Acción de la Conferencia Internacional sobre la Población y el Desarollo. (2000). *United Nations, Mexico Informe.* CIPD+5.

Frias-Armenta, M., & McCloskey, L. (1988). Determinants of harsh parenting in Mexico. *Journal of Abnormal Child Psychology, 26*(2), 129–140.

Fundación Mexicana para la Planeación Famila. (2000). Retrieved July 22, 2000, from the World Wide Web: http://www.mexfam.org.mx.

Health—Americans: More children orphaned by AIDS. (1999, July 23). *Inter Press Service English News Wire.*

Huerta-Franco, R., Díaz de León, G., & Malacara, J. (1996). Knowledge and attitudes toward sexuality in adolescents and their association with the family and other factors. *Adolescence, 31*, 179–192.

Huerta-Franco, R., & Malacara, J. (1999). Factors associated with the sexual experiences of underprivileged Mexican adolescents. *Adolescence, 34*, 389.

IPPF (International Planned Parenthood Federation). (2000). Retrieved July 23, 2000, from the World Wide Web: http://www.IPPF.prg/regions/countries/mex/index.htm.

Mexfam (Fundación Mexicana para la Planeación Familia). World Wide Web address: http://www.mexfam.org.mx.

Molina y Verdia, E. (1996, January 17). Population: Social development or family planning. *Inter Press Service English News Wire.*

Molina y Verdia, E. (1997, May 29). Population: Church, state disagree on birth control. *Inter Press Service English News Wire.*

Oropesa, R.S. (1997, June 1). Development and marital power in Mexico. *Social Forces, 75*(28), 12–91.

PAHO. (Pan American Health Organization). (1998). Health in the Americas. Washington, DC (electronic version).

Pick, S., & Palos, P. (1995). Impact of the family on the sex lives of adolescents. *Adolescence, 30*(9), 6–67.

Pilar, F. (1999, March 28). Health: Quality of life passes by Mexican children. *Inter Press Service English News Wire.*

Po, Z. (1997, May 26). Population: Reproductive rights lacking in Latin America. *Inter Press Service English News Wire.*

Ross-Fowler, G. (1998, March). Reports on reproductive rights. *Off Our Backs.* New York: Center for Reproductive Law and Policy.

Shen, C., & Williamson, J. (1997, December 1). Child mortality: Women's status, economic dependency, and state strength: A cross section of less developed countries. *Social Forces.*

Singh, S. (1998). Adolescent childbearing in developing countries: A global review. *Studies in Social Planning, 29*(2), 117–137.

Vidales, M. (1998, December 23). Mexico—Labor: No Mother's Day for Mexican women workers. *Inter Press Service English News Wire.*

Walker, L. (1995, September 8). Machismo has put Mexico in a family way. *San Diego Union Tribune,* p. A2.

Weil. T. (1991, January 1). Mexico: Social mobility. *Countries of the world* (electronic version), chapter 5B.

11

NIGERIA

Andrew L. Cherry

PROFILE OF NIGERIA

Nigeria is not a large country in terms of land area. The population density is 310 people per square mile (120 persons per square kilometer). The population increased by approximately 37 million people between 1990 and 2000, growing from 80 million to over 120 million. By 2025, the population is expected to reach 200 million people. Of these, 100 million will be younger than 15 years of age.

The birthrate in Nigeria is 42 births per 1,000 women. The death rate is 13 per 1,000 people. Nigeria's population is growing at an average rate of 3% annually. This rate has remained more or less constant since the 1970s.

The average woman in sub-Saharan Africa will give birth to six children in her lifetime. Women in Nigeria want, on average, eight children; Nigerian men want, on average, 13 children. Among more educated women in Nigeria the rate is much lower (Metz, 1991).

In the year 2000, slightly over 40% of Nigerians live in an urban area, twice the number that lived in cities in 1970. Nigeria has a long history of urban development, particularly in northern and southwestern Nigeria. Many of these urban areas were important cities many centuries before the Europeans arrived. The largest cities are Lagos, Ibadan, and Kano. Lagos was colonial Nigeria's capital and is today the leading port city. It is also one of the largest cities in the world (Metz, 1991).

Nigeria's three major ethnic groups are the Hausa-Fulani, the Yoruba, and the Igbo. Together they make up slightly over 70% of the population.

In most of Africa, ethnic labels are often inexact and obscure important differences. The remaining 30% belong to the 250- to 300-plus ethnic groups that inhabit Nigeria.

The Hausa live mostly in the far north and are the largest of Nigeria's ethnic groups. The majority of Hausa are Muslims and work in agriculture, commerce, and small-scale industry.

The Yoruba of southwestern Nigeria consist of several subgroups that have a tribal chief and live in the same city. The majority of Yorubas live in cities that predate the arrival of Europeans. They are farmers or tradesmen.

The Igbo live in the southeastern region of Nigeria. They have tradition- ally lived in small independent villages with an elected council rather than a chief. Igbo society has been, and continues to be, highly stratified along lines of wealth, achievement, and social rank. Overcrowding and exhausted farm soil have forced many Igbo to migrate to nearby cities, other parts of Nigeria, and Africa to find work to support their families in their ancestral homelands (Metz, 1991).

Most Nigerians speak several languages. English is the country's official language and is widely spoken among the educated. Estimates vary, but around 400 native Nigerian languages have been identified (Metz, 1991).

Islam, Christianity, or one of a number of indigenous religions is practiced by most Nigerians. In the 1963 census (the last best count of these religious groups), it was estimated that 47% of Nigerians were Muslims and 35% Christians. Many Muslims and Christian Nigerians also adhere to beliefs and practices associated with indigenous religions.

Islam is dominant in the northern part of Nigeria. Consequently, Islamic fundamentalist practices such as the seclusion of women and strict fasting tend to be observed in northern cities. Islamic fundamentalists in these areas have also become more vocal and militant. There have been numerous bloody clashes between some of these Islamic fundamentalists and other Muslims, Christians, and the state of Nigeria in the late 20th century.

Before the arrival of Europeans, Nigerian children were taught about their culture, work, survival skills, and social activities by family members. In Is- lamic communities, students studied the Qur'an (Koran). The better stu- dents went on to higher Islamic studies and became teachers, clerics, or legal scholars.

By the 1920s, northern Nigeria had some 25,000 Qur'anic schools. A large number of Islamic schools are still in operation. Adult literacy is esti- mated to be about 67% for Nigerian men and 47% for women. In 1996, Nigeria had 37 universities. In 1994, the total enrollment in Nigerian uni- versities was 208,000.

Government education reforms in the 1970s were almost universally ac- cepted by 1980. The primary school enrollment increased to 90%. However, this was a fragile increase. By 1990, government cutbacks, rising school fees, the deterioration of school buildings, inferior instruction, and poor prospects after graduation dropped the percentage of children attending the compulsory first six years of school to 72% (Odimegwu, 1999). This drop was largely among girls—in part, because many parents in the rural north remain skeptical about schooling for girls. In 1996, girls made up 34% of adolescents enrolled in secondary schools (Odimegwu, 1999).

Today extended families are fragmented, and for the most part, elders who traditionally were responsible for preparing young people for sexuality and parenthood are no longer involved in the process. The schools and courses on Family Life Education have been developed to replace traditional approaches to learning about sex and childbearing (Odimegwu, 1999). However, the low rate of school attendance, particularly among girls, diminishes these Family Life Education program efforts.

Although more girls are going beyond the compulsory first six years of school, there is still strong normative pressure for girls to become parents at a young age.

Nigerian society varies greatly across ethnic and religious lines and levels of education. Even so, Nigerians share a strong attachment to their family and especially to their children. Within the family, there are clear and distinct roles for men and women. This distinction is also strongly reflected in Nigerian society—a society organized around a hierarchical social structure where religion shapes community values.

Nigerian society is highly patriarchal. Men exercise broad control over the lives of women, even though women work far longer hours than men. Women do all the housework and child care and often work at a job that pays a wage, or they work on a farm. In a few southern states, women are merchants and traders and have considerable influence on local and state politics. In the north, within Muslim communities the seclusion of women from public places, known as *purdah*, is very common. However, like other Muslim women in *purdah*, the women participate in the underground trade of craft articles, prepared foodstuffs, and other goods. Children are used as go-betweens and couriers.

Some of these Muslim women have their own social tradition based on the *bori* (a cult that includes being possessed by spirits). *Bori* rituals provide women with an institution that is nearly free of male control. The *bori* offers women explanations and remedies that help them cope with tragedies such as the death of a child.

Polygyny is still practiced among many Muslims. It is also practiced among people that adhere to some indigenous religions and even among some Christians who belong to Christian African churches that are independent of mainstream European religious groups.

Muslims, as a rule, disapprove of drinking alcohol. In northern Nigeria, Muslims prefer tea and soft drinks. The rest of Nigerians drink commercially brewed beer, traditional drinks such as beer made from sorghum or millet, or a palm wine. Drinks from the Kola nut (a strong stimulant and source of caffeine, used in drinks like Coca-Cola and Pepsi Cola) are used widely in the northern Muslim communities as a stimulant.

Young Nigerians are fervent sports fans. At the 1996 Olympic Games, Nigeria's national team, the Green Eagles, won the gold medal in soccer. It was, and is, a source of national pride.

The distribution of wealth and power in Nigeria is a serious and long-standing problem. On the one hand, the vast majority of Nigerians are struggling day to day just to earn a living. They have few possessions and almost no chance of improving their lives. On the other hand, politicians, high-ranking civil servants, rich merchants, and tribal chiefs have accumulated massive fortunes that they display ostentatiously.

The economic inequality has a severe effect on the health of children and adolescents. In Nigeria, the health care for children and adolescents is the worst on the continent of Africa. Nigeria's per capita health spending is $9 (U.S. dollars) per person a year. In contrast, Kenya spends $14 a year per person on health. Health spending accounts for 2.7% of the yearly gross domestic product (GDP) in Nigeria and 4.3% in Kenya.

In Nigeria, about 20% of children die before they reach the age of five. These deaths are usually from treatable diseases such as malaria, measles, whooping cough, diarrhea, and pneumonia. Malnutrition affects over 40% of children under the age of five. Less than 50% of infants are immunized against measles.

Families and adults are also affected by inadequate public services such as water and sewage. About 80% of rural Nigerians and 47% of urban Nigerians do not have safe water to drink. Some 65% have no access to health care because they live too far from a treatment center. Others cannot pay the fees charged by clinics.

Stable, good-paying jobs are rare in Nigeria, even for those with an education. Food is expensive. Housing, in spite of its primitive construction, is also expensive. Many poor people build basic houses in shantytowns on the outskirts of Nigerian urban areas. Few cities have modern sewage disposal systems, which has resulted in the pollution of streams, wells, roadside drains, and most other bodies of water in Nigeria. The lack of clean drinking water increases the spread of infectious disease. Worldwide, in developing countries, the lack of drinkable water is a serious concern (Eberstadt, 1997).

INTRODUCTION

The African continent is generally divided into two parts: the north, which is above the Sahara Desert, and the sub-Saharan countries that are below the Sahara Desert (the world's largest desert). The majority of Africans live in sub-Saharan Africa. Sub-Saharan Africa includes such countries as Ethiopia, Somalia, Uganda, Angola, Cameroon, Ghana, Nigeria, the Democratic Republic of the Congo, South Africa (including the homelands: Botswana,

Lesotho, Namibia, Transkei, and others), and a number of islands, the largest of which is Madagascar.

Nigeria has the largest population of any country in Africa, an estimated 125 million people. This chapter will focus on Nigeria, although other sub-Saharan countries will be included to provide a better picture of adolescent pregnancy in sub-Saharan Africa.

In the mid-1980s, there was widespread concern that the population explosion taking place in sub-Saharan Africa would destabilize the entire continent of Africa. The number of adolescents giving birth was far too high for both wed and unwed adolescent girls in the majority of the sub-Saharan nations. At that time, great emphasis was placed on programs that provided effective contraception methods to slow down population growth (Metz, 1991).

In 2000, there was continued concern over the high number of adolescents becoming pregnant; however, of greater concern was the widespread HIV/AIDS (human immunodeficiency virus/acquired immunodeficiency syndrome) infection, especially among adolescents and teenagers. Botswana, the country in the sub-Sahara with the world's highest HIV infection rate, reports that 36% of adults were infected in the year 2000. Deaths from AIDS dropped the life expectancy of people born in Botswana from 71 to 39 years of age. It was also the first time that the U.S. Census Bureau predicted that a country's population would drop because of AIDS (Haney, 2000).

In Nigeria, HIV/AIDS infections are not nearly as high as in other sub-Saharan countries; nevertheless, Nigeria is like a human timebomb that will likely explode with high levels of HIV/AIDS if sexual behaviors do not change. Young married men in the sub-Saharan nations who relocate to urban areas to work to provide for their wives and children tend to return home every two or three weeks with their earnings. However, over time, the men tend to return home less frequently, and they often begin sexual relationships with women in these urban areas. Unprotected sex leads to contracting sexually transmitted diseases (STDs) and HIV. If these diseases are taken back home to their wives, future children are subsequently infected.

In a 1995 study of young women between the ages of 17 and 19 living in southeastern Nigeria, researchers found that 82% had a vaginal discharge, 26% had clinical evidence of candidiasis, 11% had trichomoniasis, and 11% had a chlamydial infection. Additionally, 10% of all Nigerian girls have a baby before they reach the age of 15. Typically, this level of STDs (82%) and this number of births before the age of 15 are indicative of high levels of sexual activity among girls between the ages of 10 and 19 in that society (Offor & Okolo, 1997).

In Nigeria and other sub-Saharan countries, teenagers are trying to find a place for themselves in the world and someone to love or someone to be their companion in life, the most natural of all human behaviors. However, because a barrier method, such as condoms, is rarely used by Nigeria's sexually active teens (and the rest of the sub-Saharan sexually active teens), the number of cases of HIV/AIDS among young people will continue to grow at an alarming rate into the 21st century (Houlder, 1999).

Vignette

After becoming pregnant, Alusa was forced to quit school. School policy did not allow a girl to attend school when pregnant. Although she had dreamed of someday becoming a teacher, her pregnancy ended that dream. Her parents had arranged her marriage when she reached puberty. Childbirth was difficult for Alusa, who was 14 when she went into labor. Her small body, stunted by a childhood of malnutrition, was torn badly during the delivery of a stillborn baby boy. Left weak from hemorrhaging, she soon developed a serious infection. Her family took her to the local clinic, and she recovered. At that time, the doctor told her husband that she would never be able to have additional children because of the damage from the birth and the infection. Her husband turned away from her in disgust and demanded the return of the *bride-price* (the money given to the bride's family by the husband to be).

In Nigeria, 64% of all infertile women are victims of infections from abortion, sexually transmitted diseases, or unhygienic child delivery.

Overview of Teen Pregnancy

As we begin the 21st century, in Africa, as elsewhere, more teenage girls are enrolled in school and delaying the birth of their first child. With the increase in urbanization in the sub-Saharan, large families are more of a burden than help. Even so, in rural areas large families with four to ten children are still the norm. Traditional values based on an agrarian lifestyle have been replaced with urban attitudes and ideas. In the past, adolescent childbearing was confined to marriage; today, early childbearing increasingly occurs outside of marriage.

Rapid social changes as a result of Western influence and worldwide communication have convinced large numbers of teenage girls in sub-Saharan Africa that adolescent pregnancy could be hurtful to their health and future and to the future of the child they may deliver. Consequently, although sexual activity has increased slightly, births among adolescent girls are not increasing in most sub-Saharan African countries. The rate of unintended births has either leveled off or is dropping. Nevertheless, as a region, most sub-Saharan African nations still have the highest rates of adolescent pregnancies in the world (Amazigo, Silva, Kaufman, & Obikeze, 1997).

In rural areas, social conditions limit educational and job opportunities for adolescent girls. Marrying at a young age and having children while still

Table 11.1
Maternal Deaths in 1996 (causes related to pregnancy and childbirth)

Sub-Saharan	South Asia	Europe/U.S.	Canada
1 in 13	1 in 35	1 in 3,200	1 in 7,300

Source: Data from Crossette, 1996.

in her teens is a social expectation and may seem a more certain route to social standing than education. However, having children early can have negative consequences because young mothers are often physiologically immature and lack access to adequate health care. In rural sub-Saharan Africa, high fertility is still highly valued in a woman.

In urban areas, social conditions encourage girls to continue their education and delay marriage. Childbearing is discouraged because it may hurt a schoolgirl's future education and employment opportunities. However, because safe, legal abortions are generally not available in Africa, a young girl's decision to end her pregnancy by abortion puts her life at risk (Amazigo et al., 1997).

To date, much of the focus on adolescent pregnancy in sub-Saharan Africa has concentrated on the health and educational consequences of early childbearing among unmarried adolescent girls enrolled in school. However, in sub-Saharan Africa, married adolescents girls have higher birthrates than unmarried adolescents do. These young married girls, because of their age and the health services available to them, suffer from the same medical complications that unmarried teens struggle with when pregnant. Because of rapidly changing circumstances and expectations, these young married girls have become a concern to health officials (Amazigo et al., 1997).

Maternal Risk

Worldwide each year about 585,000 women die during pregnancy or because of giving birth; most die needlessly. An additional 18 million women suffer injuries or debilitating illnesses. The majority of girls and women who die from pregnancy or birth complications are healthy and in the prime of their lives.

A 1996 UNICEF (United Nations Children's Fund) report on maternal risks noted that sub-Saharan Africa had the highest risk of maternal injury and deaths in the world (Table 11.1). Limited obstetric care in many sub-Saharan nations is at the root of the problem. Each year, about 75,000 women die of botched abortions. About 75,000 more suffer brain damage or kidney damage or die in eclampsia. There are at least 40,000 women who die of blood poisoning, 40,000 who die from obstructed labor, and another 140,000 women die from hemorrhaging (Crossette, 1996). These are all common health risks faced by adolescent girls who give birth in Nigeria and most of sub-Saharan Africa.

Contraceptive Needs

Contraceptive use is increasing almost universally in all regions of the developing world including sub-Saharan Africa. This is occurring in sub-Saharan Africa because the number of married and unmarried females who wish to control the number of children they give birth to has risen slowly but steadily since the 1970s. By the 1990s, 20% to 40% of women in the sub-Saharan were using some form of birth control. Even so, this percentage is far below the rest of the world, which is somewhere between 40% and 60%. However, the low number of women using birth control in Nigeria is misleading; a growing number of married women in most sub-Saharan African countries would like to stop having children but have no real access to modern methods of contraception (Westoff & Bankole, 2000).

A study of 2,290 women aged 15 to 49 in the predominantly rural nation of Transkei found an exceptionally high prevalence of contraceptive use. It was an unexpected high usage of contraception by women from a poor sub-Saharan African nation. Transkei is a self-governing black African homeland in southeast South Africa. It is located on the coast along the Indian Ocean. It was designated as a semiautonomous territory in 1963 during apartheid. It gained nominal independence in 1976 and has an estimated population of 2 million people.

In this study, researchers found that over 60% of women had used a contraceptive method, and 42% were currently using one. Even more striking, 58% of the women who were using a contraceptive method were using the highly effective method of injectable implants. The pill was used by 30%. Among women who have never used a modern contraceptive method, 90% plan to use an injectable or the pill in the future to control the number of children they give birth. Almost 50% of the women surveyed had heard of condoms, but they reported that the use of condoms was rare. In this study, contraception methods were used more often by teenage girls and never-married women (53%) than by married women (34%).

Almost 80% of the women who use a contraceptive method in Transkei obtain it from a government clinic. The majority of women who use contraceptives say they wish to stop childbearing (43%), space the births of their children (33%), or postpone the birth of their first child (21%).

Other studies support the Transkei findings and suggest that in the sub-Saharan region births have been declining for three decades. This trend is evident both in wealthy urban areas and in impoverished rural areas.

Contraceptive knowledge is highest among women who are younger than 30 and well educated. Contraceptive use ranges from 16% among the least-educated women to 67% among the best-educated. Women who are employed outside the home know more about and use contraceptives more often than women who work in the home.

TEEN PREGNANCY TODAY

Marrying in her early teens and having several children before the age of 20 has historically been a common life experience for the vast majority of women around the world and is still common in sub-Saharan Africa.

Political Views and Public Policies

The widespread use of injectable contraceptives and the pill, which is common among sub-Saharan African women, is in great part due to the limited range of methods provided by government programs. In the past, government services promoted methods that required minimal education, little client involvement, and few follow-up services.

In one recent study, oral contraceptives were used by 43% of 15- to 19-year-old girls. Use of oral contraceptives fell to less than 20% among women 30 to 44 years of age. In contrast, reliance on injectable implants increases with age. About 65% of women in their thirties use injectables.

This change in sexual behavior (high-level contraceptive use) raises the question as to what conditions in the social environment resulted in the widespread use of these highly effective contraceptive methods by these poor rural women (Harnden, 1995). The limited range of methods provided by government programs explains the types of methods used, but this does not explain the decision by poor rural females to use a modern contraception method.

A major force behind the decision to use only one method of birth control can be attributed to the economic and political policies that were devised to ensure a pool of cheap labor for South African mines, industries, and commercial agriculture. The money these men sent back to their homeland had a major impact on the socioeconomic structure, family life, and reproductive behavior in rural areas. This increase in wealth in rural areas upset the marriage market and created a scarcity of marriageable men. Finally, these policies put considerable strain on the sexual faithfulness of married couples.

These public policies were far-reaching. The widespread use of birth-control methods in marital relationships, by nonmarried couples, and those involved in extramarital sexual relationships became increasingly tolerated.

A general result of this situation was a lessening of norms governing nonmarital and extramarital sexual relations. One specific effect is that never-married women in their late twenties or older who engage in sexual relations and have a child suffer from less stigma.

Another effect was the increase in the number of marital and nonmarital households led by women in the men's former homelands. In effect, the migrant labor system gave many women economic and conjugal autonomy. In this context, rural women in sub-Saharan Africa see and use contraceptives as part of a socioeconomic adjustment strategy.

In cases where girls and women need economic support from their male partners, adult and teenage women may engage in sexual intercourse, but they also tend to use contraceptives. In these situations the girls and women are more likely to choose a method that is highly effective and can be used in secret. These preferences help explain the popularity of injectables (Chimere-Dan, 1996).

Social Views, Customs, and Practices

In northern Nigeria, in Muslim and other traditional African societies, the majority of girls enter marriages that are arranged by their family. The bride could be as young as nine years old, but most often the girls are closer to puberty. In the south, among the better-educated families, girls tend to marry when they are in their late teens or early twenties.

In rural Nigeria, men tend to be older when they marry, especially if their family is poor and unable to afford the high cost of a wedding and the bride-price. Adolescent girls are often involved with more than one male partner before marriage.

In the growing urban areas, it is clear that marriage has lost its role as a prerequisite for socially accepted sexual relations. Having said that, it is also clear that many Nigerian adolescents and young people are acting responsibly and successfully by using contraceptives.

The 1996 study in Transkei found 70% of never-married teenagers were sexually active. Of those, some 95% reported using a contraception method to prevent pregnancy. Even so, many teenagers reported visiting the family planning service centers after several sexual encounters, a very high risk behavior (Mfono, 1998).

THE FUTURE OF TEEN PREGNANCY

Policies designed to increase the use of condoms need to be strengthened in all sub-Saharan African nations. The people of the sub-Saharan region have changed their sexual behavior to include modern contraceptive methods. Sub-Saharan people, if given the opportunity, will use a barrier method such as the condom to prevent HIV/AIDS and other STDs. These programs should also promote a better understanding of contraception and barrier methods and encourage more cooperation between spouses and sexual partners when using a barrier method.

Programs need to emphasize that family planning gives parents control over the number of children they wish to have. In countries where contraceptive use is already high, the emphasis needs to be on increasing access and helping women, young and old, practice contraception more effectively (Westoff & Bankole, 2000).

CONCLUSION

The young people of Nigeria face many struggles. But for the young Nigerian girl who successfully gives birth before she is 15, her life is pretty much socially scripted. She can expect to give birth to between six and eight children during her lifetime. This is provided she lives through childbirth, and her child lives through infancy. She can also expect to be poor, unless she and her husband live apart while he is working in another region of Nigeria or Africa.

Although Nigeria has more resources than most other sub-Saharan nations, the wealth of this oil-rich country is in the hands of a few. Little money is left for social services or family planning.

In many sub-Saharan countries, contraceptives and condoms are difficult for unwed adolescents to get without a prescription from a medical doctor. Yet by all accounts they manage to find a way to acquire modern, effective methods of contraception. The next step among Nigerian teens (and among all sub-Saharan African teens) needs to be a sexual behavior change that includes both effective modern contraceptive use and condom use.

State policies need to address the threat of HIV/AIDS, which disproportionately affects young people. For their sake, family planning programs need to promote condom use in the same way they promote the use of injectables and the pill. Widespread condom use will save millions of lives in Nigeria and the sub-Saharan, including the lives of millions of adolescent moms and their babies.

REFERENCES

Amazigo, U., Silva, N., Kaufman, J., & Obikeze, D.S. (1997). Sexual activity and contraceptive knowledge and use among in-school adolescents in Nigeria. *International Family Planning Perspectives, 23*, 28–33.

Chimere-Dan, O. (1996). Contraceptive prevalence in rural South Africa. *International Family Planning Perspectives, 22*(1), 4–9.

Crossette, B. (1996, June 11). UNICEF cites pregnancy toll: 585,000 women die yearly. *New York Times* (National Edition), p. A1.

Doppenburg, H.J.A.T. (1993). Contraceptive choices for teenagers. *Fertility Control Reviews, 2*(3), 10–13.

Eberstadt, N. (1997). World population implosion? *The Public Interest, 1* (129) (electronic version).

Haney, D.Q. (2000, July 11). AIDS toll in Africa to soar, experts say. *Miami Herald*, p. A1.

Harnden, T. (1995, August 24). Women having fewer children. *Daily Telegraph*, p. 7.

Houlder, V. (1999, September 23). UN trims its estimate for population growth. *Financial Times Limited*. (London), p. 4.

Metz, H.C. (1991). *Nigeria, a country study*. Library of Congress, Federal Research Division. Retrieved August 2, 2000, from the World Wide Web: http://lcweb2.loc.gov/frd/cs/.

Mfono, Z. (1998). Teenage contraceptive needs in urban South Africa: A case study. *International Family Planning Perspectives* 24(4), 180–183.

Odimegwu, C.O. (1999). Family planning attitudes and use in Nigeria: A factor analysis. *International Family Planning Perspectives*, 25(2), 86–91.

Offor, E., & Okolo, A.A. (1997). HIV seroprevalence in women of childbearing age in Benin City, Nigeria. *African Journal of Reproductive Health*, 1(2), 36–40.

Rubinson, L., & De Rubertis, M.S. (1991). Trends in sexual attitudes and behaviors of a college population over a 15-year period. *Journal of Sex Education & Therapy*, 17(1), 32–41.

Westoff, C.F., & Bankole, A. (2000). Trends in the demand for family limitation in developing countries. *International Family Planning Perspectives*, 26(2), 56–62, 97.

12

RUSSIA

Andrew L. Cherry

PROFILE OF RUSSIA

Even after the breakup of the Soviet Union, the Russian Federation (Rossiskaya Federatsiy), in geographic size, is still the largest country in the world. Russia covers more than 11% of the earth surface (17,075,200 square kilometers/6,592,770 square miles). Of that, only 7.8% is arable land. Russia extends north to the Arctic Ocean and stretches east to the Pacific Ocean. This location gives Russia the longest continuous coastline (37,650 kilometer/23,400 miles) of any country in the world. Even so, Russia has almost no year-round oceanic ports because most of the coastal waters are frozen for most of the year.

Permafrost, or permanently frozen subsoil, is found throughout the northern region, providing limited sustenance to plants. Forests cover 45% of Russia. These forests account for nearly 25% of the world's forest area.

Russia contains the greatest mineral reserves of any country in the world. It is especially rich in mineral fuels, including petroleum and natural gas.

The majority of the 146,861,022 people (1998 estimate) live in European Russia. Although more than 100 nationalities make up the population, Russians account for 82%. The official language is Russian. Minorities include Tatars, Ukrainians, Chuvash, Belarussian, Bashkir, and Chechen.

Russian Orthodox Christianity is the primary religion, with an estimated 35 million adherents. The Russian Orthodox Church has played a major role in Russian history that goes back more than 1,100 years.

The Russian population has been shrinking since 1992; it could fall to about 120 million by 2050. It fell by nearly 500,000 in 1996 (McRae, 1997). Population figures in mid-1995 released by the Ministry of Labor indicate that between 1960 and 1995 about 66% of Russia's small villages (those with fewer than 1,000 residents) disappeared. Of the 24,000 that remained in the mid-1990s, more than 50% of the population was older than 65 years of age (Traynor, 2000).

The Russia Federation inherited a well-developed system of education from the Soviet Union. The Soviet government operated virtually all the schools in Russia. It had an extensive network of preschool, elementary, secondary, and postsecondary schools. The Soviet educational philosophy was simple. The teacher's job was to transmit standardized materials organized around socialist ethics. The student's job was to memorize those materials.

Soviet Communist ethics stressed the primacy of the collective over the interests of the individual. Consequently, creativity and individualism were not valued in the Soviet system of education. Even before the fall of the Communist Russia, the educational reform programs in the 1980s called for new curricula, textbooks, and teaching methods. The idea was to develop schools that could better equip Soviet students to deal with a modern, technologically driven economy that Soviet leaders believed would be the trend in the future. However, because of a lack of funding, educational facilities generally were inadequate, overcrowding was common, and equipment and materials were in short supply. The schools and universities could not supply the skilled labor needed in almost every sector of the economy.

At the same time, Russian young people became increasingly cynical about the Marxist-Leninist philosophy, as well as the stifling of self-expression and individual responsibility.

The collapse of the Soviet system and glasnost did what the education reforms in the 1980s could not do. The collapse opened the door for change in the curriculum. These changes included the teaching of previously banned literary works and a reinterpretation of Soviet and Russian history. In 1995, 2.21% of government expenditures went to education.

Russia's economy was severely crippled when it moved from the Communist system, where prices are controlled by the central government, to a market economy, where prices are determined by industry and the supply and demand of the products. Although the move toward a market economy was met with widespread resistance, it did not stop the economic change from taking place.

As the market system developed, many people found themselves out of work. Unemployment in 1996 was reported to be 9.3%. Another 46.5 million people (31%) had incomes below the poverty level. The gross domestic product (GDP) per person in 1996 was $2,980 (U.S. dollars) (Bureau of European Affairs, 2000).

During this period, many Russians experienced unemployment for the first time. In particular, middle-aged workers found it difficult to adjust to the loss of the cradle-to-grave social security provided by the Soviet system. The gap between Russia's "haves" and "have-nots" continues to grow. In the new economic system, the haves were distinguished by skills, audacity, and connections to influential people (Bureau of European Affairs, 2000).

Russian law provides numerous protections that meet the needs of adolescent mothers and all women of childbearing age. This legislation merges family policy and employment policy to assist mothers and families. Women who are employed are entitled to paid maternity leave from 70 days prior to giving birth until 70 days afterward. Despite what may look like generosity from the state, maternity leave salary and benefits are based on the Russian minimum wage, not on a woman's current wage. This increases the cost of childbearing to the mother and family.

A portion of Russian workers have entitlements to housing, child care, and paid vacations, regardless of their rank within a company. Housing entitlements involve either outright provision of a low-rent apartment or cash or in-kind housing. Furthermore, occupants obtain an ownership right to the apartment extending beyond their employment and into retirement. They may also have the legal title to the apartment transferred to their own name without paying any purchase price.

The Social Insurance Fund that administers the payment of benefits is managed by the largest union organization in Russia, the Federation of Independent Trade Unions of Russia (Federatsiya nezavisimykh profsoyuzov Rossii—FNPR). Employers contribute 5.4% of the total payroll to fund the benefits.

At the end of 1995, some 8.2 million people were registered as unemployed. The true number is thought to be much higher. In 1998, about 5 million people were unemployed. The "new poor," according to the World Bank, far exceed the resources available in Russia for social welfare. The Communist system, with all of its problems, provided universal employment. Without a job, able-bodied citizens did not have access to social security benefits. In post-Communist Russia, unemployment and the lack of funding for basic social services are openly acknowledged (Bureau of European Affairs, 2000).

Because of the unemployment and related despair, Russia's rate of alcohol consumption has always been among the highest in the world and increased throughout the 1990s. Alcoholism, particularly among men, is the third leading cause of death after cardiovascular diseases and cancer. Periodic government campaigns to reduce alcoholism have resulted in thousands of deaths from the consumption of illegal alcohol called *samogon* (homemade vodka similar to the American moonshine version).

The last campaign to reduce alcoholism was undertaken by Mikhail Gorbachev's administration between 1985 and 1988. Government efforts failed, and public anger over the restrictions on the amount of vodka one could purchase as well as an increase in cost contributed to Gorbachev's failure to win reelection. By 1987, the production of *samogon* had become a large-scale industry, depriving the state of tax revenue. When restrictions were eased in 1988, alcohol consumption exceeded the pre-1985 level. One study suggested that between 1987 and 1992 the annual per capita consumption of alcohol rose from about 11 liters of pure alcohol to 14 liters in 1992. Consumption in the late 1990s was estimated to be 15 liters of pure alcohol per Russian. The World Health Organization standards suggest that over 8 liters of pure alcohol per person per year is likely to cause major medical problems. In 1994, about 53,000 Russians died of alcohol poisoning, an increase of about 36,000 over the number of deaths in 1991 (Bureau of European Affairs, 2000).

In 1994, Russia as a nation averaged 84 murders a day. Many of those were contract killings attributed to criminal organizations. In 1995, the national crime total exceeded 1.3 million crimes, including 30,600 murders. Crime experts predicted that the murder total would exceed 50,000 before the 21st century.

Crime statistics from Moscow in 1995 listed a total of 93,560 crimes. There were 18,500 white-collar crimes—an increase of 8.3% over 1994. Swindling increased 67.2%, and extortion increased 37.5%. Murder and attempted murder increased 1.5%; rape, 6.5%; burglaries, 6.6%; burglaries accompanied by violence, 20.8%; and serious crimes by teenagers, 2.2%.

After the collapse of the USSR, Russia became a major conduit for the movement of drugs, contraband, and laundered money between Europe and Asia. In 1995 an estimated 150 criminal organizations with transnational links were operating in Russia (Bureau of European Affairs, 2000).

Labor camps are strict-regime camps where inmates work at the most difficult jobs, usually outdoors, and receive meager rations. The system of corrective labor came to be viewed by Soviet authorities as successful because of the low rate of recidivism. But prison reforms in 1989 emphasized rehabilitation and attempted to "humanize" the Gulag system. Nevertheless, there were few changes in the treatment of most prisoners in the Gulag system.

In 1994 the estimated prison population was more than 1 million. Of these, about 600,000 were held in labor camps. Of those in labor camps, about 21,600 were women, and about 19,000 were adolescents. About 50% were imprisoned for violent crimes, 60% were repeat offenders, and better than 15% were alcoholics or drug addicts. Presently, the population of Russian prisons exceeds the capacity of those facilities by an average of 50% (Bureau of European Affairs, 2000).

Since the fall of the USSR, while average Russians have gained greater individual freedoms from arbitrary government intrusion, they have been plagued by a crime wave that gets worse each year. Lacking effective law enforcement, Russian society continues to be targeted by criminals world-wide.

INTRODUCTION

Teenagers in Russia have been living through some of the most extreme and rapid changes any group of teens has ever experienced. The collapse of the Soviet Union was followed in 1991 by a decade of deteriorating infrastructure, a major increase in poverty, and an overall decrease in the quality of life. Facing social instability, social disorganization, and economic uncertainty, teens in Russia search for their identity and a future in a country where prospects are poor. In this climate, many adolescent girls who try to find love and security will become pregnant.

In almost all of the industrialized countries in the world, adolescent childbearing—and for the most part, pregnancy—has been on the decline for 25 years. However, in Russia and the United States they have just recently begun to drop. Hence, Russia and the United States lead the industrial world in the number of teens who become pregnant and give birth. About 101 per 1,000 adolescent Russian girls become pregnant each year. In the United States, around 85 per 1,000 adolescent girls become pregnant. Russia's and the United States' teen pregnancy and birthrates are similar to several eastern European countries, including Bulgaria (Alan Guttmacher Institute, 2000).

Vignette

Larisa, 16, found out she was going to have a baby when she was three months pregnant. She said that she and her boyfriend had been seeing each other for a long time and had not used "protection." "I always wanted a baby. They are precious to me. When I found out I was pregnant I wanted to keep my baby. But, the way I was treated at the prenatal clinic was the worst experience in my life."

Larisa's experience is very typical for pregnant adolescents who go to the prenatal clinics in Russia—in many cases, even married teenagers. "The moment they looked at me, I wanted to run. They talked to me with such hate. One of the staff asked if I was a tramp who did not know the name of my baby's father. Another woman on staff asked why I needed a baby."

The staff at the clinic assumed Larisa would have an abortion. "They were really surprised when I told them I wanted to keep my baby. The Doctor shouted at me, 'Have you no conscience girl?' They gave me a week to think about my decision."

Larisa did have her child, a healthy girl. The birth was not typical of babies born in Russia in 1998 in that the baby girl was born healthy. Larisa was luckier than the vast majority of teen moms. She discovered the existence

Table 12.1
Pregnancy, Abortions, and Births per 1,000 Girls Ages
15 to 19

Pregnancy Rate	Abortion Rate	Birthrate
101.7	56.1	45.6

Source: Data from Singh & Darroch, 2000.

of Tesna, a clinic that serviced "pregnant schoolgirls," which had just opened. Larisa was allowed to stay at the crisis center for twenty-four days free of charge. She received assistance from a professional psychologist and gynecologist and attended several courses that were designed to help her become a good mother. Larisa said, "They made me feel that, even if I am only sixteen, my baby is wanted."

Even so, Larisa was realistic: "I want all the best for my baby," she said. "Times are always tough in Russia. That's not enough of a reason not to have my baby."

Overview of Teen Pregnancy

High levels of adolescent and teenage childbearing are typically found in developing countries. In these countries, the number of women who have their first child by age 19 is often between 33% and 66%. In contrast, among developed nations, about 10% of girls the same age give birth before age 20 (The Economist, 2000).

Russia and the United States are the glaring exceptions. Both countries have very high adolescent pregnancy and birth rates (Tables 12.1 and 12.2). The reasons for these rates differ in some ways, but they are similar in other ways. *Poverty* in both countries (e.g., in the United States among African Americans) fuels the high numbers. A lack of educational and job opportunities (e.g., in the United States among African Americans) results in girls and boys seeking other paths to self-fulfillment. There are inadequate *health services for the poor* in both countries but especially in Russia. In addition, in Russia teens face inadequate *family planning services* and receive little school-based *sexuality education* (Associated Press, 1997).

In Russia, there is also a lack of choice between effective birth-control methods. Abortion has traditionally been the way Russian teenage girls and women have controlled their reproductive lives. A mass reeducation campaign will be needed to make them aware of other options (Cohen, 1997).

Sexually Transmitted Diseases

Like with adolescent births, the Russian Federation and the United States led the other developed nations of the world in reports of sexually transmitted diseases (STDs) among teenagers (1970–2000) at nearly 600 cases

Table 12.2
Birthrates per 1,000, by Year

1970	1975	1980	1985	1990
29.7	34.5	43.6	55.6	45.6

Source: Data from Singh & Darroch, 2000.

per 100,000 teenagers. For instance, syphilis rates are less than 7 cases per 100,000 teens in developed countries—rates that continued to decline into the 1990s. However, syphilis rose dramatically in the Russian Federation in the 1990s (Randolph, 1992). It remained high throughout the 1990s, with over 200 cases per 100,000 teenagers per year. There are several reasons for these high numbers of STDs among teens in Russia, including a health care system that was slow to recover after the collapse of the Soviet Union. Poorly made Soviet condoms contributed to low levels of use. There was a major increase in sexual activity among adolescents in the 1990s, and many teenagers planned to use abortion to avoid unwanted births (Alan Guttmacher Institute, 2000; Charlton, 2000).

Teen Sexuality in Russia

Teens and adults receive the same reproductive services in Russia. Few official statistics are kept. However, statistics available from the Ministry of Public Health and other agencies concerning services provided and tracked by age and sex can reveal a great deal. In 1997, according to official marriage records in Moscow, 305 girls 16 years of age were married. Among 16-year-old boys, 26 were married. There were 867 Moscow girls 17 years old who were married, and 120 boys of the same age were married. These numbers suggest teenage girls tend to marry males who are older than they are (Nadezhdina, 1998; UNICEF, 1999).

According to official reports in 1997, 75 girls under the age of 15 became mothers in 1996. Girls who were 16 years of age gave birth to 315 babies. For three of the 16-year-old mothers, it was their second child. Seventeen-year-old Muscovite girls gave birth to 864 babies, and for 16 of them, it was their second child. Among Moscow girls under the age of 15, there were 71 legal abortions in 1996. Girls between the ages of 15 and 19 had 10,536 abortions the same year. This was a drop from a 1994 high of more than 12,000 abortions performed on Moscow adolescents (Kon, 1995; UNICEF, 1999).

In Russia, at least 56% of adolescent pregnancies ended in abortion in 1999. Reporting was incomplete, so the actual number was probably higher. For example, the percentage of teenage pregnancies ending in abortion was reported higher in some Scandinavian countries; in Sweden, it was 69.6% during the same period (The Economist, 2000).

According to official figures, in 1996 there were 2.7 million abortions recorded in Russia. Teenage girls accounted for about 270,000, or 10% of all abortions performed that year. These numbers do not include illegal abortions. Some experts suggest that the number of official abortions needs to be increased by as much as 25% to account for illegal abortions.

HISTORY AND SOCIAL CONTEXT

For generations, Russian women have wanted small families. A typical Russian woman who wanted only two children would have four or more abortions in her lifetime. Historically, abortion is—and continues to be—the most often used and acceptable method of birth control in Russia. Females, who bear the responsibility for family planning, do not use other methods of contraception because they are of poor quality, because they are unavailable, or because the female believes the method is carcinogenic or will harm her or her baby. Consequently, induced abortion remains the primary method of birth control in Russia (Remennick, 1991).

In 1920, Russia's law on abortion was one of the most progressive in the world. The legalization of abortions presented women with an option to terminate pregnancies at state hospitals without cost. This policy was maintained until 1936 when Stalin, in an effort to raise the birthrate to create more workers and soldiers, outlawed abortions. Without state-supported abortions and no other contraception available, adolescents girls and women of childbearing age who needed to terminate a pregnancy continued to use abortion, though now clandestine (Remennick, 1991).

The birthrate remained low because of illegal abortions. However, the harm done to the health of the women rapidly escalated (Ryan, 1993). Abortion was again legalized in 1955. Abortion was viewed as a necessary evil—necessary to prevent lethal illegal abortions and to keep women in the labor force (Kotlyar & Battin, 1999).

The first official statistics on abortion were released in September 1988. They show that 6 million to 7 million induced abortions were performed that year at Russian hospitals and clinics. However, these abortion statistics are believed to be low because illegal abortions are not included and because miniabortions, performed by vacuum aspiration or extraction, were not consistently registered as abortions. Including illegal abortion, in 1992 there were an estimated 224.6 abortions for every 100 live births (Ryan, 1993). As many as 60% of adolescent girls who become pregnant terminate their pregnancy using an abortion procedure.

TEEN PREGNANCY TODAY

During the Soviet era, all public organizations were used to promoting the ideology of the Communist Party. Women's health services, fertility, and contraception became a political battleground. When the Soviet Union dissolved, services to pregnant women, young children, and adolescents deteriorated badly. At the beginning of the 21st century, maternal and neo-natal health care had not returned to pre-Soviet-era levels.

Political Views and Public Policies

In the mid-1990s, Russian society was in the midst of a wrenching transition from a totalitarian structure to a pro-democratic system that was still developing at the end of the 20th century. As economic and civil controls were eased during the early part of the 1990s, the cost of basic necessities skyrocketed. At the same time, Russians became the victims of a malicious criminal element that had been suppressed under communism. Infectious diseases, drug addiction, homelessness, and suicide touched everyone. Growing pollution and other environmental hazards added to the general state of despair (Bureau of European Affairs, 2000).

Social Views, Customs, and Practices

The Role of Women

In post-Soviet Russia, equality among men and women is at least as problematic as it was under the Communist government. Despite Communist official ideology, Soviet women did not enjoy the same position as men in society, in employment, or within the family. One indicator of the lack of political power of women in Russia is that less than 5% of the Party Central Committee is female, and no woman has ever achieved full membership in the Politburo (Bureau of European Affairs, 2000).

Under both systems, legal protections for women have failed to address the existing conditions or have not provided adequate monetary support for the regulations. In the 1990s, increasing economic pressures and shrinking government programs left women with no choice but to find employment, even though most available employment was of poor quality and jobs of any kind were hard to find. In the Soviet era, women earned, on average, about 70% of what men earned. By 1995 they were earning about 40% of what men earned doing the same job. Income disparities contributed immensely to Russia's declining birthrate and to the general deterioration of the family.

Sexual harassment and violence against women is another serious problem faced by women of all ages in Russia. In the 1990s, sexual harassment and violence against women increased at all levels of Russian society. More than 13,000 rapes were reported in 1994. Many more went unreported. Some 18,000 battered women received treatment at a hospital or clinic. Yet it is estimated that this accounts for only 15% to 20% of all battered women. Many more do not receive any medical treatment. In 1993, an estimated 14,000 women were murdered by their husbands or lovers. This is a murder rate 20 times higher than in the United States at the same time. This number of murders is also several times higher than the number of women murdered in Russia in the mid-1980s. More than 300,000 other types of crimes (not including murder and rape) were committed against women in 1994. In 1996 the state Duma drafted a law against domestic violence.

Although the 1996 law against domestic violence provides for as much as three years' imprisonment for sexual harassment, the law is rarely enforced. Approximately 300 Moscow firms have been blacklisted for sexual harassment. Demands for sex and even rape are still common on-the-job occurrences for Russian women.

The exceedingly high divorce rate is another serious problem for women and adolescent girls faced with an unplanned pregnancy. In 1993, the divorce rate was 4.5 per 1,000 people, compared to 4.1 in 1983. Consequently, the marriage rate declined from 10.5 per 1,000 people in 1983 to 7.5 in 1993. In 1992 some 17.2% of births were to unmarried adolescent girls and young women. Finally, according to 1994 Russian government statistics, about 20% of families were run by a single parent, and 94% of these single-parent families were headed by the mother. In the 1980s, the Soviet Union ranked second in the world behind the United States in the number of official divorces yearly, a number that does not include informal separations.

Poverty and economic hardship have driven some Russian adolescent girls and young women into prostitution. In the 1990s, organized crime became heavily involved in prostitution, both in Russia and in central and western Europe. Some estimates put the number at about 10,000 Russian women and girls lured into prostitution by bogus advertisements for matchmaking services or modeling agencies.

The Family

In post-Soviet Russia, the family continues to be viewed as the most important institution in society. In 1994, a survey funded by the Commission on Women's, Family, and Demographic Problems found that less than 3% of respondents thought that "living alone without a family" was the best choice for a young person. Although the number of children in the average Russian family has decreased steadily since the 1970s, nearly 80% of respondents named children as the essential element of a good marriage. At the same time, about 75% of respondents said that divorce was appropriate to terminate a bad marriage. The social and economic crises experienced by Russians have caused them to rely more than ever on their family as a source of personal satisfaction and stability. At the same time, these same crises have caused the standard of living to fall, putting more pressure on the already strained Russian family (Bureau of European Affairs, 2000).

To illustrate, the average Russian's diet during the 1990s was classified as nutritiously inadequate. Vegetables were scarce in Russia, except in rural areas where they are homegrown. Fruits have never been important to the Russian diet. Per capita meat consumption also fell in the 1990s. During that period, the population began to show the cumulative effects of malnutrition. Poor economic prospects, together with low confidence in the state's family benefits programs, discourage Russian women from having children (Bureau of European Affairs, 2000).

Health Care

In addition to the deterioration of Russia's health facilities and clinics in the 1990s, the quality of medical personnel also dropped because many of Russia's best medical people immigrated to Europe and the United States when restrictions were lifted. However, much of the poor health of the Russian people is the result of poor personal hygiene, poor diet, and a lack of exercise. Programs to educate the public about personal hygiene, proper diet, and vitamins are nonexistent (Demine & Demine, 1998).

Russia's public health budget was 1.74% of all government expenditures in 1995. As a comparison, Britain spent 6% of its budget on health care, whereas the United States spent more than 12% of its budget on health care. Such a meager outlay (1.74%) was not adequate to address Russia's major health care problems, not to mention the air, water, and soil pollution that contribute to a worsening of the public health. The current meager level of health care expenditures is insufficient even to meet the minimal needs of the Russian people. Because of the poor quality and limited availability of health services in Russia, traditional home cures became widespread in the 1990s (Digges, 2000).

Attitude about Sexuality

In the 1990s, Russian sexual values and attitudes became more liberal. In the Soviet era, the Russian attitude toward sexuality itself was simply concealed. Most Soviet philosophical, psychological, and biological reference works made little or no mention of sexuality as a major characteristic of human beings. Soviet psychology, notoriously backward and misused, almost completely ignored the influence of sexual behavior and motivation on overall psychological makeup.

Objections to the trend toward sexual liberation still come from the older generations. In surveys, younger and better-educated Russians generally voice approval. This is especially obvious among the Russian youth culture. The change in sexual attitudes over time has lessened the commitment of young Russians to long-term relationships and affected their views of relationships. In surveys in the mid-1990s, younger males had a much stronger perception of sex being associated with pleasure, whereas young females associated sex with love.

Sex Education

Russia has a strong tradition that is opposed to sexuality education being taught in school. Consequently, when Russian teens embraced the new sexual freedom in the late 1980s, they had little information about barrier methods of contraception. Condoms were of poor quality and difficult to find. Though contraceptives were increasingly available in Russia in the late 1990s, they are still mistrusted or misunderstood (Charlton, 2000). Thus, the rates of STDs have become among the highest in the world. Scientists fear that the high STD rate could be the forerunner of a major HIV/AIDS (human immuno deficiency virus/acquired immuno deficiency syndrome) outbreak.

Sexuality education could help curb the rise in teen pregnancy and reduce STDs; however, among older adults there is still resistance to sex education in the schools. In 1997, a group of psychologists, lawmakers, and political activists lobbied to keep sex education out of Russia's schools. They believed that sex education would promote an unwholesome interest in sex among teenagers, leading "to sexual looseness and sexual excesses." "[I]t will also lead to a tremendous growth of psychological pathologies and spur drug addiction and alcoholism." As the 21st century begins, sex education is still not found among subjects in the official education curriculum (Associated Press, 1997).

Birthrate

Many people within and outside of Russia point out that as a country, as a culture, and as a people, Russian society is slowly dying out. There are two major reasons for these observations: rising death rates among middle-aged men and a low birthrate. The low birthrate is clearly associated with the rise in job opportunities for women. The greater the chances that women have of earning a good income, the greater the cost of taking some time off to have a family. There may be some lag here in the response of the rest of society. The labor market for women has grown faster than the social infrastructure that underpins it: everything from childcare to the willingness of male partners to pitch in with running the home (McRae, 1997).

The Russian birthrate began to fall dramatically in the 1960s. It dropped from 23.2 births per 1,000 women in the 1960s to 14.1 births per 1,000 by 1970. The birthrate recovered slightly in the early 1980s, with 17.3 births per 1,000, stimulated by state incentives to have larger families. However, by 1993 the rate was only 9.4 births per 1,000. According to the projections of the Center for Economic Analysis, after reaching its lowest point (8.0 per 1,000) in 1995, the birthrate will rise gradually to 9.7 per 1,000 by 2005. In 1999, a survey of women of childbearing age found that 25% did not intend to become mothers.

The fertility rate had dropped in both urban and rural areas. Roughly half as many children were born in 1993 as in 1987. In 1994, the population of Russia fell by 920,000.

Between 1989 and 1993, the number of women in the prime childbearing age group decreased by 1.3 million, or 12%, making a major contribution to the 27% decline in births during that period. Adding to this decline, between 1990 and 1994, the government estimated that infant mortality rose from 17.4 deaths per 1,000 live births to 19.9 deaths per 1,000 births. Other experts suggest the rate is about 25 deaths per 1,000 live births. Between 1992 and 1995, the official maternal mortality rate also rose from 47 to 52 deaths per 100,000 births.

Maternity and Infant Care

Poor overall health care, lack of medicines, especially in rural Russian areas, and poor diet drive up the number of infants that die each year. An estimated 40% to 50% of infant deaths are caused by respiratory failure, infections, parasites, accidents, injuries, and trauma. In other developed countries, infant deaths range from 4% to 17%. The poor health and diet of new mothers were obvious in the numbers. Less than 50% of new mothers can breast-feed. This in turn undermines infant health.

Unwanted adolescent pregnancies are common because of the limited availability of accurate and confidential information on contraception, the substandard quality of contraceptives, and a reluctance to discuss sexual issues openly at home or to provide sex education at school. However, no social stigma is attached to children born out of wedlock to adolescent girls, and unmarried mothers receive similar maternity benefits as married mothers.

Western advances in birth control—and all modern means of birth control—were systematically kept from women in the Soviet Union because the state could not afford them. As a result, Russian gynecologists lacked the training to advise women on contraception. Even in Moscow in the mid-1990s, most contraceptives were paid for by international funds and charities. International charities, however, could not nearly meet the need. By the early 1990s, only 22% of women of childbearing age were estimated to be using contraceptives, relying solely on abortion to control their fertility. The child mortality rate (under five) was 25 deaths per 1,000 live births in 1996.

After giving birth, most mothers, even adolescent mothers, need to return to work. However, placing an infant in a child-care center puts the child at greater risk of contracting contagious diseases. Illnesses such as cholera, typhoid fever, diphtheria, pertussis, and poliomyelitis, which have been virtually eradicated in other advanced countries, are widespread among Russia's children. Basic vaccines are not available or are in short supply. Even when immunizations are available, parents often refuse them for fear their children will be infected from dirty needles (Bureau of European Affairs, 2000).

The medical journal *Meditsinskaya Gazeta* reported in 1999 that only one Russian baby in ten was born in good health. The authors said, "Pregnancy and child-bearing are about 10 times more dangerous for Russian mothers than, for example, a mother in Germany." In the decade after the collapse of the Soviet Union, the birthrate in Russia fell by 50% (Charlton, 2000).

HIV/AIDS

In 1987, after the first case of AIDS was confirmed in the Soviet Union, the strictest anti-AIDS law in the world was passed by the Soviet Union. The law made the transmission of the infection a criminal offense punishable by up to eight years in jail. Nonetheless, AIDS transmittal increased because of a chronic shortage of condoms (which Soviet medical officials euphemistically called "Article Number 2") and because of hospitals and clinics that repeatedly used poorly sterilized needles rather than disposable hypodermic syringes to save money.

In late 1995, the Ministry of Health reported that 1,023 Russians, including 278 children and adolescents, were officially registered as having HIV. By 1995, 160 Russians, of whom 73 were children, had died of AIDS. Before 1992, several mass infections of children occurred in medical facilities. The number of people officially diagnosed with HIV increased 50% from 1993 to 1994.

AIDS sufferers face a great deal of intolerance in Russian society. HIV/AIDS is associated with foreigners and homosexuals. A survey of adults found that homosexuals are the most hated group in Russia (Kon, 1995).

Social Orphans

There are more than half a million children officially classified as orphans in Russia. Most of them have a father or mother, but they are either alcoholics, criminals, or single parents unable or unwilling to look after their children. These children are known as social orphans. They account for 95% of all children who live in homes or are reared by foster parents.

"We are doing our best to create a family-like environment for our young charges," said Natalia Novikova. But Serova's orphanage, officially called Boarding School Nr. 36, is badly overcrowded with 250 children sleeping in cramped dormitories with 14 to 17 beds per room. A staff of 62, including teachers, care assistants, and a psychologist, look after the children, whose ages range from 6 to 15. Natalia Novikova found it sad that "the children have almost no personal possessions" (Landwehr, 1995, p. 381).

More than 70,000 orphans live in homes or other institutions scattered across Russia. In 1994, some 200,000 children were placed in foster homes, and 135,000 were adopted. The orphaned children remain in foster homes as long as they are of school age. When they leave the foster home, many children move on to vocational training colleges. If they are able to get jobs, most of them lead seemingly normal lives and raise families of their own.

Others have problems, and they often put their children in orphanages (Landwehr, 1995).

THE FUTURE OF TEEN PREGNANCY

The health of children and adolescents in Russia should be considered a crisis of such proportion that it is a threat to its national security. Russia needs to take emergency measures just to stop the deterioration of the health of its children and adolescents. Of special concern are the continuously high rates of infant and child mortality; the rising morbidity among children beginning in the postnatal period in practically all disease categories; teenage pregnancy; teen alcoholism, tobacco use and drug abuse/use; and the deterioration of the general health of girls and young men.

The situation as it relates to the reproduction and health status of the new generation is aggravated by the social economic and political instability in Russia. The declining quality of mother and child care is attributed to a drop in the standard of living of the overwhelming majority of families with children under 18 years of age.

The failure to implement universal and accurate sex education in school has left many adolescents unprotected and unarmed in an increasingly dangerous sexual world. The general destruction of health education and promotion facilities for children and adolescents has added to their worsening health (Demine & Demine, 1998).

In large cities, private-pay pediatric and health promotion services, which are illegal, continue to grow despite the cost. Most Russians believe or hope private medical services will be better than that provided by the government.

The increase in infectious diseases among children and STDs among adolescents is attributable to poor public health standards and inadequate financing. Improving sanitary standards at facilities for children would go a long way in reducing outbreaks of serious epidemics. The health of young children and adolescents is compromised in regions of ecological distress and because of iodine deficiency (Demine & Demine, 1998).

Unless these various levels of health threat are dealt with in a comprehensive way, these factors will continue to impair the mental and physical development of Russian children and adolescents—and the babies to which adolescent girls give birth.

CONCLUSION

Sadly, the people of Russia are experiencing the most wrenching social, political, and economic changes in modern history. This is particularly hard on adolescents, who have grown up in this country deprived, in many cases, of the basic necessities of life. Besieged by massive corruption at all levels of Russian society, the infrastructure and the people continue to pay dearly for Russia's move to a market economy.

Given the conditions in Russia at the beginning of the 21st century, as an adolescent or teenager, becoming pregnant in the Federation of Russia is a perilous enterprise. The future teen mother is at risk of contracting any number of STDs and may become HIV-infected. In several studies, researchers have reported that as many as 80% of adolescents have some type of sexually transmitted disease. If a girl becomes pregnant and avoids STDs and HIV, she will have to fight to keep from having an abortion, much like teenage girls in the United States fight to get an abortion. If she does carry her child to term, and the baby is born healthy, there is a good chance she or her baby will contract a contagious disease at the hospital. If the baby lives long enough to be vaccinated, the child could be infected with a syringe already used on other children or adults. If the newborn survives all of these hazards, the child faces a future of malnutrition and hardships. If it is a boy, the teen mother can expect to outlive her son.

REFERENCES

Alan Guttmacher Institute. (2000, February 24). *United States and the Russian federation lead the developed world in teenage pregnancy rates.* Washington, DC: Author. News Release.

Associated Press. (1997, November 22). Russians protest sex education. *Toronto Star Newspapers, Ltd*, 2nd ed., p. L5.

Bureau of European Affairs. (2000, May). *Background notes: Russia.* Washington, DC: U.S. Department of State.

Cohen, S.A. (1997). *The role of contraception in reducing abortion.* Washington, DC.: Alan Guttmacher Institute.

Charlton, A. (2000, July 29). Fertility problems, abortions aggravate Russia's demographic decline. *Associated Press*, International News. Dateline: Moscow.

Demine, A.K., & Demine, I.A. (1998). *A vision of health for children, adolescents and youth in Russia.* Moscow: Russian Public Health Association, (electronic version).

Digges, C. (2000, July 2). Drugs fuel AIDS epidemic in Chelyabinsk. *The St. Petersburg Times*, (electronic version).

The Economist. (2000, February 26). Teen pregnancy. *The Economist* (U.S. edition), (electronic version).

Kon, I.S. (1995). *The sexual revolution in Russia.* New York: Free Press.

Kotlyar, J.O., & Battin, M.P. (1999). Abortion in Russia. *University of Utah's Journal of Undergraduate Research, 7*(1), 11–23.

Landwehr, S. (1995, March 8). More than half-a-million orphans in Russia. *Deutshe Presse-Agentur* (Hamburg, Germany), (electronic version).

McRae, H. (1997, June 11). The strange case of falling birth rates in the West. Infonautics Corporation. Newspaper Publishing P.L.C., p. 21. Retrieved July 25, 2000, from the World Wide Web: http://www.infonautics.com.

Nadezhdina, N. (1998, January 16–22). SOS against a background of love. *Trud* (Moscow), p. 7.

Randolph, E. (1992, February 23). Free love in the Soviet Union. *St. Petersburg Times*, p. 7D.

Remennick, L. (1991). Epidemiology and determinants of induced abortion in the USSR. *Social Science Medicine, 33*(7), 841–848.

Ryan, M. (1993). *Social trends in contemporary Russia.* London, England: Macmillan Press.

Singh, S., & Darroch, J.E. (2000). Adolescent pregnancy and childbearing: Levels and trends in developed countries. *Family Planning Perspectives, 32*(1), 14–23.

Traynor, I. (2000, June 30). Russia dying of drink and despair. *Guardian Unlimited* (electronic version).

UNICEF. (1999). *AFTER THE FALL: The human impact of ten years of transition.* The United Nations Children's Fund. Retrieved July 30, 2000, from the World Wide Web: http://www.unicef-icdc.org.

13

SWEDEN

Annulla Linders

PROFILE OF SWEDEN

Sweden is a small and highly developed northern European democracy of less than 9 million people. By the end of the 20th century Sweden's population base was being sustained more through immigration than "natural" reproduction. It emerged in the mid 20th century as one of the forerunners of the modern welfare state. Guided by a deeply ingrained social democratic ideology, the Swedish welfare state is built on the principles of equality and universality. Universal services are services that everyone, rich or poor, can receive. To support welfare services, Sweden has a progressive tax system, a nationalized and universal health care system, a nationalized public school system (including higher education), a well-developed union system, and a wide range of universal and some need-based benefits. Despite its recent economic crisis, Sweden still is counted among the nations with the highest standard of living.

Sweden's family policy has a well-developed support system that includes a generous system of parental insurance, child allowances, and free prenatal, maternity, and child health care (including free medical and dental treatment for children), and it offers a range of need-based subsidies and services (e.g., housing and child care). The Swedish commitment to family planning and voluntary parenthood goes well beyond the nation's borders, making Sweden an active participant in family planning efforts throughout the world.

INTRODUCTION

Teenage pregnancy is currently not a serious problem in Sweden. Teenage pregnancy rates have steadily declined since the mid-1970s, as has the teenage abortion rate. Since there is no evidence that teenagers have become less sexually active, the Swedish decline in teen pregnancy can only be explained in terms of relatively efficient contraceptive use among teenagers.

To say that teenage pregnancy is not a serious problem in Sweden does not mean that it is not a concern. Adolescent sexuality, in all its various forms, emerged as a social and political concern in Sweden in the early 20th century. The overarching principle guiding the approach has been the prevention of unwanted pregnancies.

Numerous public agencies, at both state and local levels, are charged with tasks related to teen sexuality. The school system also occupies a prominent position in providing preventive services. Other youth and women's organizations are actively involved in helping, teaching, and disseminating information about sexuality, contraceptives, and intimacy issues. If teenage pregnancy were to suddenly increase, this massive social apparatus that monitors teenage sexuality could be mobilized.

In Sweden, although there was widespread social and political backing for prevention programs to reduce teenage pregnancy, the debate over the methods to achieve this goal was highly contentious, pitting "moral" (abstinence) against "rational" (contraception) concerns. Nevertheless, with the growing dominance of the Social Democratic Party in the 1930s, and the repeal of the law against contraceptives in 1938, all serious discussions about sexuality (teenage or otherwise) is conducted with reference to contraceptives. Abstinence, consequently, has all but disappeared as a feasible policy alternative, and with it has gone the notion that teenage sexuality is inappropriate, problematic, or even unfortunate. Instead, Swedish policy acknowledges teenage sexual activity, while at the same time placing a strong emphasis on the distinction between "good" and "bad" expressions of that sexuality. The Swedish approach to teenage sexuality, in short, amounts to an effort to coax teenagers toward "good" sexual behavior (loving, caring, safe, and preferably stable relationships) and away from "bad" sexual behavior (hasty, thoughtless, temporary, and unsafe relationships). From this point of view, the lowering of the birth and abortion rates among teenagers indicates that the Swedish model has been quite successful.

In Sweden, the concerns about teen pregnancy are formulated almost entirely around the age of the mother, not her marital status. What this means is that the determination of whether or not a pregnancy is appropriate for an adolescent is no longer determined by her marital status but instead determined by her level of maturity (Lewin et al., 1998). However, given the Swedish emphasis on sex as fundamentally a "natural" and "healthy" form of behavior throughout the life cycle, maturity is viewed as being needed to navigate the social landscape of sex and intimate relationships. In order to gain the requisite maturity, however, some form of sexual experimentation is expected and even considered advisable. From this perspective, then, teenage sexuality remains a major social concern.

Another source of concern is the socioeconomic status of teenage mothers and parents. Child rearing at a young age, even if morally unproblematic, is more likely to bring financial hardship. This is a long-standing concern in Sweden and has over time generated a multifaceted policy that provides economic benefits (a parental support system) aimed at erasing the economic differences between rich and poor, married and unmarried parents. Although no one would argue that there are still families that are poorer than other families, the inequalities are much less pronounced, and less devastating, than they would have been without the parent support system policy. Hence, teenage parenting in Sweden is not as intimately linked to poverty as it is in some nations (the United States, for example), and accordingly it does not trigger the same kinds of concerns. It should be noted, however, that the parental support system is not designed to promote childbearing among teenagers, and in some ways, it actually discourages early parenting. The amount of parental insurance is based on the income of the parent who is staying at home, and young people typically have had less chance to gather the skills that would bring them a higher-income job. Although probably a very small factor in a teenager's decision to have or not have a child, it is most likely a significant factor in adult women's decisions and may have contributed to the general delay of childbearing in Sweden.

Vignette

Lena works as a counselor at a public youth clinic. She spends most of her time in sessions with individual clients, but every so often, she meets with visiting school classes. She likes her job and is convinced her discussions with adolescents are important, but there are still aspects of her job that she finds frustrating. The clients are overwhelmingly girls in their midteens who come to seek contraceptive advice (but that's only part of it, since many want to talk about their relationships). In most cases she recommends birth-control pills, a solution the girls usually agree with (it helps that the cost of the pill is heavily subsidized, at least in her county). Although it seems to be getting better, she is still frustrated that so many of these girls wait until *after* their sexual debut to secure birth control. It is a consolation, though, to know that in many cases the girls' partners used a condom.

Some of the girls, quite a few actually, come in when they suspect they might be pregnant. It is not that she resents counseling the girls on abortion; on the contrary, she herself often thinks that it would be the best solution. What she finds frustrating is to be reminded of how naive and ignorant some of these girls are and how difficult it is for them to translate what they learn into safe and satisfying sexual experiences.

It makes her wonder about the state of sex education in their schools. For example, a 16-year-old girl should know that withdrawal is not a reliable method to prevent pregnancy. In general, however, the work is satisfying, and the girls are easy to work with.

It is a different story with the boys. First of all, boys almost never come for counseling, although some show up to pick up condoms. When they do come in, it is almost always because they have a sexually transmitted disease (STD). That is good, of course, but she simply refuses to believe that boys have no trouble with either relationships or their own sexuality. In this regard, she feels vindicated: The clinic's new question-and-answer Web site is bombarded with questions, many of which come from boys. There is no doubt it would be better if the boys came into the center. However, the Web site can answer some of their questions, which makes it less threatening since there is no personal contact. If that helps them develop a more responsible attitude toward sex and intimacy, then she is happy.

Overview of Teen Pregnancy

Apart from a slight increase in teenage pregnancy in the late 1980s and early 1990s, the birthrate for Swedish teenagers ages 15 to 19 has steadily declined since the mid-1970s, from a birthrate of 29 per 1,000 in 1975 to about 9 births per 1,000 in 1998 (see Table 13.1). (The brief period of increased birthrates for all teen groups in the late 1980s and early 1990s corresponds with a more general increase in the birthrate and therefore cannot be viewed as a distinct youth phenomenon.) The decline is equally sharp for all age groups, but the rate varies extensively between the teenage groups. In 1998, for example, the birthrate for 15-year-old girls was 0.6 per 1,000, whereas the rate for 19-year-old girls was 16.5 per 1,000 girls.

An examination of the teenage birthrate obviously does not tell the whole story about teenage pregnancy, since a number of pregnancies are terminated through abortion (and, to a lesser extent, miscarriage). Considering the potential relationship between births and abortions, the abortion issue occupies a particularly significant role in discussions about teenage pregnancy. Fortunately, available evidence from Sweden suggests that the relationship between births and abortions is largely a positive one; that is, a low birthrate corresponds with a low abortion rate (Jones et al., 1986). For this reason, a high teenage abortion rate in Sweden is generally viewed as an indication of the ineffectiveness of services and programs aimed at reducing unwanted teenage pregnancies. Since abstinence is not a part of the official Swedish approach to teen sexuality, the fact that teenagers *do* expose themselves to the risk of pregnancy by having sexual intercourse is not viewed as an indicator of the ineffectiveness of these programs.

Table 13.1
Teenage Birthrate for 15- to 19-Year-Olds, Plus Total Birthrate, 1975–1998
(per 1,000 women)

Year	15	16	17	18	19	15-19	Total 15-44*
1975	2.3	8.2	22.8	41.8	67.6	29.0	65.5
1980	0.9	3.6	10.9	28.4	42.9	16.5	58.0
1985	0.4	2.0	6.4	24.1	29.7	13.2	57.2
1986	0.6	2.1	6.2	24.3	30.5	13.2	58.8
1987	0.4	2.3	6.0	28.1	30.5	13.4	60.4
1988	0.7	2.5	6.8	30.3	32.7	14.4	64.6
1989	0.7	2.9	7.7	30.6	34.9	15.4	66.8
1990	0.8	3.0	8.5	30.8	37.7	16.5	71.5
1991	0.8	2.7	7.8	28.7	34.4	15.4	71.7
1992	0.5	3.0	7.9	24.6	31.3	14.1	71.6
1993	0.6	2.3	6.6	24.0	28.0	13.0	69.0
1994	0.4	2.2	5.8	21.7	25.6	11.5	65.7
1995	0.7	2.1	5.8	20.2	22.7	10.3	60.7
1996	0.6	2.1	5.3	21.2	20.8	9.9	56.2
1997	0.6	2.1	5.3	22.6	19.4	10.0	53.8
1998	0.6	1.5	4.4	22.4	16.5	9.2	53.1

Mother's age columns span 15–19.

*This rate does not include births to women less than 15 years old and over 44 years old.
Sources: Data from Socialstyrelsen, 2000; Statistiska Centralbyrån, 2000.

Since the 1960s, Swedish girls have been experiencing sexual intercourse at a younger age than their mothers (see Table 13.2). Among women 18 to 30 years old in 1996, almost 40% had experienced their first intercourse before the age of 16. In 1967, only 8% of women in the same age group had their first sexual experience before 16 years of age (Lewin et al., 1998).

It is important to note that the age of sexual initiation is currently about the same for boys and girls; the median age for first intercourse is currently 16.5 years of age for girls and 16.8 for boys (Folkhälsoinstitutet, 2000). In Sweden, the similar age for first sexual intercourse for boys and girls is generally taken as a positive sign of greater gender equality. It indicates a shedding of the old double standard that imposed greater sexual restrictions on girls than boys.

After an initial increase in abortions, after the liberalization of the abortion law in 1974, the abortion rate for teenagers sharply declined, whereas the abortion rate among adult women remained fairly stable (see Table 13.3). An increase in the abortion rate, including the teenage abortion rate, followed the birthrate increase in the late 1980s and early 1990s. This increase is generally attributed to a range of factors that, taken together, brought about an increase in the number of women who became pregnant against

Table 13.2
Percent of Men and Women Ages 18 to 30 Who Had Their First Intercourse
at a Certain Age, 1967 and 1996

Age at first	1967		1996	
Intercourse	Women	Men	Women	Men
13 or younger	1%	2%	5%	5%
14-15	7	17	33	29
16-17	36	38	35	33
18-19	38	28	19	21
20-24	17	13	8	12
25 or older	1	1	0	0

Source: Data from Lewin et al., 1998, p. 154.

their wishes. These factors include a decline in the use of birth-control pills
(in part related to growing concerns about side effects and in part because
of cost considerations); an increase in the portrayal of sex as "dangerous,"
leading to more technical and scare-oriented educational packages
(prompted in part by human immunodeficiency virus [HIV] concerns); and
finally, a system of contraceptive counseling and services that was generally
inadequate (SoU04, 1990–1991).

After this temporary increase, the abortion rate once again started to decline, and for teenagers, it reached an all-time low of 16.5 abortions per
1,000 in 1995. Since then, the teenage abortion rate has inched upward.
However, whether this increase is a significant shift in the pattern of teenage
pregnancy and abortion or if it simply reflects a temporary fluctuation is yet
to be determined (Socialstyrelsen, 2000).

Even though the abortion rate is low for young teenage girls, most teenage pregnancies in Sweden end in abortions. Among 15-year-old girls, for
example, almost 93% of all pregnancies in 1998 ended in abortion, whereas
less than 60% of the pregnancies among 19-year-old girls ended in abortion.
Judging from the relatively high proportion of pregnancies that end in abortion, one might be tempted to conclude that contraception practices among
teenagers are lacking. Such a conclusion, however, is premature and is not
supported by the available evidence.

The fact that most teenagers are able to avoid pregnancy, even as they
are sexually active, suggests that effective contraceptive practices are widespread. A recent government-sponsored report on youth and sexuality con-
firms a pattern of increasing and consistent contraceptive use among
teenagers (Folkhälsoinstitutet, 2000). In fact, in contemporary Sweden it is
teenagers and young adults that are most likely to engage in "safe sex."
Several studies have shown that among teenagers in the late 1990s somewhere between 60% and 76% used some form of contraceptive during their

Table 13.3
Abortion Rate for Women 15 to 19 Years Old, in Comparison with the Total
Abortion Rate for Women 15 to 44 Years Old, 1975–1998 (per 1,000
women)

Year	Woman's age					Total 15-19	Total 15-44
	15	16	17	18	19		
1975	16.1	29.2	33.7	32.9	31.3	28.7	20.2
1980	10.1	17.0	21.2	28.4	30.0	21.0	20.6
1985	6.5	12.8	17.4	24.1	25.8	17.7	17.7
1986	7.2	14.4	19.8	24.2	29.2	19.2	18.9
1987	8.4	15.4	21.2	28.1	32.2	21.1	19.7
1988	9.8	18.8	25.0	30.3	34.4	23.6	21.4
1989	9.9	19.3	25.9	30.6	34.3	24.0	21.5
1990	10.0	18.3	25.2	30.8	34.4	24.0	21.3
1991	8.9	17.5	21.4	28.7	33.2	22.3	20.5
1992	8.3	14.8	20.8	24.5	29.0	29.9	20.1
1993	6.9	13.7	18.8	24.0	26.4	18.4	19.8
1994	7.1	13.1	17.8	21.7	26.4	17.4	18.7
1995	7.2	13.3	16.3	20.2	25.2	16.5	18.3
1996	7.6	14.5	18.8	21.2	24.0	17.2	18.8
1997	7.3	13.7	18.0	22.2	24.7	17.3	18.5
1998	8.4	14.1	19.5	22.4	24.4	17.9	18.3

Sources: Data from Socialstyrelsen, 2000; Statiska centralbyrån, 2000.

first sexual intercourse. This is an increase from about 50% to 60% in the
1980s. When the question refers to the *latest* rather than the first intercourse, contraceptive use is even higher, reaching between 69% and 84% in
1999 (Folkhälsoinstitutet, 2000). Among sexually active young women, the
dominant (and most widely recommended) contraceptive method is the
birth-control pill. When it comes to the first sexual intercourse, however,
the condom is the most commonly used method (Folkhälsoinstitutet,
2000).

HISTORY AND SOCIAL CONTEXT

Teenage pregnancy cannot be analyzed in isolation from other social issues. Sweden's history is intertwined with a number of issues and problems,
including sexuality, abortion, birth control, and contraceptives. At a more
general level these issues are linked in various ways to larger state interests
in population issues, social welfare, public health, and social order. Seen in
this light, the issue of teenage pregnancy comprises an uneasy and tenuous
mix of individual and state concerns.

The history of Swedish public policy related to teenage sexuality reflects a continuous effort to reach a balance between individual and state needs, both of which have undergone major transformations during the last century. Nevertheless, at the core of the tension between personal and public concerns has always been the question of reproductive control.

In order to understand how Sweden arrived at its current approach to teenage pregnancy, it is necessary to review some of the conflicts over public policy in a historical perspective. Swedish policymakers early on managed to stake out a position on teenage pregnancy that was not intrinsically hampered by the moral quagmire that had traditionally surrounded adolescent sexuality in other countries.

Adult-sanctioned teenage sexuality has deep cultural roots in Sweden (Persson, 1972). In many rural regions, especially in the north, the rituals of teenage courtship included nightly visits during which boys and girls talked and shared a bed together (a practice called "bundling"). While this practice did not overtly or explicitly sanction premarital sexual intercourse, it could accommodate it, provided that the union was eventually formalized in marriage. (In wealthier regions where the older generation had a greater material stake in the consequences of their children's love interests, premarital liaisons were less tolerated and hence subject to more parental control. Among the emerging urban middle class, similarly, premarital sexual relations were subject to severe moral condemnation. In addition to extramarital births, the practice of premarital sexual relations in 19th-century rural Sweden resulted in an unknown number of children conceived prior to marriage but born within marriage.) In other regions, the notion of "engagement children" (*trolovningsbarn*) captures the general acceptance of sexually consummating a relationship prior to the actual marriage. As a result, a significant number of children were conceived, and sometimes born, outside of marriage without community uproar. The tolerance of extramarital sexuality that these practices tolerated was later extended to the growing urban working class, especially in the big cities. Working-class young people frequently formed unsanctioned but marriagelike unions, popularly referred to as "Stockholm marriages." (According to available statistics, the proportion of extramarital births increased steadily throughout the 19th and early 20th century, even as the absolute birthrate started to decline around 1914. The extramarital birthrate for youths ages 15 to 20 during the same period *increased* from 4.14 [1871–1880] to a high of 13.39 [1911–1915] and remained fairly stable after that [SOU, 1936, 59]. The extramarital birthrate for all women started to increase again in the late 1960s [Hoem, 1992], and in 1995, 53% of Swedish children were born out of wedlock [Fürst, 1999].)

If the lack of community condemnation in these cases often clashed head-on with official ideology (which remained focused on sin and moral decay until the 1920s), the ideological distance between the state and the populace narrowed in the context of temporary sexual liaisons outside of married, marriagelike, or soon-to-become married unions. Thus, the response to "promiscuous" extramarital sexuality remained harsh and unforgiving throughout the nineteenth and early twentieth century. Not surprisingly, it was the woman who was forced to bear the brunt of the moral burden, thereby suggesting a strong motive for the rapid increase in the abortion rate among unmarried women of all ages (Edin, 1934). These cultural roots, in combination with the social and political upheavals of the early 20th century, provide the context in which Sweden formulated the approach to teenage sexuality and pregnancy that still tends to guide official policy.

The modern Swedish approach to teenage sexuality and pregnancy took shape during the 1930s. In general, there was a shift from moral condemnation and harsh penalties for sexual transgressions to one that emphasized the state's responsibility in providing a socioeconomic environment to make it possible for all wanted children to be born—and all unwanted children never to be conceived. (The major interest organization in Sweden in the area of sex and reproduction was formed during this decade. The National Association for Sex Education [Riksförbundet för sexuell upplysning (RFSU)] was founded in 1933 and has served a prominent and highly visible role ever since [Ottesen-Jensen, 1986].)

This policy shift was formulated in response to the most pressing political concern at the time: the "population crisis" (Myrdal & Myrdal, 1934). Against a backdrop of declining birthrates and a low marriage rate, and with the average age of marriage moving upward, a massive political effort was set in motion to combat the dropping birthrate, which was widely perceived as a fatal threat to the Swedish nation (Carlson, 1990; Hirdman, 1989; Kälvemark, 1980). It was this political effort that laid the foundation for the ambitious policy programs that have come to characterize the Swedish welfare state. Originating in population concerns, it might seem paradoxical that one consequence of this policy effort was the legitimization of the notion of birth control, including contraceptives and, to a lesser extent, abortion. These changes were made, according to policymakers at the time, because a healthy and viable population not only requires "many" citizens, but it also requires "good" citizens (Linders, 1998).

Against this background, Swedish population politics took two different complementary paths. On the one hand, the state sought to *promote* childbearing through a policy package that aimed to remove or lessen the socioeconomic obstacles to childbearing. Under the assumption that women typically did not avoid childbearing because they shunned motherhood, this package was composed of an array of laws, benefits, and services that were designed to make it easier for women (and to a lesser extent men) to marry and have children. This support package is composed of (1) various child and family benefits (cash allowances), (2) various forms of parental insurances (related to pregnancy, childbirth, and the care of sick children), and (3) a well-developed and high-quality child day-care system. It is worth noting, perhaps, that the current parental cash benefits in connection with childbirth (or adoption) can be received for a period of 450 days, by either the mother or the father; for 360 of those days, the parent is paid at a rate of 80% of the qualifying income, whereas the additional 60 days are paid at a lower level that is the same for everyone (Ministry of Health and Social Affairs, 2000).

On the other hand, the state sought to *prevent* childbearing among those who were in no position to bear and raise children. To this end, a series of measures were implemented with the aim of improving people's birth-control practices (e.g., advisory services, information campaigns, sex education). As well, the law against abortion was partially reformed (1938), allowing for the termination of pregnancy for eugenic, humanitarian (rape and incest), and sociomedical reasons. (In 1946, a sociomedical indication was added, and in 1963, a fetal "damage" indication.) In combination, these policies established the state as an active participant in people's sexual and reproductive lives and thus transferred part of the responsibility for, and the consequences of, sexual behavior from the individual to the state.

Although childbearing within marriage was clearly the goal of the policy, it is significant to note that marital status per se was not the ultimate measuring rod. Rather, observing the practice of cohabitation among working-class couples and the reluctance of many young people to enter into marital unions (primarily for economic reasons) convinced most policymakers to redefine the definition of marriage. While continuing to try to coax people into marriage, the traditional understanding of appropriate sexual behavior was liberalized in state policy (SOU, 1936, p. 59).

This change in policy resulted in three important and interrelated consequences. First, the veil of sin and embarrassment that had driven sexual practices from view was lifted. It was replaced with a spotlight that emphasized sex as a natural and healthy human activity. Second, abstinence was firmly and irrevocably abandoned as a feasible policy alternative. Finally, the "double standard" of "wed" and "unwed" mothers came under heavy criticism. Consequently, it became increasingly possible for unmarried women to bear and raise children. The change in policy also removed a prominent motive for illegal and dangerous abortions (e.g., Svenska fattigvårds—och barnavårdsförbundet, 1942). It is the insistence on and persistence of this "rational" approach to sexuality (including teenage sexuality) that eventually gave Sweden the reputation of being a "promiscuous country." As a commentator in the 1960s makes clear, however, from a Swedish perspective there is a clear and important distinction between promiscuity and permissiveness. To accept and tolerate sexual expressions among people who love and care for one another (permissiveness) is a far cry from condoning and encouraging promiscuous sex that, from a Swedish point of view, can flourish only in social environments characterized by an adherence to the double

standard, the idealization of virginity, sexuality laden with shame and secrecy, and the pervasive presence of prostitution (Linnér, 1967).

Although teenagers were not directly targeted by the policies developed
in the 1930s (teenagers were not considered a distinct social group), the
problems associated with "youths" were significant in the debates over how
services would be provided (Ariès, 1962; Karp & Yoels, 1982). In the conservative view, the danger of abandoning the punitive approach to reduce
teen pregnancy would result in the loosening of family ties. It would promote various forms of urban entertainment such as bars, alcoholism, secu-
larization, prostitution, and lewd publications. Under these circumstances,
the conservatives argued, to remove the legal markers of social disapproval
was not only morally inadvisable but outright dangerous. They believed it
would amount to a tacit approval, even encouragement, of sexual miscon-
duct. Rather than discarding this argument entirely, those favoring birth
control and family planning invoked the distinction between "healthy" and
"unhealthy" relationships and emphasized the need to counterbalance the
destructive influence of prurient commercial interests—especially on the
young—with "rational" information and education (e.g., SOU, 1938,
p. 19). (If the punitive approach was abandoned in the context of sexuality
and contraceptives, it was retained in the context of illegal abortion. As the
decades progressed, however, the penal focus shifted from the woman to
the abortionist.)

It was out of this broader ideological framework that sex education in the
Swedish national schools came about. The fact that such an educational
program was not implemented as a compulsory subject until 1956 (although
introduced in 1944) is an indication of the lingering resistance to exposing
children to the "secrets of sex." Primarily, for these reasons, the first round
of sex education in Swedish schools was focused primarily on the biological
elements of reproduction (Jones et al. 1986). It also "contained norms and
moralistic evaluations that did not correspond with the reality of youths"
(SOU, 1983, pp. 31, 87, my translation). Nevertheless, the insistence that
it was the state's responsibility to provide young people with the knowledge
and tools necessary to make informed sexual choices paved the way for the
more comprehensive sexual education curriculum. The official Swedish position was that "knowledge doesn't mean temptation" (Linnér, 1967,
p. 49). On the contrary, only through knowledge can people, including
young people, navigate the temptations and pitfalls of the sexualized marketplace.

It is important to remember that the early advocates of sex education did
not envision a world in which teenagers could (or should) have sex freely
and safely. Rather, sex education was viewed as a preventive measure, aimed
at preparing the young for the future. Once sex education became a formal
element of the national school curriculum, despite the limitations of the

initial program, it was modified and transformed to meet the needs of new generations without a major policy shift.

It was not until the 1960s that the notion of teen sexuality emerged as a concern distinct from the more general problems associated with sexuality, family planning, abortion, and birth control. The calls for sexual liberation, women's rights, and free abortion (among a whole range of other political demands) reverberated throughout Sweden in the late 1960s and early 1970s, as well as in many other parts of the Western world. The subsequent changes firmly established the notion that young people were not so much a group of incomplete adults as a social group (and social force) in their own right (cf. Hines, 1999).

This enduring concern around teenage sexuality is visible in the controversy surrounding the decriminalization of abortion. The debate eventually resulted in a policy package that was designed exclusively for teenagers. The goal was, and still is, to ensure that every teenager has sufficient information, knowledge, and resources to make responsible decisions in the realm of sexuality and intimacy. To meet this goal, Swedish policymakers pursued two strategies—counseling and contraceptives. Family planning services were already integrated into the maternal and child health care provided by primary health care centers.

While many teenagers, especially girls, had utilized these centers to secure birth-control services, the debate surrounding the abortion law led to the recognition that adolescents might have needs that are not best met at the general health care centers. As a result, a system of contraceptive clinics especially for adolescents was designed to offer both counseling/advice (including advice on abortion) and actual contraceptive services. During the first 15 years the number of such clinics rose from 2 to 128. The overwhelming majority of these clinics are operated under the auspices of local government (SoU04, 1990–1991). Even so, this number of youth clinics still does not reach all teenagers (SoU04, 1995–1996).

Since 1975, the state has taken responsibility for the provision of contraceptives, which means that advisory services are provided free to all who want them, and the cost for contraceptives (and abortion) is heavily subsidized. However, when it comes to teenagers, the goal is to provide *all* contraceptives, free of charge (Jones et al., 1986). The system of distributing free condoms, in schools and at many youth clinics, is fairly well established. Most recently, subsidized oral contraceptives have been provided.

The lowering of the teenage abortion rate during the first half of the 1990s was attributed to contraceptives distributed by the state, but when abortion began to increase, new demands were made to evaluate the relationship between free pills and abortion (Folkhälsoinstitutet, 2000; SoU18, 1994–1995).

The goal of the clinics was to ensure that all teenagers have access to contraceptive services, even those with parents who may not approve of premarital sexual relations. When counseling teenagers on contraceptives, counselors are prohibited by law from informing the parents (Jones et al., 1986).

In addition to these efforts at providing contraceptive counseling and services to teenagers, the system of sex education has been revised extensively, now encompassing the broader issues of intimate relations (*samlevnad*) instead of the previously more narrow focus on sexuality. Despite a long and firmly established tradition of sex education, the educational effort still varies extensively between schools (and between individual teachers). Nevertheless, teenagers often report that school is their primary source of information regarding sexuality, contraceptives, and STDs (Folkhälsoinstitutet, 2000).

TEEN PREGNANCY TODAY

Contraceptive services (including abortion) remains a central piece of the overall policy goal of preventing unwanted teenage pregnancies. In this view, teenage sexuality emerges as a factor, because teen sexuality is considered "risky" behavior. To be understood properly, these concerns must be seen in light of some larger social developments, among them the economic crisis in the early 1990s, the rise of a multicultural society, and the communications revolution.

A long-standing assumption in Swedish family policy has been that childbearing drops during harsh economic times, and the recent decline in the overall birthrate is generally attributed to the worsening of economic conditions (Ministry of Health and Social Affairs, 2000). When it comes to teenagers, however, this relationship is less clear. In fact, it may be reversed; available evidence suggests that teenagers who are socioeconomically disadvantaged are somewhat more likely to engage in "risky" sexual behavior, but the differences in pregnancy rates are not clear (Folkhälsoinstitutet, 2000).

The relationship between socioeconomic background and "risky" sexual behavior is not a direct one but operates through factors like family instability, trouble in school, and early sexual initiation. Of these, the latter has recently been examined in some depth; girls whose sexual debut took place prior to the age of 15 are more likely to have had sex on the "first date," to have had more sexual partners, and to have somewhat greater experience with STD and abortion, but they are as likely as other teenage girls (about 81% in this study) to have used some form of contraception during their "latest" intercourse (Folkhälsoinstitutet, 2000).

The rise of a multicultural society has prompted a range of concerns associated with the "clashes" between traditional Swedish ideologies and practices. In the context of teenage sexuality, these concerns are increasingly centered around norms and practices that appear to challenge the long-standing Swedish emphases on sexual tolerance and gender equality.

The value that some immigrant groups place on (female) virginity, for example, has given rise to concerns about the return of a more restrictive role for women but not for men. (Moreover, there is some evidence that the virginal ideology makes young women *more*, not less, vulnerable to pregnancy [Folkhälsoinstitutet, 2000; Lewin et al., 1998].) As a result, teenagers from these cultural backgrounds might be less able to learn from and take advantage of the schools' sex education programs (Östlund, 1996).

The rapid expansion of new communications technology has given rise to a new set of concerns around the ability of the state to counterbalance the potentially negative influences on youths that come from sources such as videos, cable-TV, and the Internet. The fear is that these media will eventually come to overshadow the educational efforts of school and community. Not only might the balance between maturation and sexual experimentation among teenagers be tilted in an unfortunate direction, but the work toward gender equality might be set back by an onslaught of sexual imagery that misrepresents, objectifies, and subordinates women.

Political Views and Public Policies

Despite these recent changes, the Swedish approach to teenage sexuality remains essentially intact. New political initiatives are formulated almost entirely around improving and expanding existing programs and services that target youths. Hence, during the last few years legislative bills have demanded improved sex education programs in schools (including better teacher education), an expansion of contraceptive programs and the system of youth clinics, increased state subsidies for birth-control pills, and improved abortion prevention programs (SoU12, 1997–1998; SoU10, 1998–1999; SoU09, 1999–2000).

Social Views, Customs, and Practices

Since the 1930s, family planning services have been developed and designed in close collaboration with the scientific community. The "scientific" approach to sexuality that has grown out of this collaborative effort is essentially devoid of the traditional moral concerns associated with "illicit" sexuality. That does not mean, however, that the scientific approach is amoral; on the contrary, the strong emphasis on "healthy" sexuality has a moral/normative component that is as strong as traditional moral positions. Seen in this light, the remaining gap between the official approach and social practices is no longer about whether, when, with whom, or how people should conduct their sexual lives but instead about doing it "right." What is understood by the term "right" is an amalgam of factors associated with maturity, identity, self-reliance, intimacy, security, and love. Consequently, the current tension between the official and social view originates in the state's efforts to arrange social life in such a way that people live healthy and productive lives (Hirdman, 1989).

In the context of youth sexuality, these tensions, as we have seen, have produced a massive effort to educate young people in healthy sexuality, to train them to behave responsibly in sexual interactions, and to coax them away from unhealthy influences (or, at the very least, to provide them with the knowledge necessary to reject those influences). In spite of that, stubborn and persistent practices like teen abortions, unsafe sex, rape and sexual abuse, pornography consumption, and various forms of sexual harassment serve as a constant reminder of the remaining gaps between social practices and official policy goals. Still, evidence suggests that most policy measures do have an impact on social practices, and without such policies, the gap might be considerably larger.

THE FUTURE OF TEEN PREGNANCY

Since there are no indications that the number of teen births is increasing in Sweden, it is unlikely that prevention and educational programs will be changed. It seems likely that the concerns of policymakers will continue to generate debate and research efforts—particularly, I suspect, because of the new forms of media and the increasingly heterogeneous Swedish population. Moreover, it is quite possible that the future Swedish approach to teenage pregnancy and teenage sexuality will be influenced by Sweden's membership in the European Union. Exactly how these changes will impact teenage pregnancy in Sweden is not yet entirely clear.

One major impact on teen sexuality has been the Internet. The rapid expansion of the Internet will emerge as a major competitor to the school's role as the primary sex educator, thus raising concerns about the negative influences of unrealistic, tantalizing, and possibly pornographic images. It is also possible that the Internet will help bring marginalized and troubled teens into support networks. Judging from the overwhelming positive response to newly established question-and-answer Swedish Web sites developed by adolescent clinics, services of this kind appear to tap into a real need. Furthermore, the site attracts boys and young men to a much greater extent than do the clinics.

In the words of a Swedish expert: "Society has taken [up] the responsibility for the sexual education of young people. In order to fulfill this responsibility, one must also have knowledge of the realities of the young" (Bo Lewin, quoted in Folkhälsoinstitutet, 2000, p. 91; my translation).

It is difficult to imagine a set of strategies to prevent teenage pregnancy that would work better than those guiding the Swedish policy approach. However, because the number of teenage pregnancies continues to fluctuate over time, the calls for expanded policy efforts during periods of increased teen pregnancy are probably well founded. Judging from the type and range of questions that teens themselves ask, it is evident that the level of preparation that the schools (and various other programs and outreach efforts) are providing is uneven. With the new emphasis on "intimate relations," young people need to learn a lot more than about reproductive functions and contraceptives. For example, the fact that young people are less likely to practice safe sex the first time they engage in intercourse suggests that knowing *about* contraceptives is no guarantee that young people will be able to negotiate their use in the "heat of the moment" (Folkhälsoinstitutet, 2000; cf. Thompson, 1995). Hence, it is neither the biological nor technical aspects of sex and birth control that are the keys to "safe" and "healthy" sexual relations but rather the social ones.

CONCLUSION

In Sweden, both the sexual practices of teenagers and the social responses to those practices have undergone major changes over the last century. Although linked in various ways, the relationship between practices and state responses is considerably more complex than teen pregnancy rates alone would reveal. However, the fact that Sweden has one of the lowest teenage pregnancy and birthrates in the world suggests that—although not perfect—the family planning services provided to adolescents is meeting most of their reproductive needs and has had a positive impact on teenagers and their sexual practices.

REFERENCES

Airès, P. (1962). *Centuries of childhood: A social history of family life*. New York: Vintage Books.
Carlson, A. (1990). *The Swedish experiment in family politics*. New Brunswick, NJ: Transaction Publishers.
Edin, K.-D. (1934). *Undersökning av abortförekomsten i Sverige under senare år*. Malmö: Fahlbeckska Stiftelsens Strifter, Nr. 21.
Folkhälsoinstitutet. (2000). *Ungdom och sexualitet—en presentation av aktuell svensk kunskap*. Stockholm.
Fürst, G. (1999). *Sweden—the equal way*. Stockholm: Swedish Institute.
Hatje, A.K. (1974). *Befolkningsfrågan och Välfärden*. Stockholm: Allmänna Förlaget.
Hines, T. (1999). *The rise & fall of the American teenager*. New York: Avon Books.
Hirdman, Y. (1989). *Att lägga livet till rätta*. Stockholm: Carlssons.
Hoem, B. (1992). Early phases of family formation in contemporary Sweden. In M.K. Rosenheim & M.F. Testa (Eds.), *Early parenthood and coming of age in the 1990s*. New Brunswick, NJ: Rutgers University Press (electronic version).
Jones, E.F., Forrest, J.D., Goldman, N., Henshaw, S., Lincoln, R., Rosoff, J.I., Wes-

toff, C.F., Wulf, D. (1986). *Teenage pregnancy in industrialized countries.* Alan Guttmacher Institute. New Haven, CT: Yale University Press.

Kälvemark, A.-S. (1980). *More children or better quality? Aspects on Swedish population policy in the 1930s.* Stockholm: Almqvist and Wicksell International.

Karp, D.A., & Yoels, W.C. (1982). *Experiencing the life cycle: A social psychology of aging.* Springfield, IL: Charles C. Thomas.

Lewin, B., Fugl-Meyer, K., Helmius, G., Lalos, A., & Månsson, S.-A. (1998). *Sex i sverige: Om sexuallivet i sverige 1996.* Stockholm: Folkhälsoinstitutet.

Linders, A. (1998). Abortion as a social problem: The construction of "opposite" solutions in Sweden and the United States. *Social Problems, 45,* 488–509.

Linnér, B. (1967). *Sex and society in Sweden.* New York: Pantheon Books.

Ministry of Health and Social Affairs. (2000, January). Swedish family policy. *Fact Sheet,* no. 2 (electronic version).

Myrdal, A., & Myrdal, G. (1934). *Kris i befolkningsfrågan.* Stockholm: Bonniers.

Östlund, H. (1996). En lagom oskuld. *Socialpolitik* Nr 1–2.

Ottesen-Jensen, E. (1986). *Livet skrev: Memoarer 1886–1966.* Stockholm: Riksförbundet för Sexuell Upplysning: Ordfronts förlag.

Persson, B. (1972). Att vara ogift mor på 1700—och 1800—talet. In K. Westman Berg (Ed.), *Könsdiskriminering förr och nu.* Stockholm: Bokförlaget Prisma.

Socialstyrelsen. (2000). Aborter i sverige 1999, January–December: Preliminär sammanställning. Sveriges Officiella Statistik. Hälsa och sjukdomar.

Socialutskottets betänkande. (1990–1991). Hälso—och sjukvårdsfrågor. SoU04.

Socialutskottets betänkande. (1994–1995). Fosterdiagnostik, abort m.m. SoU18.

Socialutskottets betänkande. (1995–1996). Barn och ungdom. SoU04.

Socialutskottets betänkande. (1997–1998). Hälso—och sjukvårdsfrågor. SoU12.

Socialutskottets betänkande. (1998–1999). Hälso—och sjukvårdsfrågor m.m. SoU10.

Socialutskottets betänkande. (1999–2000). Hälso—och sjukvårdsfrågor m.m. SoU09.

SOU. (1936) Betänkande i sexualfrågan. Avgivet av befolkningskommissionen. Stockholm.

SOU. (1938) Yttrande med socialetiska synpunkter på befolkningsfrågan. Avlämnat av befolkningskommissionen. Stockholm.

SOU. (1971) Rätten till abort. Stockholm.

SOU. (1983) Familjeplanering och abort: Erfarenheter av en ny lagstiftning. Betänkande av 1980 års abortutredning. Stockholm.

Statistiska Centralbyrån. (2000). Vad händer efter grundskolan? *Pressmeddelande* Nr 2000:002.

Svenska fattigvårds—och barnavårdsförbundet. (1942). Hur hjälper samhället mor och barn? *Socialmediciniska sektionens ströskrift* nr 15.

Thompson, S. (1995). *Going all the way: Teenage girls' tales of sex, romance, and pregnancy.* New York: Hill and Wang.

14

UNITED STATES

Andrew L. Cherry, Mary E. Dillon, and Douglas Rugh

PROFILE OF THE UNITED STATES

The United States of America is one of the most powerful nations on earth. It has great wealth in natural resources, and many of its citizens have accumulated vast personal fortunes. Even so, this enormous wealth has not translated into benefits for many of its citizens who are poor and disadvantaged. Although leading other nations in production of manufactured goods, technology, higher education, and military hardware, the United States usually lags behind other industrial nations in providing for the social needs of its citizens, especially its poor.

The population in the United States in 1998 was 270, 311, 758, with a labor force of 134, 125, 342. Roughly 75% of the people live in urban areas. People of European descent constitute about 84% of the population; those of African descent, about 12%; Asians and Pacific Islanders, about 3%; and Native Americans, about 1%. Hispanics, who may also be counted among other groups, make up about 9%.

The gross domestic product (GDP) in 1995 was $8.5 trillion, $31,500 per person. In 1997, the military consumed 3.4% of the national gross domestic product (GDP). (The GDP measures the value of all goods and services produced in a country. It is calculated by adding personal spending, government spending, investment, and net exports [exports minus imports].) In the same year, the active troop strength was 1.55 million.

There are 146 million passenger cars and another 59 million commercial vehicles in use in the United States. This is one vehicle for 1.3 persons; 834

airports with scheduled flights; one television set per 1.2 persons, and two radios for each person; and one telephone per 1.7 people in the United States.

Life expectancy at birth in the United States in 1996 was 73 years of age for males and 79 years of age for females. There were 15 births per 1,000 people and 9 deaths per 1,000 people. There is one hospital bed for every 223 people, and one physician for every 391 persons. Infant mortality is 7 per 1,000 live births, but it is much higher for some minority groups and the poor.

In the United States, 86.5% of the population are Christian (Baptist, Episcopalian, Lutheran, Methodist, Roman Catholic, and other Christian religious groups). Jewish religious groups make up 1.8%; Muslim, 0.5%; and Buddhist and Hindu, less than 0.5%.

Elementary and secondary education is free and compulsory. The duration of compulsory education is 10 years between the ages of 7 and 16. Approximately 96% of people in the United States are officially literate.

INTRODUCTION

If you are an adolescent and poor in the United States and you have a child out of wedlock, it is likely that you will stay poor. Almost surely, you will *not* get a good education, and you will *not* find employment that pays enough to support a middle-class lifestyle. Moreover, because of your poverty, it is unlikely that your children will have a future that is any different from yours. In the years between 12 and 16 they, too, may find themselves expecting a child or fathering a child—and the cycle will continue.

Conservative groups often sight teenage pregnancy in the United States as a social problem that has developed because of the disintegration of the traditional family. The increase in child neglect and abuse, juvenile delinquency, and domestic violence are examples of the other problems that are believed to be the result of the declining role of the family in the care and education of children.

The numbers seem to support their concerns until the late 1990s. Teenage births decreased from 656,460, the highest number per year in 1970, to 505,513 teen births in 1996 (see Table 14.1). This 24% drop in 1996 was the lowest number of teen births since the 1960s. At the end of the 20th century, about 80 out of every 1,000 adolescents were becoming pregnant a year. Of this group, about 30 were aborting the pregnancy, and about 50 girls gave birth (Child Trends, 1997; Holden, Nelson, Velasquez, & Ritchie, 1993).

This was an unexpected drop in teen births in the United States, and it took time for some skeptics to accept the idea that teen pregnancy began dropping in 1990 and it continued an overall decline in the 1990s. However, the numbers of teen births are still the highest in the developed world.

Although the number of teen births declined in the 1990s, so did teen births around the world, even in most underdeveloped countries. Therefore, although politicians in the United States tend to take responsibility for the decrease, the truth is that the United States benefited from a change in teen sexual behavior around the world.

How and why teenage pregnancy became a social issue in the United States in the 1980s and 1990s is a story of changing cultural norms, public policy, and a capricious economy. Steps taken to curb the increase in teen pregnancy is a story that reveals as much about the United States and its view of social responsibility as about the children and teenagers who became pregnant.

A recent Child Trends review of the factors associated with teen parenthood in the United States identified four major risk factors: (1) early school failure, (2) early behavior problems, (3) family dysfunction, and (4) poverty. Female teenagers who experienced none of these risk factors had the lowest rate of pregnancy. The more risk factors faced by the teenager, the higher the likelihood of the teenager becoming pregnant and giving birth (Child Trends, 1997).

Vignette

Tamara Smith became pregnant at age 11 after being raped by her mother's boyfriend over several weeks. Tamara recalls being startled awake by a 200-pound man pinning her to her bed with his body. He had his hand over her mouth and threatened to kill her and her mother if she cried out or told anyone. She recalled the pain, the blood, and the shame. Several weeks later, when she worked up the courage, she told her mother what had happened. Her mother began screaming and slapping her. After her mother calmed down, the mother kicked her boyfriend out of the house.

Tamara had her first child when she was 12 years old. She and her child continued living with her mother, grandmother, and several sisters and brothers in a small rental house in the Liberty City area of Miami. Liberty City can be described as an inner-city ghetto. Almost all the residents in this community are extremely poor; and almost all of the residents were born, grew up, and went to public school in that community.

After giving birth to her first child, a daughter, Tamara attended an alternative school for girls where she was attempting to continue her education. However, she dropped out of school when she became pregnant a second time at age 14. She had her second child at 15 years of age.

An example of Tamara's immaturity as a mother can be illustrated by an event that happened after she gave birth to her second child. Her social worker gave her baby clothes and toys for her two-year-old and her baby. When Tamara was presented with the gifts for her children, her response was, "Why didn't you bring something for me?" Although her response sounds selfish, it is a typical response for a 14-year-old child who had grown up deprived of the most basic necessities that other children in the United States take for granted.

Tamara comes from a family of long-term welfare recipients. She grew up in a household that has a history of teen pregnancy (Tamara's mother and one sister), substance abuse problems, sexual and physical abuse, school dropout, truancy, and delinquency problems. Her mother is receiving a small welfare check for Tamara and her three children. Tamara is not old enough to receive welfare in her own right.

Overview of Teen Pregnancy

In the United States, the traditional markers of adulthood, such as full-time employment, economic independence, marriage, and childbearing, generally occur at later ages for most children than it did 50 years ago. However, at the same time, the majority of adolescents initiate sexual activity much earlier than their parents (Gibbs, 1993). Consequently, early sexual activity puts the teens at risk of dropping out of school and failing to develop employable skills. It puts them at risk of contracting sexually transmitted diseases (STDs) and HIV/AIDS (human immunodeficiency virus/acquired immunodeficiency syndrome). They may also experience unintended pregnancies, abortions, and out-of-wedlock births (Brecher, 1997; Franklin, 1988; Ladner, 1971; Olson, 1993; Williams, 1991).

Teenage Sexual Activity

By the early 1990s, over 33% of 15-year-old males living in the United States reported having had sexual intercourse, and approximately 27% of 15-year-old females reported having had intercourse. This was a 19% increase since 1982 (Gibbs, 1993). In 1995, according to data from the Youth Risk Behavior Survey, over one-half of high school students have engaged in sexual intercourse before graduation. Estimates appear to be higher for males, minority adolescents, and adolescents of lower socioeconomic status. For example, 81% of African American and 62% of Hispanic males in high school report engaging in sexual intercourse. Among females, 67% of African American and 53% of Hispanic females in high school report engaging in sexual intercourse. Comparable rates for high school students who identify themselves as white is the same for both male and female students, about 49% (Miller, Forehand, & Kotchick, 1999).

Births to Teens in the United States

The United States has one of the highest rates of teenage pregnancy in Western industrialized countries, and the rates are rising among unmarried 14- to 16-year-old females. Over 1,011,000 children were born to children and teenagers in the United States in 1996 (Miller et al., 1999).

What is the most disturbing to policymakers and the public is the doubling of birthrates among girls younger than 15 years of age between 1960 and 1996. In 1960, the birthrate for girls under 15 was 6,780. By 1994, the birthrate had increased to 12,901. For many, this was an alarming increase—especially when compared to the birthrate among older teenagers. For instance, the birthrate for teenage females between 18 and 20 years of age has declined after reaching a high in 1970. The birthrate among some age groups declined or was about the same between 1960 and 1996. The birthrate for 18- and 19-year-old females actually dropped by 15%. The birthrate among girls between 15 and 17 years of age has remained pretty much the same. Again, the most disturbing trend was among girls under 15 years of age. The birthrate among these children almost doubled in the same time period (see Table 14.1).

Out-of-Wedlock Births to Teenagers in the United States

From 1960 to 1996, the birthrate among married teens declined substantially. In 1960, there were 531 births to married teens per 1,000 females between the ages of 15 and 19 years of age. By 1995, there were 362 births to married teens per 1,000 females between the ages of 15 and 19 years of age. This was a 32% drop in the number of married teens giving birth. During the same time period, the number of reported out-of-wedlock births tripled. In 1996, there were 386,371 nonmarital births and 119,142 marital births. About 76% of children born to teenagers were out-of-wedlock births.

Births to Teenagers by Race and Ethnicity

Teen births for Hispanics in the United States increased until 1991 and stabilized. Births to African American and white teens decreased over the same period, reaching its lowest level for African American teens in 50 years (see Table 14.2). However, some conservative groups pointed out that although births among African American teenagers were down, the rate of African American babies born out of wedlock had increased. In 1960, the rate of African American out-of-wedlock births was 23%; in 1990, the rate was 62%. Others point out that if the birthrate among married African American women had remained the same in 1990 as 1960, the real increase in out-of-wedlock births would have been about 6% higher than in 1960.

Although the reduction in African American teen births is dramatic and good news, the African American adolescent birthrate is still as high as many adolescent groups found in the developing nations in the world. We would suggest that the high rate of African American and Hispanic teen births is the result of many factors faced by African American and Hispanic children and adolescents that are faced by children and adolescents in many developing nations: poor health care, poor educational opportunity, poor job opportunity, and institutional discrimination.

Table 14.1
Number of Births to Females under Age 20

Ages	1960	1970	1980	1990	1992	1993	1994	1995	1996
Under 15	6,780	11,752	10,169	11,657	12,220	12,554	12,901	12,242	11,242
15-17	182,408	223,590	198,222	183,327	187,549	190,535	195,169	192,508	186,762
18-19	404,558	421,118	353,939	338,499	317,866	310,558	310,319	307,365	307,509
Under 20	593,746	656,460	562,330	533,483	517,635	513,647	518,389	512,115	505,513

Source: Data from Child Trends, 1997.

Table 14.2
Teen Birthrate (births per 1,000 females ages 15–19), by Race/Ethnicity

Race/Ethnicity	1980	1986	1990	1991	1992	1993	1994	1995
Hispanics	82	80	100	107	107	107	108	107
African American	105	104	116	119	116	111	108	99
Whites	41	36	43	43	42	40	40	39

Note: 1980 data on Hispanic ethnicity are reported for 22 states, accounting for 90% of Hispanic births; 1986 data are for 23 states and DC; 1990 data are for 48 states and DC; 1991 and 1992 data are for 49 states and DC; 1993–1995 data are for all states and DC.

Source: Data from Child Trends, 1997.

Repeated Teen Births

Teenagers giving birth to a second and third child surpasses the concern over teenagers becoming pregnant and giving birth. The birthrate for teens having a second or third child stayed fairly stable between 1980 and 1996 (see Table 14.3).

There are several factors that have been found to be associated with reducing the risk of a second or third pregnancy. Both involvement in work or school activities after the birth of the first child and receipt of a high school diploma or its equivalent were strongly associated with postponing a second teen birth.

The Cost of Teen Pregnancy

Politicians and the public at large have come to realize that programs that deal with teen pregnancy are going to be costly. However, they have also come to believe that the results of prevention and support programs for teen parents and their children may offer tremendous savings in both human and economic terms. Low-birth-weight babies who do survive, for example, do so at great cost. The average cost is $30,000 during the first two months of life (Alan Guttmacher Institute, 1994). The U.S. federal government spends over $30 billion a year in health and human services on adolescent parents and their children (Gleick, Reed, & Schindehette, 1994). This sum does not include state and local government expenditures.

Medical and Social Complications

There are a number of serious medical and social problems associated with adolescent childbirth in the United States: premature birth, higher rate of

Table 14.3
Percentage of Teen Births That Are Second Births or Higher

Percentage of Teen Births That Are Second Births or Higher									
Age	1980	1986	1990	1991	1992	1993	1994	1995	1996
15-19	21%	23%	25%	25%	25%	24%	22%	21%	22%

Teen Birthrates (births per 1,000 females ages 15 to 19), by Birth Order									
Birth Order	1980	1986	1990	1991	1992	1993	1994	1995	1996
1st Birth	41.4	38.8	45.1	46.5	45.3	45.3	45.8	44.6	42.7
2nd Birth or Higher	11.6	11.4	14.8	15.6	15.4	14.3	13.1	12.2	12.0

Source: Data from Child Trends, 1997.

infant mortality, low birth weight resulting in developmental disabilities, and malnutrition related to poverty and a lack of prenatal care. The social economic consequences are also severe: school failure, economic dependency, poverty, and social and developmental deficits for both the mother and her child or children (Combs-Orme, 1993; Forste & Tienda, 1992).

Many of these complications are being prevented or somewhat mitigated by federal, state, and local government programs that provided adequate prenatal and neonatal care to pregnant teens and their children. These health and developmental programs are needed. Teenage mothers are only half as likely as adult pregnant women to see a doctor for prenatal care.

HISTORY AND SOCIAL CONTEXT

The public attitude in the United States toward childhood and teenage pregnancy is based in part on the religious and moral principals brought over by settlers from western Europe in the 1600s. The most important sanction was not children or teenagers giving birth but whether the young girl was married. Early colonial church records indicate that if a young woman became pregnant out of wedlock, she would confess her transgression and marry the father if possible (Ravoira & Cherry, 1992).

By the early 1800s in the United States, among the growing middle class and the well-to-do, the view of children began to change. It was believed that "early introduction into the adult world not only affronted adults but harmed children" (Aries, 1962, p. 130). This was a period where children of the opposite sex were not to sleep together in the same room. A period when girls and women dressed in modest clothing that covered all but their faces. When children should not be exposed to songs—"dissolute passions should be neither sung nor heard" (p. 130).

During the 1800s, the majority of births to unwed teens were handled within the family. A teenage girl of a middle-class or upper-class family who became pregnant would more than likely leave her community and go to a distant home of a relative until she gave birth. Then a relative or friend of the family would adopt and raise the child. The young woman would then return to her community and resume her life as a teenager. For the poor unwed teen mother, there was the public or religious home for unwed mothers.

Until the 1970s, teenage pregnancy was not the issue that concerned politicians and the public in the United States. They were concerned about out-of-wedlock pregnancy and illegitimacy (Ravoira & Cherry, 1992). Public policy in the United States was harsh on women who became pregnant out of wedlock. Legal treatment was based on English common law. Public policy attempted to protect the community from financial liability by putting the cost of caring for and raising the child entirely on the mother. It was 1934 before unmarried women became eligible for federal welfare benefit (Young, 1954). With the Kinsey Report in the early 1950s, it became clear that premarital sex was widespread and fairly typical in the United States (Kinsey, Pomeroy, Martin, & Gebhard, 1953). However, when it was known that a teenage girl had given birth, she was stigmatized in her community for the rest of her life. The child would also suffer the same cruel stigma and disdain from his peers and the adults in the community.

This view and response to out-of-wedlock pregnancy and their children changed rather rapidly during the sexual revolution in the late 1960s and early 1970s. Many long-held ideas and attitudes began to change. There was also a shift in the view of pregnant teens. Instead of teen pregnancy being viewed as a moral issue, policymakers, service providers, and the public began to view it as a technical issue (Arney & Bergen, 1984).

However, the negative views of unwed pregnant teens continued. During the 1960s, teen parenthood was identified as a cause of poverty and inter-generational welfare dependency (Johnson, 1974). This approach led to the availability of additional social services to teen mothers. In many cases, this support made it possible for some teen mothers to support themselves and their baby if she chose to keep her baby.

Another major influence on teen pregnancy in the United States was the legalization of abortion in 1973 (*Roe v. Wade* [1973]). This gave pregnant teens access to legal abortions without parental consent. By the end of the 1900s, this right of teenage girls to an abortion without parental consent was being scaled back by both federal and state legislation. The public over-whelmingly wanted to require a teenage girl to obtain consent from a parent before receiving an abortion.

A great deal of stigma is still associated with being a teen mother in the United States as we begin the 21st century. The public and political concern for teen motherhood is reflected in policy and programming as a concern for the long-term consequences for the teen mother and her child. Because of this concern and the services provided, many of the long-term conse-quences that have been associated with teen pregnancy have been reduced.

TEEN PREGNANCY TODAY

Political Views and Public Policies

Prevention Programming

Prevention efforts were intensified in the early 1990s. The most common prevention programs include general encouragement for use of birth con-trol; school-based clinics; condom distribution; sexuality and contraception education in and out of school; enhancing life options; and encouraging teens to delay sexual initiation. Although different approaches to pregnancy prevention generate tremendous public and political debate and disagree-ment, there is not adequate research evidence suggesting the most effective. The National Council's *Risking the Future* found that encouraging contra-ceptive use for sexually active teenagers has the most empirical support (Hayes, 1987).

Evidence exists that programs that are comprehensive tend to be the most successful. Some evidence does suggest that exposure to innovative pro-grams geared toward pregnancy prevention, such as peer counseling/ad-vocacy and peer theater troupes, promotes the utilization of health services.

Contraceptive Use among Teens

Among teens that are sexually active, the contraceptive trends are mixed. Contraceptive use rose during the 1970s, preventing an even greater in-crease in teen pregnancies. The average time between initiation of sexual activity and the first use of birth control by a teenager is about one year. This lapse has been a consistent finding since the early 1970s.

Several factors are positively associated with teens using birth control. They include: older age of initiation of sexual activity; stability of the rela-tionship with a single partner; knowledge of sexuality, reproduction, and contraception; higher academic aspirations; less inclined toward personal risks; greater acceptance of one's own sexuality; and the presence of parental supervision and support.

Underlying many of these factors is the degree of an adolescent's cognitive development. In general, a 17-year-old is better able to comprehend the consequences of an action and anticipate the future than a 12-year-old. Many teens believe that they are personally invulnerable to harm. This common developmental characteristic (as well as other aspects of working with adolescents) should be considered when designing pregnancy prevention programs in both educational and health care settings.

Teen Abortion

One of the concerns of many who oppose abortion for children and teenagers is that abortion will be used as a prophylactic to reduce the rate of teen births. Data on the number of abortions to teens are available from the Centers for Disease Control and Prevention (CDC) through 1994. These data indicate a decline in abortion. Abortion rates from the Alan Guttmacher Institute are also available through 1992, and estimated rates are available through 1994. They indicate that the rate of abortion declined slightly during the early 1990s. Thus, available data indicate that a decline in the teen birthrate is not driven by an increase in abortion.

Programming to Help Teenage Fathers

In recent years, attention has shifted to include young men in efforts to prevent pregnancy and promote more responsible teen behavior. Many programs that serve young fathers or boys at risk of parenthood have been thwarted by the difficulty of attracting clients to female-oriented programs. In addition, studies attempting to identify specific characteristics of these young men are limited by sample selection problems—a significant group of boys will not admit to authority figures that they are fathers.

Despite a great deal of public attention being given to programs for teen parents and mounting evidence of their effectiveness, the number of new young parents who participate in these programs is very small. Access is limited by the fact that these programs are inadequately funded to serve all who need their services; also, programs are often not well known in many communities.

Social Views, Customs, and Practices

An early pregnancy that is unwanted generally is a crisis not only for the young woman but also for her family and the baby's father (Maracek, 1987). Scientists found that a pregnant adolescent's choices about pregnancy resolution are influenced in part by her own attitudes toward abortion, her perceptions of the attitudes of parents and friends, parents' and her own aspirations, and how close she is to her boyfriend. This suggests that the process of resolving an unplanned pregnancy should include significant individuals in the teen's life whenever possible. A comprehensive approach should allow the pregnant teen to review all of the options available, including whether to proceed with the birth, whether to keep the baby, whether to marry or remain single, and (if she keeps the child) how to obtain financial and social support for parenting.

Poverty among Teen Parents and Their Children

Many of these pregnant and parenting adolescent females are likely to come from poor, low-income, single-parent households headed by mothers. They are more likely to drop out of school, thus diminishing their chances for economic self-sufficiency. Because of their youth and disadvantaged background, these adolescents continue to rely on their families and public assistance programs to help defray the cost of raising a child, for assisting them in completing their education, and in finding a job. These negative consequences of pregnancy and childbearing are severe and often irrevocably disrupt the adolescent's life cycle.

In the United States, children in single-parent families make up 21% of children who are living in poverty. However, 75% of children living in a family with a single teenage parent are growing up in poverty.

Despite the odds, the fate of teenage girls and boys who become parents is by no means sealed upon becoming a parent. Mediating factors such as completing education and receiving support services can significantly improve life chances for teenage parents and their children. Teen parents vary considerably in the support they need in order to avoid the worst consequences of teen parenthood. For those who need assistance, programs for teen parents are showing some success based on program evaluations and longitudinal studies. In general, programs that offer comprehensive services (e.g., day care, educational support, and/or vocational placement) are most effective.

THE FUTURE OF TEEN PREGNANCY

Over the years, there has been a great deal of debate about public programs that are intended to help pregnant and parenting teens. The concern is that such programs may be unintentionally encouraging teens to become sexually active and pregnant and give birth. However, everyone agrees that the children of teen parents should not pay the consequences of their parents' behavior. The following recommendations are designed to interrupt the cycle of poverty among teenage parents.

Policy 1: Access to quality medical, mental health, dental care, and case management services for teen parents and their children.

The first element in a comprehensive policy to reduce or eliminate the consequences of a teen pregnancy is to provide access to medical, mental health, dental care, and case management services for pregnant teens, teen parents, and their children. This policy requires federal leadership and federal subsidies.

Policy 2: Provide parent skills training for teen parents.

The second policy considered to be a part of a comprehensive policy is parent training. In the past, most parents in the United States learned parenting by modeling themselves after their parents, uncles, aunts, and grandparents at home or nearby. As they grew up, they learned how to care for younger siblings because they were expected to. The isolated nuclear families in U.S. society today often cannot provide children with these modeling experiences. Under such circumstances, parenting education must be included in public education programs and as a part of a comprehensive care program for teen parents and their children.

Policy 3: Access to quality day-care services for the children of teen mothers.

The third element in a comprehensive policy is to assure access to quality day-care services for the children of teen mothers. This policy requires federal standards mandating high-quality care and federal subsidies to pay for the services. Quality infant day care is simply unaffordable, even for teen mothers who earn the average full-time wage for their age group. A graduate system of subsidies indexed to family income is needed to meet the expense of quality day-care and case management services.

Policy 4: Support for teen parents to finish high school, vocational school, or college.

Policy 5: Supplementary income and subsidized housing that provides an adequate level of living for the child and parents—this is the right of the child.

The fourth and fifth elements of a comprehensive policy are to protect young mothers and their children from the damaging experiences of poverty. It is not single parenthood alone but the poverty associated with it that accounts for much of the pathology in the children of teen parents.

Policy 6: After-school prevention programs for all children through high school.

A sixth element of a comprehensive policy to protect children of teen parents from the negative consequences of teen pregnancy is after-school programs during childhood and adolescence. After-school programs have been shown to reduce school failure, teen pregnancy, and juvenile delinquency and to provide early detection of child neglect and abuse.

CONCLUSION

By the 1970s, teenagers in the United States were more sexually active earlier than ever in recorded U.S. history. However, because of the structure of the U.S. economy in the last half of the 20th century, it was difficult to become a successful teen parent. Successful parents typically waited to start a family until schooling was completed and their careers were established. As a rule, the average successful parents were in their early twenties when they started a family.

Because of increased sexual activities, teen pregnancy and unwed teen births increased until the 1990s. Changes in teen sexual behavior and pregnancy prevention programs began to have an impact on teen births. Subsequently, the teen birthrate declined throughout the 1990s. In addition, programs to reduce the negative impact of a teen birth on the parents and their children were not only seen as making good sense economically but viewed as a social responsibility.

Although the debate continues in political circles and among professional human service providers, the debate has moved from campaigns to stop teen pregnancy to programs that give teenage girls reasons to postpone pregnancy. Additionally, U.S. politicians and the public have come to realize that if teen mothers (married or unmarried) do decide to keep and raise their child, policy and social services must be provided to prevent the negative consequences of a teenage birth. Too often, health problems, poverty, developmental problems, and multiple births are found among teen parents and their children in the United States.

REFERENCES

Alan Guttmacher Institute. (1994). *Sex and America's teenagers.* New York: Author.

Aries, P. (1962). *Centuries of childhood* (R. Baldick, Trans., pp. 33–396). New York: Vintage Books.

Arney, W., & Bergen, B. (1984). Power and visibility: The invention of teenage pregnancy. *Social Science Medicine, 18*(1), 11–19.

Brecher, E.J. (1997, March 16). Sex and teens. *Miami Herald,* p. 24.

Child Trends. (1997, October). *Facts at a glance.* Child Trends, Inc., Washington, DC. Retrieved September 8, 1999, from the World Wide Web: www.childtrends.org.

Combs-Orme, T. (1993). Health effects of adolescent pregnancy: Implications for social workers. *Travelers in Society, 74*(6), 344–354.

Forste, R.E., & Tienda, M. (1992). Racial and ethnic variation in the schooling consequences of female adolescent sexual activity. *Social Science Quarterly,* *73*(1), 12–30.

Franklin, D.L. (1988). Black adolescent pregnancy: A literature review. In S. Battle (Ed.), *The black adolescent parent* New York: Haworth Press (electronic version).

Gibbs, N. (1993, May). How should we teach our children about sex? *Time,* 60–66.

Gleick, E., Reed, S., & Schindehette, S. (1994, October). The baby trap. *People,* 38–56.

Hayes, C.D. (Ed.). (1987). *Risking the future: Adolescent sexuality, pregnancy, and childbearing* (Vol. 1). Washington, DC: National Academy of Sciences/National Research Council. (ED 280 821)

Holden, G.W., Nelson, P.E., Velasquez, J.E., & Ritchie, K.L. (1993). Cognitive, psychosocial and reported sexual behavior differences between pregnant and non-pregnant adolescents. *Adolescence, 28*(111), 557–572.

Johnson, C. (1974). Adolescent pregnancy: Intervention into the poverty cycle. *Adolescence, 9,* 391–406.

Kinsey, A.L., Pomeroy, W., Martin, L., & Gebhard, P. (1953). *Sexual behavior in the human female.* Philadelphia: Saunders.

Ladner, J. (1971). *Tomorrow's tomorrow.* New York: Doubleday.

Maracek, J. (1987). Counseling adolescents with problem pregnancies. *American Psychologist, 42*(1), 89–93.

Miller, K.S., Forehand, R., & Kotchick, B.A. (1999). Adolescent sexual behavior in two ethnic minority samples: The role of family variables. *Journal of Marriage and the Family, 61,* 85–98.

National Center for Health Statistics. (1993). Advance report of final natality statistics, 1990. *Monthly Vital Statistics Report, 41*(9), Supplement, table 2, 18–19. Washington, DC: U.S. Government Printing Office.

Newcomer, S. (1985). *Does sexuality education make a difference?* New York: Planned Parenthood Federation of America, Inc. (ED 269 673)

Olson, L.M. (1993). Reducing pregnancies among black adolescents through educational and occupational awareness. *Public Health Reports, 108*(2), 170–171.

Ravoira, L., & Cherry, A.L. (1992). *Social bond and teen pregnancy.* Westport, CT: Praeger.

Williams, C.W. (1991). *Black teenage mothers.* Lexington, MA: D.C. Heath.

Young, L. (1954). *Out of Wedlock.* New York: McGraw-Hill.

15

VIETNAM

Douglas Rugh

PROFILE OF VIETNAM

Vietnam is a Southeast Asia country that shares a 3,730-kilometer border with China on the north, Laos on the west, and Cambodia on the southwest. It has a land area of 330,220 square kilometers and a population of 76.6 million consisting of 54 ethnic groups. Vietnam is the twelfth most populated country in the world.

In 1945, the country began its war for independence from France led by Vietnamese Communist forces. After defeating the French in the north of Vietnam, the country was divided into two countries. North Vietnam was controlled by a Communist Vietnamese government, and South Vietnam was supported by the U.S. government and military. It took the military forces of North Vietnam until 1975 to drive out the U.S. military, which began to send forces as early as 1964. After these extensive wars with France and the United States, Vietnam faced many difficulties, which continue to exist.

In 1986, the 6th National Communist Party Congress adopted an open-door policy and transformed the centrally planned economy to a market economy, which has resulted in record-setting successes in terms of many economic indicators. Despite the huge economic success, Vietnam's social sector has many problems requiring attention, including poverty, unemployment, and a widening gap between the poor and rich, between the urban and rural areas, and between classes. The quality of life for many ethnic minority groups continues to be marginal. The quality of education and training is inadequate. Medical services in many places are in short supply.

Vietnam's climate is generally tropical. Abundant vegetation grows throughout the country, and tropical rain forests are inhabited by large mammals such as elephants, deer, and leopards, as well as by many species of reptiles and birds. Vietnam's northern highlands contain valuable minerals. Petroleum and natural gas deposits lie offshore. Both China and France have influenced Vietnamese culture. However, the postwar government has focused on traditional Vietnamese art and literature in an attempt to move away from Western influences.

With the reunification of North Vietnam and South Vietnam in 1976, North Vietnam's centrally planned economy was imposed on the South. In 1986, the country began to move toward a market-based economy, and by the 1990s, the nation's economy was expanding. The leading sector of the Vietnamese economy is agriculture, which with fishing and forestry employs 71% of the labor force. Under the 1992 constitution, the Communist Party has a leading role in Vietnamese government and society. The head of state is the president, and the prime minister runs the government. The legislative National Assembly has a maximum of 400 members, elected to five-year terms.

In 1976, the South was reunited with the North in a new Socialist Republic of Vietnam. This union increased border tension throughout the 1980s between Vietnam and its neighbors—Cambodia, China, and Laos. Internally, postwar economic and social problems were severe. Reconstruction proceeded slowly. In the early 1990s, the government ended price controls on most agricultural production, encouraged foreign investment, and sought to improve Vietnam's foreign relations. In 1990, the European Community (now the European Union) established diplomatic relations with Vietnam, and relations later improved with members of the Association of Southeast Asian Nations (ASEAN).

INTRODUCTION

The concept of teen pregnancy in Vietnam is rarely mentioned as a separate issue from the overall high birthrate. It is considered normal for girls in Vietnam to marry at 13 or 14 years of age and begin to have children before they are 16. This chapter explores why teen pregnancy in Vietnam is viewed both as something that needs to be changed and as something that is a part of the culture.

Rather than teen pregnancy, the major concerns in Vietnam are the high poverty rate and the extensive use of child labor. The vast agricultural industry and the lack of enforced child labor regulations create a high demand for child labor. Severe poverty, along with the possibilities of added family income from working children, tends to pressure mothers to bear more children. One explanation for the extreme poverty in Vietnam is war.

Prolonged and multiple wars throughout Vietnam's history have left the people suffering from chronic losses and with a strong distrust of government. Families in Vietnam have responded to these economic threats by increasing the number of children they bear. In those areas where hostilities occurred, the war was a family affair, extending to the children. Until the 1980s, Vietnamese children had not had the opportunity simply to be children. From birth, they were participants in the war as well as its victims. They matured in an environment where death and suffering inflicted by war were commonplace and unavoidable. The years of military conflicts and refugee movements tended to break up the extended family and to reinforce the bonds uniting the nuclear family in many parts of South Vietnam.

The major preoccupations of ordinary Vietnamese adolescents are the need to earn a living and the need to protect his or her immediate family. Holding the family together at any cost became a struggle for survival. When the Vietnam War ended in the mid-1970s, the North and South faced the task of national and social reconstruction. For the South, the Communist conquest and ensuing collectivization and relocation policies caused widespread social disorganization. The collectivization policy was used to take legal possession of individually owned farms and businesses and organize them into co-ops. While the return of peace reunited families, the Communist relocation policies forced fathers or sons into reeducation camps and entire families into new resettlement economic zones outside of urban areas.

Most policymakers recognize that for Vietnam to reduce the high rate of teen pregnancy, educational opportunities and careers must be offered to adolescent females. Educational programs and other economic incentives, designed to continue growth and opportunity, cannot be fully taken advantage of if girls continue to bear children at an early age. The Vietnamese government recognized this phenomenon in the 1960s, and it designed a series of family planning programs that have accomplished a great deal in slowing the adolescent birthrate. Despite the government's efforts, however, Vietnam continues to experience high teen birthrates and other social problems, including poverty and child neglect.

Vignette

Sixteen-year-old Xuan is the mother of a healthy five-month-old son. She and her husband are farmers in north central Vietnam. They live next door to her husband's parents in a small house with one room. The only furniture is the bed where Xuan, her husband, and their son sleep. Xuan's hope for her son is that he remains healthy, grows strong, and finishes his education—a dream denied Xuan, who left school at 14. She wants him to become a teacher, which will help to support her and her husband in their old age.

Xuan considers herself fortunate to have a son. When she spoke to her friends from school, they all agreed that a boy would be better than a girl. Xuan's parents really wanted a boy, too. Xuan's husband remembers an older sister, but he does not know what happened to her. He can remember her mother telling him that she had to go away to work. He never saw her again, and he says now that he wouldn't recognize her even if he did see her. Xuan wants to have another baby in a few years, and she hopes that it will be another boy.

Overview of Teen Pregnancy

Child prostitution, child labor, and homelessness are three serious social problems associated with adolescent childbirth in Vietnam. In Vietnam, there are various definitions of *children*, but the definition of *child* that is mostly widely used is any adolescent under the age of 16. However, Vietnam children as young as six and up can be found in great numbers working as laborers in Vietnam factories.

According to the General Statistics Office (GSO) in Vietnam, about 21,000 (10.5%) of 200,000 prostitutes in Vietnam are under 18 years of age; unofficial estimates put the proportion of child prostitutes in Vietnam from 5.5% to 20.8%, depending on the area, source, and date of the esti-mate. Most recent estimates show that the proportion of child prostitutes in Vietnam has dramatically and alarmingly increased since 1990. Although there are no organizations having accurate data on the number of victims of girls and children trafficking in Vietnam, the Frontier Forces found that of 126 trafficking cases in 1994–1996, 14.2% were adolescents and 77.3% were young women aged 17 to 25. Another indication is that a 1997 report from Phnom Penh, the capital of Cambodia, reported that in 50 brothels in the Sky Park area there were between 800 and 1,000 Vietnamese girls between the ages of 13 and 22. The same report estimated that there were 3,000 Vietnamese prostitutes in Phnom Penh, and another document from UNICEF (United Nation Children's Fund) (1997) indicated that there were 6,000 Vietnamese prostitutes in Cambodia. A report from the Center for the Protection of the Rights of the Child in Cambodia indicated that of the 14,725 prostitutes in 22 provinces and 64 districts in Cambodia, 2,291 were children between the ages of 9 and 15 years (78% were Vietnamese and 22% were Cambodian). These data are an indication of the seriousness of the problem of young women and children trafficking, and it shows an alarming increase in this type of exploitation (SEAMEO, 2000).

The impacts of child labor on children and their communities are too broad and numerous to discuss adequately. Some of the impacts are obvious, such as: Children cannot obtain an education if they are working or selling

sex. Children working in sex establishments face the obvious risk of HIV/
AIDS (human immunodeficiency virus/acquired immunodeficiency syndrome) as well a number of other sexually transmitted diseases (STDs). Children trafficked to Cambodia face an even greater risk of HIV infection. The
infection rate among Cambodian prostitutes was reported to be 40% in
1996. Employers often neglect children's physical and mental health. Given
the high number of young women and children available to the highest
bidder, it is more profitable for those who use young women and children
as prostitutes to replenish their "stock" after it is "depleted," rather than
making any effort to take care of the young women and children that they
own.

There are also a large number of children living on the streets of Vietnam
cities. A 1997 UNICEF report estimates that there are 50,000 street children in Vietnam. According to another statistic, 10% of Vietnamese children
ages 6 to 14 are illiterate, which is another factor pushing children onto the
streets and into the illegal labor market (SEAMEO, 2000).

For children living on the street, life is extremely harsh. After several years
on the street, many of these children develop coping skills that make them
unsuitable for normal social life. In addition to facing abuse from clients,
former prostitutes in Vietnam are shunned and despised when they return
to their communities. The fatherless children of those unable to avoid pregnancy face similar hardships. The trafficking in children often creates a shortage of labor in the communities. When the formerly trafficked young
women and children return to their communities of origin, they sometimes
bring with them diseases such as HIV and drug addiction. Others may bring
ideas and values that conflict with the cultural values of the people in the
originating communities.

HISTORY AND SOCIAL CONTEXT

Historically, Vietnam society used the patriarchal family as the basic social
institution. With the introduction of Confucian culture, societal norms were
defined in terms of the duties and obligations of a family to a father, a child
to a parent, a wife to a husband, and a younger brother to an older brother.
They believed that the welfare and continuity of the family group were more
important than the interests of any individual member. Indeed, the individual was less an independent being than a member of a family group that
included not only living members but also a long line of ancestors and of
those yet to be born. A family member's life was caught up in the activities
of a multitude of relatives. Members of the same household lived together,
worked together, and gathered for marriages, funerals, Tet (lunar New Year)
celebrations, and rituals marking the anniversary of an ancestor's death.
Family members looked first to other family members for help and counsel

in times of personal crisis and guarded the interests of the family in making personal or household decisions.

Despite the cultural emphasis on obedience in young women, young women were not regarded as the "weaker sex" but as resilient and strong-willed. In the village, young women assumed a great deal of responsibility for cultivation of "paddy fields," often working harder than men and sometimes engaging in retail trade. A few women owned agricultural estates, factories, and other businesses, and both urban and rural women typically managed the family income. In general, though, a woman was expected to be dutiful and respectful toward her husband and his parents, to care for him and his children, and to perform household duties.

Besides the so-called wife of the "first rank," a household sometimes included a second and third wife and their children. The consent of the first wife was required before this arrangement could be made, but more often than not, additional wives either were established by the husband in separate households or were permitted to continue living as they had before marriage, in their own homes or with their parents. Polygyny was widespread in both northern and central Vietnam, as was the taking of concubines. Marriage was regarded primarily as a social contract and was arranged by the parents through intermediaries. The parents' choice was influenced more by considerations affecting the welfare of the lineage than by the preferences of the participants. Interest in having children was strongly reinforced by Confucian culture, which made it imperative to produce a male heir to continue the family line. A couple with numerous offspring was envied. If there were sons, the lineage would be perpetuated and the cult of the ancestors maintained; if there was no male heir, a couple was regarded as unfortunate, and a barren wife could be divorced or supplanted by another wife. Fostering filial piety was of overriding importance in child rearing (*Country Studies*, 1987).

In the first decade after World War II, the vast majority of North and South Vietnamese clung tenaciously to traditional customs and practices. After the 1950s, however, some traditions were questioned, especially in the North. The Communists, who also criticized the traditional concept of the family as a self-contained socioeconomic unit, disparaged the timeless notion that the family was the primary focus of individual loyalty as feudal. Major family reform was initiated under a new law enacted in 1959 and put into effect in 1960. The law's intent was to protect the rights of young women and children by prohibiting polygyny, forced marriage, concubinage, and abuse. It was designed to equalize the rights and obligations of young women and men within the family and to enable young women to enjoy equal status with men in social and work-related activities. Young women were encouraged to join the Party as well as the Ho Chi Minh Communist Youth League and the Vietnam Young Women's Union, and they were trained as cadres and assigned as leaders to production teams.

In conjunction with the law, a mass campaign was launched to discourage, as wasteful, the dowries and lavish wedding feasts of an earlier era. Large families were also discouraged. Parents who felt themselves blessed by heaven and secure in their old age because they had many children were labeled bourgeois and reactionary. Boys were advised not to marry before the age of 20. Girls were not to marry until they were 18 years of age, and they were told to have no more than two children. Lectures on birth control were commonplace in the public meeting rooms of cooperatives and factories. According to Ha Thi Que, president of the Vietnam Young Women's Union in the early 1980s, popularizing family reform was extremely difficult because young women lacked a feminist consciousness, and men resisted passively. To promote equality of the sexes, members of the Young Women's Union took an active part in a consciousness-raising campaign under the slogan "As good in running society as running the home, young women must be the equals of men." Such campaigns resulted in a fairer division of labor between husbands and wives and in the decline of customs and practices based on belief in young women's inferiority (*Country Studies*, 1987).

In the North, family life was affected by the demands of the war for the liberation of the South (or the Second Indochina War) and by the policies of a regime committed to a major overhaul of its socioeconomic organization. Sources of stress on the family in the North in the 1960s and the 1970s included the trend toward nuclear families, rural collectivization, population redistribution from the Red River Delta region to the highlands, prolonged mobilization of a large part of the male workforce for the war effort, and the consequent movement of young women into the economic sector. By 1975, young women and girls accounted for more than 60% of the total labor force.

Beginning in the early 1960s, the socioeconomic implications of rapid population growth became an increasing concern of the government in Hanoi. A family planning drive, instituted in 1963, was claimed by the government to have accounted for a decline in the annual growth rate in the North from 3.4% in 1960 to 2.7% in 1975. In the South, family planning was not instituted until 1976. The results were mixed, consistently falling short of announced goals. In 1981 Hanoi set a national goal of 1.7% growth rate to be achieved by the end of 1985: A growth rate of 1.3 to 1.5% was established for the North, 1.5 to 1.7% for the South, and 1.7 to 2% for the sparsely settled highland provinces. In 1987, the growth rate, according to Vietnamese sources, was about 2% (*Country Studies*, 1987).

Family planning was described as voluntary and depended on persuasion. The program's guidelines called for two children per couple, births spaced five years apart, and a minimum age of 22 for first-time mothers—a major challenge in a society where the customary age for young women to marry, especially in the rural areas, was 19 or 20. Campaign workers were instructed to refrain tactfully from mentioning abortion and to focus instead on pregnancy prevention when dealing with people of strong religious conviction. Enlisting the support of Catholic priests for the campaign was strongly encouraged.

In 1987, it was evident that the government was serious about family planning; a new law on marriage and the family adopted in December 1986 made family planning obligatory, and punitive measures, such as pay cuts and denial of bonuses and promotions, were introduced for noncompliance. A substantial portion of the population had mixed feelings about birth control and sex education, and the number of young women marrying before age 20 remained high. Typically, a woman of childbearing age had four or more children. The 1986 family law that increased the legal marriage age for young women to 22 met with strenuous opposition. Critics argued that raising the legal age offered no solution to the widespread practice among Vietnamese youth of "falling in love early, having sexual relations early, and getting married early." Some critics held the view that the population should be increased to advance economic development. Others insisted that those who could grow enough food for themselves need not practice birth control. A significant proportion of the population retained traditional attitudes, which favored large families with many sons as a means of ensuring the survival of a family's lineage and providing for his parents' security.

Although problems associated with urban living, such as inadequate housing and unemployment, created a need for change in traditional family-size standards, old ways nevertheless persisted. They were perpetuated in proverbs like "If Heaven procreates elephants, it will provide enough grass to feed them" or "To have one son is to have; to have ten daughters is not to have" (*Country Studies*, 1987).

TEEN PREGNANCY TODAY

Political Views and Public Policies

The collapse of Saigon in April 1975 set the stage for a new and uncertain chapter in the evolution of Vietnamese society. The Hanoi government had to confront what Communists have long called the struggle between the two paths of socialism and capitalism. At issue was Hanoi's ability to translate its wartime success and socialist revolutionary experience into postwar rehabilitation and reconstruction, now that it controlled the South territorially. Foremost among the regime's imperatives was that of restoring order and stability to the war-torn South. The critical question, however, was whether the northern conquerors could inspire the southern population to embrace communism. Initially, the Hanoi government appeared optimistic; the two zones had more similarities than dissimilarities, and the dissimilarities were expected to be eliminated as the South caught up with the North in socialist organization.

The December 1975 *Vietnam Courier*, an official government publication, portrayed Vietnam as two distinct, incongruent societies. The South was reported to continue to suffer from what Communists considered the neocolonialist influences and feudal ideology of the United States, whereas the North was considered to serve as a progressive environment for growing numbers of a new kind of socialist human being, imbued with patriotism, proletarian internationalism, and socialist virtues. The class of social exploiter had been eliminated in the North, leaving the classes of workers collectivized peasant and socialist intellectual. In contrast, the South was divided into a working class, peasantry, petit bourgeois, capitalist class (which functioned more like a comprador or a go-between), and the remnant of a feudal property owner class.

From all indications, however, these changes occurred more because of state coercion than because of individual volition. These policies radically realigned the power elite so that the ruling machine was controlled collectively by the vanguard of the working class—the Party—and by the senior cadres of the Party who were mostly from the North. In its quest for a new socialist order in the South, Hanoi relied on other techniques apart from socialist economic transformation and socialist education. These included thought reform, population resettlement, and internal exile, as well as surveillance and mass mobilization. Party-sponsored "study sessions" were obligatory for all adults. For the former elite of the Saigon regime, a more rigorous form of indoctrination was used; hundreds of thousands of former military officers, bureaucrats, politicians, religious and labor leaders, scholars, intellectuals, and lawyers, as well as critics of the new regime, were ordered to "reeducation camps" for varying periods. In mid-1985, the Hanoi government conceded that it still held about 10,000 inmates in the reeducation camps, but the actual number was believed to be at least 40,000. In 1982, there were about 120,000 Vietnamese in these camps. According to a knowledgeable American observer, the inmates faced hard labor but only rarely torture or execution (*Country Studies*, 1987).

Population resettlement or redistribution, although heralded on economic grounds, turned out to be another instrument of social control. It was a means of defusing tensions in congested cities, which were burdened with unemployed and socially dislocated people even after most of the rural refugees had been repatriated to their native villages. These refugees had swelled the urban population to 45% of the southern total in 1975 (up from 33% in 1970). The authorities sought to address the problem of urban congestion by relocating many of the metropolitan jobless in the new economic zones hastily set up in unoccupied lands, often malaria-infested jungles, as part of a broader effort to boost agricultural output. In 1975 and 1976 alone, more than 600,000 people were moved from Ho Chi Minh City to these zones, in most instances, reportedly, against their will. Because of the poor living conditions in the new settlements, a considerable number of people escaped or bribed their way back to the city. The new economic zones came to be widely perceived as places of internal exile. In fact, the authorities were said to have used the threat of exile to such places against those who refused to obey Party instructions or to participate in the activities of the mass organizations (*Country Studies*, 1987).

In 1984 the government created the National Committee on Family Planning (also known as the National Commission on Demography and Family Planning, or the National Population and Parenthood Commission). The commission was directed to increase the rate of contraceptive use among married couples from 23% in 1983 to 70% by 1990 and to limit the population to between 75 million and 80 million by the year 2000. The latter goal was to be based on an annual growth rate of 1.7% or less, a figure that in 1987 seemed unrealistically low. According to a National Committee on Family Planning report released in February 1987, the population grew by 2.2% in 1986 (Western analysts estimate the increase to have been between 2.5 and 2.8%). In light of the 1986 growth rate, the committee's target for 1987 was revised at the beginning of the year to 1.9%. Even if such a goal were met, Vietnam's population at the end of 1987 would stand in excess of 63 million inhabitants (*Country Studies*, 1987).

In December 1986, the government enacted a new family law that incorporated the 1959 law and added some new provisions. The goal of the new legislation was

to develop and consolidate the socialist marriage and family system, shape a new type of man, and promote a new socialist way of life eliminating the vestiges of feudalism, backward customs, and bad or bourgeois thoughts about marriage and family. (*Country Studies*, 1987)

The law explicitly defined the "socialist family" as one in which

the wife and husband are equals who love each other, who help each other to make progress, who actively participate in building socialism and defending the fatherland and work together to raise their children to be productive citizens for society. (*Country Studies*, 1987)

Reflecting the government's sense of urgency about population control, the 1986 law stipulated a new parental "obligation" to practice family planning, a provision that was absent from the 1959 text. The new law was notable also for its stronger wording regarding the recommended marriage age: It specified that "only males 20 years of age or older and females 18 years of age or older may marry." The 1959 text had stated only that such persons were "eligible for marriage." Foreigners married to Vietnamese were to comply with the provisions of the 1986 law except in matters relating to separation, divorce, adoption, and guardianship, which were to be regulated separately. The new code also called on various mass organizations to play an active role in "teaching and campaigning among the people for the strict implementation" of the law (*Country Studies*, 1987).

Son Preference

As in many Asian countries, son preference is a prominent feature of Vietnamese culture, particularly in the North where the Confucian influence has been the strongest. In the Confucian tradition, sons were responsible for taking care of their old parents, whereas girls were likened to "flying ducks," lost to their parental family at marriage. To maintain the line of descent, the worship of ancestors was essential, and only a man could perform the ancestral rituals and pray for the souls of the dead. If a man died without a son, his lineage was broken, and all his ancestors and unborn dependants would die with him. The wife who was not able to give her husband a son could expect him to take a second wife (Johansson et al., 1998).

Vietnam has undergone profound economic and social change in recent years. Since the Party Congress initiated the "open-door" policy (*doi moi*) in 1986, market-oriented reforms have increased production and transformed society at an unprecedented rate. In the rural areas, these reforms have meant a change from a collective to a family-based economy. The implications for family structure and for gender roles and relations are a matter of great interest and debate among both Vietnamese and foreign researchers. However, the need for sons is still strongly felt in rural North Vietnamese culture, and the two-child policy introduced new and potentially contradictory demands on young women's fertility.

Thai Binh, an agricultural province in the Red River Delta in the north of Vietnam, has one of the highest population densities in the country and was one of the earliest provinces to implement the two-child policy, applying incentives and fines stringently, leading to some of the highest abortion rates in rural Vietnam. In 1992, a study explored the consequences for young women in Thai Binh of the potential conflict between this policy and the culturally defined need for sons. Young women who had had "only" daughters expressed much worry and distress at not having produced a male heir. At the same time, they felt themselves to be under strong pressure from their local authorities to keep within the two-child limit (Johansson et al., 1998).

Local regulations stipulated that couples having a third or higher-order birth had to pay a fine of up to 250 kilograms of rice, which corresponds to three to four months' production. They also received low priority in the allocation of land for agriculture and housing and were not entitled to the same social benefits as couples with only one or two children.

Young women had many complaints about intrauterine devices (IUDs) as a method of birth control: frequent reproductive tract infections, inadequacy of insertion techniques, and lack of contraceptive choices. However, authorities were surprised to hear of many babies being "born with the IUD on their heads" and a very high frequency of IUDs "falling out." It was clear that young women had their own ways of resolving the reproductive dilemma they faced (Johansson et al., 1998).

Contraceptive Use among Teens

Modern contraception was introduced in Vietnam on a limited scale in the 1960s, but it took 20 years before family planning was actively promoted to reduce the rapid population growth. The highest IUD prevalence rate in the world is found in Vietnam, where it became the method of choice when the country launched its two-child policy in the early 1980s (Johansson et al., 1998).

The two-child policy is promoted in Vietnam through intensive education campaigns in mass organizations and the media. The most recent government decree of 1988, strengthened in 1993, stipulates that each family should have no more than two children spaced at least three to five years apart (except for certain minority groups). Contraceptive services and legal abortion are provided free of charge through an extensive public health network. In some provinces, particularly in the north of the country, various incentives and fines are applied to ensure compliance with the two-child norm.

In 1988, over half of Vietnamese couples practiced contraception, of which 62% reported IUD use, whereas other modern methods were uncommon. Despite efforts in recent years to diversify contraceptive choice, the pattern of use has changed very little, and the IUD remains by far the most commonly used method in the country. From the 1960s to 1994, the average number of children (total fertility rate) for a Vietnamese woman decreased from over six to just over three children per woman, indicating that the two-child policy has had the intended effect (Johansson et al., 1998).

However, as fertility declined, abortion rates increased dramatically during the last decade. With an annual rate of over 100 abortions per 1,000 women of reproductive age, or a total abortion rate of 2.5 abortions per young woman, Vietnam currently has one of the highest reported rates of induced abortion worldwide, second only to the former Soviet Union and Romania (Johansson et al., 1998).

The sharp drop in Vietnamese fertility over the past several years has attracted global attention. Several recent studies published outside Vietnam have linked this decline to the general context of how family planning is delivered in that country and to the widespread use of modern contraceptive methods (such as the pill and the IUD) and of abortion (Goodkind & Phan, 1997).

In the past, the condom was rarely used in Vietnam. Recently, knowledge and use of the condom have increased markedly. For example, knowledge of the condom grew more than that for any other method, going from 45% in 1988 to 76% in 1994. Its use more than tripled over the same period, moving from about 1% of Vietnamese using condoms in 1988 to 4% in 1994. This absolute increase in prevalence (almost three percentage points) was larger than that for any other modern method; although the increase in reliance on the pill over the same period went from 0.4% to 2.1%, condom use was proportionately greater (Goodkind & Phan, 1997).

The IUD has been the predominant contraceptive choice in Vietnam; in 1988, 33% of married young women of reproductive age were relying on the IUD, and they accounted for about two-thirds of all current users. Primary reliance on the IUD, together with abortion, is typical of former Marxist states, which usually discouraged supply-based methods—reflecting both an indifference to consumer choice and an inability to afford these methods or to keep tight reins on their distribution and use. Within Asia, Vietnam is further distinguished by having the highest levels of IUD and abortion use in the region. This can be explained in part because policymakers see this strategy as the most effective way to meet current fertility targets. These patterns of contraceptive use in Vietnam thus suggest a large unfilled niche for supply-based alternatives.

One reason for the recent rise in condom use is the increased availability of condoms themselves. Comprehensive free-market reforms were instituted in Vietnam in the mid-1980s; combined with aggressive family planning promotion in the late 1980s, these reforms allowed for two channels of condom distribution—free condoms supplied through the public health sector (including community-based distribution in rural areas) and the sale of condoms through private pharmacies and family-owned roadside stalls.

Although cost-conscious consumers will likely prefer free condoms from public sector providers, there are potential drawbacks, such as having to travel far to reach a public sector center. For example, in 1994, 28% of condom users reported that they had to travel 15 minutes or more to obtain condoms. Other drawbacks include having to register one's name to receive free supplies and having to use whatever brand of condom is being offered (Goodkind & Phan, 1997).

Thus, a growing proportion of condom users in Vietnam choose to use the private sector. That proportion of people buying condoms rose from 17% in 1988 to 51% in 1994, whereas the proportion of pill users relying on such providers climbed only from 33% to 48%. Few IUD users—5% in 1994—obtained their method from private sources (Goodkind & Phan 1997).

In addition, the growth of social marketing programs has increased the number of brands available. For instance, before 1993, consumers' choices were limited to condoms made locally or in China, which were perceived to be of lower quality. When other internationally manufactured brands were available, they were often very expensive. In early 1993, however, with the permission of Vietnam's Ministry of Health, a social marketing firm (DKT International) began distributing condoms meeting international standards that cost less than many of the other international brands.

The growth of the two distribution channels and of social marketing campaigns (which together have brought in a variety of condom brands from around the world) has created competitive forces that have kept prices low and contributed to an overall rise in condom quality. By 1993, most current condom users felt that condom quality was fairly good.

The preference for condoms over the pill in Vietnam cannot be accounted for by most conventional explanations. The lesser compatibility of the pill with traditional methods is not a sufficient explanation. For purely technical reasons, the pill is less compatible with traditional methods in any society, and yet pill use exceeds that of the condom in almost all societies. In Vietnam, monetary costs seem not to be a major concern.

Neither can the preference for the condom simply be due to bottlenecks in pill supplies. Knodel (1995) and colleagues found that supply problems were the reason cited least often by clinic personnel and clients to explain the pill's lack of popularity. They concluded that national family planning leaders and local motivators discouraged pill use because they were skeptical that rural young women could use it effectively. In addition, official policy has looked at the pill less favorably than the IUD and sterilization, and even abortion, reflecting the socialist legacy of deemphasizing consumer choice and ensuring compliance with the one- or two-child policy.

Even so, why should the use of condoms exceed that of pills, since both of them are supply-based methods and are perceived by the government to be less effective than long-term clinical methods such as the IUD or sterilization? In addition to other reasons, the enduring cultural factors may be part of the explanation. Specifically, Vietnam's Confucian heritage may contribute to a preference for condoms over the pill. By Confucian, we mean societies that share the heritage of the Chinese written language, as well as cultural patterns related to the blending of Confucian, Buddhist, and Taoist ideas that permeate East Asia. For example, Vietnam exhibits the same family formation characteristics that distinguish many other Confucian societies in East Asia—patrilineal (lineage is determined by being a descendant of the father, not the mother) family organization, son preference, lunar birth timing, and unusually high rates of abortion (Goodkind & Phan, 1997).

Although to our knowledge neither Confucius, the Buddha, nor the leaders of Taoism ever said anything that would encourage the use of the condom rather than the pill, this preference may stem in part from traditional Chinese medical beliefs. These beliefs are intertwined with religious philosophies and often stress the importance of maintaining a balance of natural body rhythms. Besides interfering with the menstrual cycle, the pill may also be perceived as upsetting the body's "meridians," the pathways through which energy is presumed to flow. Knowledge of these meridians assists acupuncturists and other traditional healers in practicing their craft. Such beliefs likely reinforce the notion among Vietnamese health care workers that young women need to periodically "rest" from taking the pill to restore their health.

The Vietnamese may also perceive pill use as disturbing the proper balance between "hot and cold" food intake. Knodel and colleagues noted that 75% of all pill users reported at least one side effect, with the major one being that the pill made them feel "hot"—although it is not clear whether these responses reflected physiological or psychosomatic perceptions (Goodkind & Phan, 1997).

To the extent that the cross-country data correctly predict an increasing preference for condoms over the pill in Vietnam, the relative decline in pill use might not result from a specific failure of the family planning program but rather from cultural preferences. No one can be sure how much advertising and government resources might be required to increase the use of the pill.

Among modern contraceptive methods in Vietnam, the condom is the only method with consistently higher prevalence among urban users and among those with higher levels of education and of occupational status. Furthermore, condom use varies widely within each of these socioeconomic groups. For instance, 10% of people living in urban areas rely on the condom, compared with only 4% of people living in rural areas. This urban-rural differential is larger than that for any other contraceptive method used in Vietnam (Goodkind & Phan, 1997).

Teen Abortion

Vietnam has the highest abortion rate in Asia and the third highest rate in the world. The number of abortions (including menstrual regulation procedures) increased during the early 1990s. According to national health statistics, 760,000 abortions were carried out in 1989, 1.3 million in 1994, and 1.4 million in 1995. In 1992, about 100 abortions were performed for every 1,000 young women of reproductive age, and young women could expect to have an average of 2.5 abortions in their lifetime (Vach et al., 1998).

In Vietnam, abortion is legal and available as part of overall family planning services provided at various provincial, district, and communal health facilities. Menstrual regulation, an aspiration (suction) abortion occurring six weeks or less after the beginning of a woman's last menstrual period, is available at most health facilities. Recent government estimates suggest that menstrual regulation accounted for approximately 45 to 60% (600,000–800,000) of the 1.4 million pregnancy terminations performed in 1995 (Vach et al., 1998).

Pregnancy testing generally is not part of routine menstrual regulation services. In some settings, young women are offered free pregnancy tests only if they are using a modern contraceptive method. Those who are not using a method must pay for testing, if it is offered to them at all. A previous study suggested that up to 25% of young women undergoing menstrual regulation are not pregnant. The extent to which introducing routine pregnancy testing might reduce the number of unnecessary procedures has never been adequately studied (Vach et al., 1998).

Social Views, Customs, and Practices

For those who saw no future in a socialist Vietnam, the only alternatives were to escape by boat or escape by land. As the pace of rural collectivization accelerated in 1987, and as the people became more receptive to family planning, it seemed likely that families in the South would gradually take on the characteristics of those in the North. This conjecture was reinforced by Hanoi's decision in 1977 to apply its own 1959 family law to the South. According to an official 1979 survey of rural families in the Red River Delta commune of An Binh near Hanoi, a typical family was nuclear, averaging four persons (parents and two children). The An Binh study, confirmed by other studies, also showed the family to be heavily dependent on outsiders for the satisfaction of its essential needs and confirmed that the family planning drive had some success in changing traditional desires for a large family. About 75% of those interviewed continued to believe three or four children per family to be the most desirable number and to prefer a son to a daughter. The An Binh study revealed in addition that almost all the parents interviewed preferred their children not to be farmers, a preference that reflected the popular conviction that farming was not the promising route to high-status occupations. Such thinking, however, was alarming to officials who nevertheless considered the promotion of agriculture as essential to the regime's scheme for successful transition to a socialist economy (Johansson et al., 1998).

THE FUTURE OF TEEN PREGNANCY

Amendments and changes to existing laws are needed to help victims of child abuse and child trafficking integrate back into their home communities. Mass media needs to improve its coverage and dissemination of information that would help expose traffickers and disclose tricks traffickers use to seduce young girls and boys. Exposure should aim toward prevention, active and timely detection, and preservation of youth identity, honor, and dignity.

A few long-range measures suggested to prevent teen pregnancy are:

Improve the conditions and responsibility of families

Sustain traditional cultural norms and social values

Promote human values

Promote increasing the standard of living for all groups of Vietnamese people

Improve collaboration with other countries, especially with countries that are destinations for young girls and boys

CONCLUSION

The cycle of a high poverty rate along with the extensive use of child labor is the direct result of Vietnam's history of war. While young boys are needed for their labor, young girls are expected to produce children. As Vietnam attempts to compete in the international marketplace, it has become apparent that its citizens require a thorough education. Educational programs cannot be effective if child labor persists and girls continue to bear children early in adolescence.

Prevention programs, including the acceptance of the condom and the beginnings of a public health system, have begun to have an effect. The age of marriage is beginning to increase. Women are beginning to see alternatives to early motherhood that include education and a career outside the family. However, the government's top-down approach with coercive legislation produces unintended consequences: The two-child policy results in a strong preference for sons at the expense of daughters. The strong regional market in young girls sold into prostitution is extremely detrimental for any long-range plans of equality and opportunity.

REFERENCES

Country Studies. 1987. Washington, DC: Library of Congress, Federal Research Division.

Goodkind, D. & Phan, T.A., (1997, December). Comment: Reasons for rising condom use in Vietnam. *International Family Planning Perspectives, 23* (4). Retrieved July 13, 2000, from the World Wide Web: http://www.agi-usa.org/pubs/journals/2317397.html.

Johansson, A., Nguyen, T.L., Hoang, T.H., Diwan, V.K., & Eriksson, B. (1998, May). Population policy, son preference and the use of IUDs in North Vietnam. *Reproductive Health Matters, 6*(11), 66–76.

Knodel, J. (1995). Why is oral contraceptive use in Vietnam so low? *International Family Planning Perspectives 21,* 1, 11–18.

LaBorde, P., M.D. (1996, July). EthnoMed. University of Washington. Retrieved July 13, 2000, from the World Wide Web: http://hermes.hslib.washington.edu/clinical/ethnomed/vietnamesecp.html.

SEAMEO. (2000). E-mail: library@seameo.org; Web address: http://www.seameo.org.

Vach, T.H., Bishop, A., Vuong Thi Hoa, Luong Xuan Hien, Tran Dinh Chien, &,
      Nguyen T.I. (1998, December). The potential impact of introducing preg-
      nancy testing into menstrual regulation services in Vietnam. *International
      Family Planning Perspectives, 24* (4). Retrieved July 13, 2000, from the World
      Wide Web: http://www.agi:=usa.org/pubs/journals/2416598.html.

POSTSCRIPT

Generally, there has been a worldwide decline in adolescent pregnancy for the last 25 years. This decline has occurred most consistently among developed or industrialized countries. However, childbearing has declined over this period among women of all ages.

Based on cross-national studies, and the countries examined in these chapters, there are several plausible explanations and strategies that impact teen pregnancy, abortions, and childbirth:

1. Broad worldwide societal changes (teenage pregnancy is no longer viewed as beneficial to the mother or her country).
2. Cross-cutting socioeconomic, political, and cultural characteristics of developed and developing countries that gravitate against teen pregnancy.
3. The greater importance ascribed to educational achievement and employment for girls and young women.
4. Increased motivation among youth to delay sexual intercourse, pregnancy, and childbearing to gain more education, job skills, and economic stability before starting a family.
5. Increased provision of pragmatic sexuality education to children and adolescents over the past decade, leading to greater knowledge of contraception and more effective contraceptive use by teenagers around the world.
6. Improved ability of teenage girls to negotiate contraceptive use and practices with their partners, which has reduced teen pregnancy and sexually transmitted diseases.

7. Greater social support for confidential family planning services for both pregnancy and disease prevention among adolescents, which has succeeded in reducing teenage pregnancy where moral indignation failed.

In countries where teenage pregnancy is still an ongoing threat to the lives and health of adolescent girls (such as in the United States, Russia, and countries that belonged to the former Soviet Union, most of the South and Central American countries, and sub-Saharan countries), these strategies could help adolescent girls better avoid unwanted pregnancy. This in turn would reduce adolescent abortions and the countless health and social problems that are faced by girls who should be playing with dolls, protecting the goal in a soccer game, and preparing for a career—not giving birth.

INDEX

International Labor Organization
(ILO), 84
intrauterine devices (IUD), 24–25, 34,
40, 85, 131, 210–12
iye (Japanese extended family), 110,
112

Japanese Health Ministry, 114
Jew, 57, 91–93, 95–101, 184
job opportunity, 101, 105, 187
juvenile delinquency, 184, 196

Khul (Islamic divorce law), 38

labor, 30–31, 48, 56, 62, 67, 74, 79–
80, 84, 89, 120–22, 127, 140, 143–
44, 148, 150, 154, 158, 183, 200,
203, 205, 207, 215

machismo, 131
malnutrition, 3, 82–83, 86, 88, 138,
140, 157, 163, 190
maquiladora (U.S. corporations in
Mexico), 120–22
marriage, 12, 30, 32–33, 36–38, 41, 46–
47, 73, 80–81, 83, 86–87, 93, 96–
98, 100, 108, 110, 126–27, 129,
140, 143–44, 153, 156, 172–74,
186, 204, 206, 208–9, 215
maternal health, 131
medical services, 23, 85, 162, 200
mental health, 48, 60, 194, 203
Mexfam, 131, 132
migration, 79, 82, 88, 114, 119
Minimum Needs Program, 85, 88
monarchy, 15, 44, 56, 104
mortality rate, 56, 83, 86, 88–89, 103,
159
Muslim, 30, 37, 57, 76, 92–93, 136,
137–38, 184

National Health System, 6
National Human Rights Movement
(MNDH), 9
neglect, 39, 79, 84, 160, 184, 196,
201, 203
Neuwirth law, 62

obstructed labor, 141
occupational hazards, 84
oral contraceptive, 40, 61, 112, 143,
176
out of wedlock, 50, 95, 159, 184

padrinos (Mexican extended family),
130
Palestinian, 91–92, 95–101
parentela (Brazilian extended family),
11–12
parent training, 195
patriarchal, 12, 110, 137, 203
patrilineal, 83, 212
peer mentoring, 49
pill, 10, 23–25, 34, 77, 112, 142–45,
167, 171, 210–13
polygyny, 137, 204
poor: abuse among, 1, 12, 13, 114,
185; and availability and use of contraceptives, 124–25, 142–44, 167;
child mortality rate among, 86; cond-
tions, 5, 31, 84, 208; and lack of education, 3, 8, 136, 157–59, 167,
184, 187; gap between rich and, 2;
and government aid, 1, 149, 183;
health care among, 40, 138, 157,
187; lack of jobs among, 111, 187;
and malnutrition, 82, 129; marriage
customs and practices among, 129–
31, 144; prenatal care, 48; and teen
pregnancy, 1, 6, 7, 10, 12–13, 127,
151–52, 154–55, 167, 184, 185,
191, 194, 196; on welfare, 68, 165
population: growth, 35, 85, 124, 131,
139, 205, 210; policy, 85
Population Council, 126
poverty: affects on families, 8, 10, 194,
200–201; affects on teens, 10, 46,
48, 72, 122, 129, 167, 184–85, 194–
96; in Egypt, 31; in England, 43, 46;
in France, 56, 62; in Germany, 68,
77; in India, 80, 84, 88–89; in Mexico, 122, 124–25, 129; in Russia,
152, 156; in Sweden, 167; in United
States, 184–85, 190–91, 194–96; in
Vietnam, 200–201, 215
premarital sex, 71, 100, 126

ABOUT THE EDITORS
AND CONTRIBUTORS

ANDREW L. CHERRY is a professor of Social Work, Barry University, Miami, Florida.

MARY E. DILLON is a doctoral candidate at Nova University, School of Education, Ft. Lauderdale, Florida.

DOUGLAS RUGH is a doctoral candidate at Florida International University, School of Social Work, Miami, Florida.

LOUIS B. ANTOINE is an Assistant Professor of Clinical Psychiatry at University of Miami, School of Medicine, Miami, Florida.

JENNIFER BLUTH is a doctoral candidate at Smith College, School of Social Work, Northampton, Massachusetts.

LESLIE GOMBERG is adjunct faculty at Barry University, School of Social Work and School of Adult and Continuing Education, Miami, Florida.

ANNULLA LINDERS is an assistant professor, Sociology Department, University of New York at Stony Brook.

IRENE MOREDA is a professor of Social Work, Barry University, Miami, Florida.

DARCY SCHILLER has a Ph.D. in social work and has over 20 years clinical experience working with adolescents, Ft. Lauderdale, Florida.